Building Lean Supply Chains with the Theory of Constraints

About the Author

Mandyam M. Srinivasan is the Pilot Corporation Chair of Excellence at the University of Tennessee. He is the author of *Streamlined: 14 Principles for Building and Managing the Lean Supply Chain* (Cengage, 2004), and coauthor of *Supply Chain Management for Competitive Advantage* (Tata McGraw-Hill, 2009). Dr. Srinivasan has many years of work experience with leading automobile manufacturing organizations, and he has consulted with a large number of industries.

Building Lean Supply Chains with the Theory of Constraints

Mandyam M. Srinivasan

New York   Chicago   San Francisco
Lisbon   London   Madrid   Mexico City
Milan   New Delhi   San Juan
Seoul   Singapore   Sydney   Toronto

The *McGraw·Hill* Companies

Library of Congress Cataloging-in-Publication Data

Srinivasan, Mandyam M.
  Building lean supply chains with the theory of constraints / Mandyam M. Srinivasan.
    p. cm.
  ISBN 978-0-07-177121-4 (alk. paper)
  1. Business logistics. 2. Lean manufacturing. 3. Quality control. 4. Cost control. I. Title.
  HD38.5.S6557 2012
  658.7—dc23

                                                                          2011038559

Building Lean Supply Chains with the Theory of Constraints

2 3 4 5 6 7 8 9 0   QVS/QVS   16 15 14 13

ISBN   978- 0-07-177121-4
MHID   0-07-177121-2

The pages within this book were printed on acid-free paper.

Sponsoring Editor	**Proofreader**
Judy Bass	Claire Splan
Acquisitions Coordinator	**Indexer**
Bridget Thoreson	Judy Davis
Editorial Supervisor	**Production Supervisor**
David E. Fogarty	Pamela A. Pelton
Project Manager	**Composition**
Patricia Wallenburg	TypeWriting
Copy Editor	**Art Director, Cover**
Jim Madru	Jeff Weeks

To my mother, Mythili;
my wife, Kanchan;
and my daughters, Tanu and Madhu

CONTENTS

FOREWORD

Throughout my 30-year career in the aerospace industry, I have witnessed unparalleled technological advancements in aeronautical systems and capabilities, as well as ground-breaking changes in our business operations. The defense technology and industrial base is now a global network with global suppliers, and our challenge is to manage the resources, skills, competencies, and tools within the network through all phases of the product life cycle.

As enterprises such as ours strive to create and deliver competitive products in this global marketplace, it is more critical than ever to develop and maintain a lean supply chain. But what is the definition of a *lean* supply chain, and how can an organization achieve this ideal? Dr. Srinivasan's book, *Building Lean Supply Chains with the Theory of Constraints*, answers this question and more because he provides an in-depth look at today's lean supply chains and offers a detailed plan on how to realize them.

Outlining a seven-step roadmap that enterprises can use on their lean supply chain journey, Dr. Srinivasan applies Theory of Constraints (TOC) concepts to supply chain management in a thought-provoking and pragmatic way. The book intimately explores building and managing a lean supply chain from an operations and logistics perspective, with Lean and TOC principles combined. Not only does Dr. Srinivasan tackle the importance of systems thinking, but he also applies TOC philosophies to throughput, meeting and anticipating customer needs, delivery requirements, collaboration, and improved visibility of the supply chain, among others.

As Dr. Srinivasan expounds on his seven-step roadmap, he lays the groundwork for what a lean supply chain should look like. Weaving in 16 Lean Supply Chain Principles, the result is a framework that enterprises can use to create and manage their lean supply chains.

In this book, lean supply chains are not assayed from one angle but are considered from multiple vantage points. The initial chapters investigate the hurdles and structure of the lean supply chain, introducing the Theory of

Constraints to enhance Lean supply chain performance. Throughout the book, Dr. Srinivasan leverages real-world scenarios to drive home the necessity of merging Lean and TOC principles.

While this book looks at an integrated approach to supply chain management and sets the expectation that industries partner with the supply chain, Dr. Srinivasan's vision never loses sight of the customer. At Lockheed Martin, our customer is our focus, and we realize that collaborative relationships are the key to our current and future successes, especially when building fifth-generation aircraft such as the F-35 with a supply chain that spans the globe. As we learn more about these relationships in the global market in which we work, we can better understand our customers' needs and plan for tomorrow.

This book is a thoughtful and comprehensive examination of how changing our views on customer needs, supply chain operations, and logistics can produce tangible, meaningful results. It is a guide not only for the supply chain management student or professional but also for anyone interested in learning key supply chain management, operation, and logistics principles.

RALPH D. HEATH
Executive Vice President of Aeronautics
Lockheed Martin Corporation

PREFACE

In the early 1990s, I began to teach in executive MBA programs and shorter executive development courses offered through the Center for Executive Education at the University of Tennessee. Having worked in the automobile industry for many years, I was eager to present cutting-edge techniques in my seminars. In particular, I wanted participants to be aware of two powerful techniques that were relatively new at that time: the Theory of Constraints (TOC) and Lean.

At that time, however, most business schools were still teaching traditional disaggregated topics such as location planning, capacity planning, and materials requirement planning. These topics were inadequate to equip professionals to manage enterprises in an increasingly competitive environment. I was unable to find a single book that covered the topics I was interested in teaching. Therefore, in 2004, I published a book entitled, *Streamlined: 14 Principles for Building and Managing the Lean Supply Chain*. *Streamlined* showed how managers could exploit the synergy between TOC and Lean to enhance the flow of products in their supply chain. The concepts and principles from the book were incorporated subsequently in numerous executive MBA programs and executive development courses.

More recently, the general consensus among the participants attending these programs is that the principles of Lean are now fairly well known. Lean applications have extended well beyond the automotive industry to other industries, such as health care and aerospace, to the extent that it almost has become commoditized. TOC, on the other hand, is still a relatively lesser known body of knowledge. The participants attending my programs invariably identify the TOC sessions as adding the most value to their learning experience. In particular, the participants want to know how to apply these TOC concepts to manage the supply chain. Such feedback encouraged me to write this book.

This book, *Building Lean Supply Chains with the Theory of Constraints*, stresses systems thinking. It uniquely integrates TOC with Lean, illustrating how these two philosophies complement and reinforce each other to create a smooth flow of goods and services through the supply chain.

What Is Unique About This Book?

While *Streamlined* was the first book to explain what a lean supply chain is in depth, it did not fully tap into the vast body of knowledge offered by TOC. TOC is arguably the world's best kept secret for managing businesses from a systems perspective. Until the early 2000s, most of the significant developments in TOC were understood and used by a few select experts in the field. The TOC body of knowledge has since become more widely disseminated in a variety of ways, through conferences, Webinars, and the Internet. This book applies the TOC body of knowledge to building and managing the lean supply chain.

This book still integrates the concepts and principles of TOC and Lean, but the emphasis is on TOC. Most of the chapters draw on the tools and techniques of TOC: Throughput Accounting, Drum-Buffer-Rope, TOC in Distribution and Replenishment, the Thinking Process, and Critical Chain Project Management. All these topics are presented in the context of building and managing the lean supply chain. The concepts presented in this book provide a clear understanding of where to apply Six Sigma and Lean methods to achieve true bottom-line results.

Flow of Material

Supply chains can be addressed from many functional perspectives— financial, marketing, operations, and logistics. This book is concerned with operations and logistics. The flow of material is organized around 16 Lean Supply Chain Principles. The first chapter presents a Lean Supply Chain Roadmap that outlines the seven steps organizations can use to build and manage the lean supply chain. Each one of these steps is presented in seven separate chapters, with each chapter presenting two of the 16 Lean Supply Chain Principles. The final chapter shows how implementation of the lean supply chain or any other project, for that matter, can be executed most effectively using a technique popularly known as *Critical Chain Project Management*, which is the approach prescribed by TOC for project management.

Who Should Read This Book

Although the original intent was to write a book for MBA students, both full time and executive, the book evolved rapidly to one a professional could use readily. It can be a guide for logistics and operations professionals to better manage their activities within the broader context of the supply chain with which they have to deal. At the same time, the book still should be valuable to students in an executive MBA or similar professional program that offers courses in operations, logistics, and supply chain management. It is also a useful reference book for educators, consultants, and practitioners who interact with any element in the supply chain.

MANDYAM M. SRINIVASAN

ACKNOWLEDGMENTS

This book is the product of my interactions with many industry professionals, colleagues, and graduate students over the past decade. These individuals have generously shared their knowledge and enriched my understanding of the supply chain. In particular, one individual, Dr. Eliyahu Goldratt, has profoundly influenced my knowledge and understanding of the concepts covered in this book.

I wish to extend special thanks to Dr. Ken Gilbert and Dr. James Holt for their insights and comments that have helped shaped some of the chapters in this book. Thanks to Dr. Dave Narasimhan for his very generous help with the figures in this book and to Dr. James Reeve for his permission to use the Integrity Motors case. My daughters, Tanushree and Madhushree, and my colleagues, Dr. Charles Noon, Kitty Cornett, and Michael May, deserve thanks for patiently reading the manuscript and providing many helpful comments and suggestions. Thanks are also due to Judy Bass, Senior Editor at McGraw-Hill Professional, for her support throughout the entire project.

Finally, and most important, I would like to thank my wife, Kanchan, who showed a great deal of patience and understanding during the past 18 months that I have worked on this project. She has been a constant source of support and encouragement.

THE SIXTEEN LEAN SUPPLY CHAIN PRINCIPLES

Lean Supply Chain Principle 1

Improving the performance of every subsystem in isolation will not improve system performance. Improvements in subsystem performance must be gauged only through their impact on the whole system.

Lean Supply Chain Principle 2

Focus on improving the performance of the Lean supply chain—but do not ignore the supply chain's business ecosystem.

Lean Supply Chain Principle 3

Time lost at a bottleneck resource results in a loss of output for the whole enterprise (entire supply chain). Time saved at a nonbottleneck resource is a mirage.

Lean Supply Chain Principle 4

Decisions should be based on a throughput world perspective. While enterprises should try to increase throughput, decrease investment, and decrease operating expenses, the focus must be on improving throughput.

Lean Supply Chain Principle 5

Focus on customer needs and process considerations when designing the product. Enterprises can gain tremendous competitive advantage through best-in-class practices that cut across industries.

Lean Supply Chain Principle 6

Maximize external variety with minimal internal variety. It is desirable to maintain inventories in an undifferentiated form for as long as it is economically feasible to do so.

Lean Supply Chain Principle 7

The role of operations strategy is to provide the enterprise with the ability to cope with changing customer preferences. Products and processes should be designed to promote strategic flexibility.

Lean Supply Chain Principle 8

Buffer the variation in demand with capacity, not inventory.

Lean Supply Chain Principle 9

Develop partnerships and alliances with members of the supply chain strategically, with the goal of delivering goods and services as quickly and efficiently as possible.

Lean Supply Chain Principle 10

Formulate supply chain performance metrics that focus on improving throughput.

Lean Supply Chain Principle 11

Use forecasts to plan and pull to execute. A system that reacts to pull signals will have less variation than a comparable system that adopts a push mode of operation.

Lean Supply Chain Principle 12

Reduce variation in the system. Reduced variation allows the supply chain to operate with higher throughput, lower investment, and lower operating expense.

Lean Supply Chain Principle 13

Focus on bottleneck resources because they control the flow. Synchronize flow by first scheduling the bottleneck resources on the most productive products; and then schedule nonbottleneck resources to support the bottleneck resources.

Lean Supply Chain Principle 14

Do not focus on balancing capacities. Focus on synchronizing the flow.

Lean Supply Chain Principle 15

Focus on project completion times rather than task completion times. To ensure timely project completions, buffer the project, not the task.

Lean Supply Chain Principle 16

To reduce bad multitasking, let the bottleneck resource pace the release of projects into the system.

CHAPTER 1

The Lean Supply Chain Roadmap

Are organizations in a better position to build and manage supply chains,* operating them more efficiently now than ever before? Or have some organizations regressed—taken a step backwards—with respect to how they build and manage their supply chains? If such a regression has taken place, how can these organizations detect it and take corrective steps?

The answers to these questions depend on your perspective. With advances in information technology (IT) and the Internet, all enterprises in the supply chain now have the ability to determine the end user's actual demand and to plan their activities accordingly. Cutting-edge management techniques have led to a quantum reduction in the time it takes an organization to fulfill customer demand. Advances in logistics have achieved similar reductions in the time products spend in storage and in transit. There is a perceptible change among supply chain members to set aside traditional arm's-length relationships and build long-term partnership arrangements in industries as diverse as aerospace, grocery retailing, apparel manufacturing, automobile manufacturing, and health care. Therefore, one answer to the questions posed earlier is, "Yes, we are now in a better position to build and manage lean supply chains."

Another answer is that for many organizations, supply chain management has taken a step backwards. These organizations are squandering some of the benefits that can be gained from improved technologies

---

*The *supply chain* for an organization is the network of enterprises that the organization uses to deliver products to the consumer. It includes the organization itself, all its upstream suppliers, any downstream enterprises that may process the products further, and possibly a distribution system that may consist of distributors, wholesalers, retailers, and logistics providers.

and techniques. Before we discuss why this is happening, let's first define the term *lean supply chain*.

A lean supply chain exemplifies the behavior of an ideal supply chain, a supply chain in which key processes are integrated among all the supply chain enterprises, and the final product or service is delivered to the end user rapidly, economically, and in a seamless manner. Since lean supply chains can better adapt to changing customer needs and deliver products quickly, the enterprises in the lean supply chain should expect a superior financial performance relative to their competitors.

A 2008 study jointly conducted by McKinsey & Company and the Georgia Institute of Technology[1] reported that organizations adopting key supply chain practices are 1.7 times more likely to have strong distribution and logistics cost performance. To quantify the impact of this finding, consider the fact that logistics-driven costs accounted for 9.22 percent of the gross domestic product (GDP) for the United States, on average, during the years 2000 to 2009.[2] Since the GDP for the United States in the year 2009 was $14.12 trillion, even a 5 percent reduction in logistics costs that year would have resulted in a saving of *$65 billion*—this is not small change. If other supply chain costs such as order processing, materials acquisition and inventory, supply chain planning, supply chain financing, and information management are considered, the potential savings from effective supply chain management would be much higher.

A detailed 2010 study from Michigan State University (MSU) classified some organizations as "top supply chain management" (top SCM) organizations.[3] The top SCM classification was based on data gathered from at least four different sources, including the AMR Research Top 25/50 Rankings from 2004 to 2008 and the Global Survey of Supply Chain Progress (2004–2008) jointly conducted by the journal *Supply Chain Management Review*, CSC, and Michigan State University. The MSU study classified organizations that appeared in at least two of these sources during the 2004 to 2008 time frame as top SCM organizations.

Next, the MSU study identified the competitors to the top SCM organizations based on the Yahoo Finance Competitor Analysis and Hoover's Competitive Report and compared the financial performance of the top SCM organizations against that of their competitors. Among other measures, the study found that the top SCM organizations had an 11 percent return-on-assets (ROA) on average compared with a 5 percent ROA for their competitors. The top SCM organizations had an average 10 percent net margin compared with 7 percent for their competitors.

Any enterprise would like to operate within a lean supply chain and to share in its benefits. However, building and managing lean supply chains present serious challenges—challenges that are discussed next.

Challenges to the Lean Supply Chain

Building and managing a lean supply chain poses a challenge owing to the highly interconnected nature of the activities in the supply chain. The present business environment is also significantly more challenging than the business environment of the *production-centric* era that prevailed for the greater part of the twentieth century. In the production-centric era, demand for goods and services often outstripped production capacity. The producers held the most clout in the supply chain, charged what the market would bear, and operated businesses to maximize the use of their own scarce capacity. Lack of global competition created, in effect, domestic cartels in many industries that dictated the price the consumer paid for the product. Organizations were able to run their businesses in relative isolation, formulating strategies that optimized their own operations with little regard for how these decisions affected other enterprises in their supply chain.

In the *customer-centric* business environment that characterizes the twenty-first century, production capacity exceeds customer demand for many industries. Prices are now determined by a different set of competitive market forces than what existed when capacity constrained the sales volume. Managers in today's global business world are well aware of the fierce competitive environment in which they must manage their enterprises. Consumers are demanding better products, and they want them cheaper and faster. To remain competitive, organizations must respond to these customer demands in a world where product life cycles are shrinking. Not only must organizations excel at *producing* the goods or services in which they are engaged, but they also must excel at *delivering* those products quickly and efficiently throughout the supply chain and ultimately to the end user (the consumer).

Let's revisit one of the questions posed at the start of this chapter. In this customer-centric era, are supply chains more efficient and responsive than they were in the past? For a large number of organizations, the answer is no, for several reasons.

The Internet and Commoditization

Consider first the potential benefits provided by the Internet and advances in IT. The Internet has provided organizations with visibility on both customer demand and the movement of goods in the supply chain. However, the Internet has proven to be a double-edged sword for these organizations because it has also enabled price-sensitive customers to easily compare prices for any product or service. Most of these products and services thus have become commoditized to some extent, resulting in some undesirable consequences, one of which is the manner in which organizations have responded to this commoditization.

Faced with increased global competition for these products and services, many organizations have resorted to cost-cutting efforts to meet Wall Street expectations on gross margins and quarterly profit and loss reports. No doubt costs must be controlled, but if cost considerations *dominate* decision making, the effectiveness of the supply chain or the product-delivery system can deteriorate. It can lead to a paradoxical situation where costs will, in fact, increase if all consequences are not carefully considered.

For example, to control costs, many organizations pursue labor and material arbitrage by *outsourcing* or *offshoring** operations. Offshoring typically increases the length of the supply chain. Offshoring may also be accompanied by an increase in the number of links in the supply chain. The net result is increased supply chain complexity. Complex supply chains typically result in costs that are either hidden or, in the words of American statistician Dr. Edwards Deming, "unknown and unknowable."[4] For example:

▲ The decision process cannot ignore the impact of outsourcing on production costs for products still manufactured in-house because these products would now bear the overhead costs previously absorbed by the outsourced product.

▲ Even if the organization carries some inventory of the outsourced product, there is a possible loss of responsiveness. The loss of responsiveness can result from the additional delays involved in trans-

---

*Both terms refer to the practice of contracting with another organization or person to perform a certain activity. Offshoring is a special case of outsourcing in which the activity is executed in another country.

porting the product, not to mention possible delays in clearing customs if these products are offshored. This strategy also makes the organization more dependent on long-term forecasts and vulnerable to the inevitable demand cycles.

▲ Since the organization is no longer intimately involved in manufacturing the product, there is a real danger that the organization will be unable to manufacture it in-house at a later date if the situation requires it. This situation is analogous to the case where the muscles in your body atrophy if they are not used.

Furthermore, managers of such complex supply chains now have to manage their service providers more effectively to make these hidden costs as low as possible while at the same time making them more predictable.

A complex global supply chain with multiple links can result in other unintended consequences. For example, members in the supply chain may not know how their products are used by their downstream partners. In one instance, a chip manufacturer thought its consignment was destined for DVD players, but the chip was instead diverted by the forwarding agent to be used in digital picture frames. Assuming that the chip worked on the digital picture frame, the customers may have benefited from this error because they got a DVD player chip for the price of a digital picture frame chip. However, the supply chain had to bear the difference in the production costs for the DVD player chips and the digital picture frame chips. Such a lack of clarity—and the accompanying costs—offsets the increased visibility provided by the Internet and lends support to the argument that some supply chains are regressing with respect to their management practices.

Manufacturing Practices

Just as the Internet has proven to be a double-edged sword for organizations, so has advances in manufacturing practices such as Just-In-Time (JIT) and Lean management. No doubt these practices have helped to remove waste from various segments in the supply chain and have resulted in faster response times at those segments, but with faster response times comes the pressure to take inventory out of the supply chain. When the safety net of "just-in-case" inventory is no longer in place, these supply chains now run a more substantial risk of performance failures or shortfalls. This problem is compounded in the more complex global supply chain. The recession of 2008–2009 exposed the weaknesses of these JIT supply chains. When demand contracted, many organizations were forced to guess at demand for their products in a shrinking market and either ended up carrying huge amounts of inventory or suffering severe stock-outs.

This discussion on Lean management is not intended to suggest that JIT supply chains do not work. It is also not intended to convey a message that removing just-in-case inventory is always a bad idea. Rather, it is intended to point out that the decision on where inventories should be reduced must be made with a systems perspective. In Chapter 2 I will introduce a management philosophy known as the *Theory of Constraints* (TOC). The TOC philosophy approaches decision making with a systems perspective, and Chapters 3 and 4 will show how this philosophy can be applied to position inventories at the right places. I will also show how the management philosophy popularly known as *Lean* can work in conjunction with TOC to produce some powerful synergies.

At this stage I will simply note that as supply chain management practices continue to evolve (or de-evolve, depending on your perspective), some fundamental principles for managing the lean supply chain are often forgotten or simply set aside, especially if cost considerations take precedence in decision making. The purpose of this book is to present or reiterate these principles. These principles are grounded in *systems thinking*. Systems thinking is based on the notion that the individual elements in a system are best understood and managed in the context of their relationships with each other and with the system as a whole rather than in isolation. The importance of systems thinking is underscored by a phenomenon known as the *bullwhip effect*.

The Bullwhip Effect

What does the telecommunications equipment industry have in common with the pasta and disposable diaper manufacturing industries? The answer is that all these industries have experienced the *bullwhip effect*. The bullwhip effect describes a phenomenon wherein minor fluctuations in demand at the end user or the retail level result in huge variations in demand at upstream organizations in the supply chain.

In the year 2000, the major telecom equipment manufacturers, including Cisco and Lucent, arrived at demand forecasts that showed increased demand for networking gear and wireless equipment. These manufacturers asked their suppliers to supply components and raw materials as fast as possible, providing the suppliers with an assurance that they would be paid for excess supplies. One of the suppliers, Solectron, supplied products to each one of these manufacturers. Solectron knew that the orders added up to a demand for telecommunications equipment that was unreasonably high, even under a best-case scenario. However, it was forced to produce at maximum throughput to meet demands from its individual customers.

In 2001, "irrational exuberance" collided with the reality of the dot-com implosion. The demand that was forecast by the software did not materialize. Instead, Cisco was forced to write off $2.2 billion in inventory and lay off 8,500 people. Many suppliers to Cisco were left with excessive inventory that had been built in response to demand from Cisco and other customers. Solectron alone was stuck with $4.7 billion in inventory. Cisco and Solectron were victims of the bullwhip effect.

It is arguable that the problems faced by Cisco and Solectron were precipitated by the dot-com implosion, but their experiences are mirrored by enterprises in almost every industry, although often not so dramatically. Enterprises experience huge variations in inventory levels, orders, and shipments at each step in the chain, with the variations typically more pronounced the further upstream the enterprise is from the end user. And it turns out that much of the demand variation is caused *by the supply chain itself*, not by the customer.

Consider the food industry and the experience of Barilla SpA, the world's largest pasta manufacturer. Barilla SpA sells to a wide range of retailers through a distribution network. In 1989, an analysis of the demand for dry food pasta at Barilla SpA's distribution centers and factories revealed extremely high variation in demand. The variation in demand observed was all the more remarkable considering that the underlying demand for pasta in Italy is fairly level.

The fast-moving consumer goods industry displays similar behavior. Consider the production and distribution of diapers. Given the consistency in diaper demand, it would be reasonable to expect the diaper supply chain to operate efficiently. Indeed, when logistics executives at Proctor & Gamble examined the demand for its diapers at retail stores, it found a relatively level demand. However, the orders Proctor & Gamble placed on its suppliers showed considerable variation.

The term, bullwhip effect, owes its origin to the fact that a slight motion of the handle of a bullwhip can make the tip of the whip thrash wildly at speeds up to 900 miles per hour, about 20 percent faster than the speed of sound, creating a sonic boom (the crack of the whip). In the context of a supply chain, the bullwhip effect manifests through increasing demand variability as you move upstream in the supply chain. Small changes to the customer demand on the retailer are magnified as the demand information is passed up the supply chain, creating increasingly higher variation in the orders received by upstream suppliers.

The bullwhip effect produces tremendous inefficiencies in the supply chain. It results in excessive inventory investment, poor customer service, lost revenues, misguided capacity plans, and ineffective transportation and production schedules. Many enterprises have gained a significant competitive advantage by understanding the underlying causes of the bullwhip effect and working with their supply chain partners to reduce it. The joint effort between supply chain partners results in reduced inventories and a supply chain that is more responsive to customer demand.

In some cases, organizations have even added inventories in a planned manner to ward off any supply chain disruptions that might result from the bullwhip effect. In 2009, Caterpillar acted proactively to restock its inventories to meet an increased demand for construction and mining equipment in the following years. Caterpillar asked its steel suppliers to plan for a 2010 demand[5] that would double the amount demanded in 2009.

Caterpillar decided on this strategy even though its own sales were very unlikely to change by a corresponding amount during the first half of the year 2010 because it wanted the suppliers to increase production gradually and thereby ameliorate the bullwhip effect. Caterpillar also visited with key suppliers in late 2009 to ensure that the suppliers had the resources to boost output quickly. In extreme cases, Caterpillar even helped some suppliers get financing.

Caterpillar's strategy appears to have worked successfully. The organization had nine straight three-month rolling periods of growth during the last nine months of 2010. Caterpillar reported that construction sales rose 49 percent in the three months ended January 2011, driven by a continuing rebound in North American demand.

The beer game simulation presents a very effective way to demonstrate the bullwhip effect and to showcase its root causes.

The Beer Game

The beer game was developed in the early 1960s as part of MIT Professor Jay Forrester's research on industrial dynamics,[6] and it illustrated the challenges faced in managing supply chains. The beer game is played assuming a serial supply chain consisting of four enterprises engaged in the production and delivery of a single blend of beer: a factory, a distributor, a wholesaler, and a retailer. Figure 1.1 illustrates this linear arrangement. The goal of each enterprise is to manage the demand placed by its customer. Each enterprise in the supply chain is managed by one or two players. Participants are usually told that the game will run for 50 weeks, although the game is terminated well before that time to avoid end-gaming strategies by the players.

Each week, an enterprise in the supply chain receives orders from its downstream customer and places orders with its upstream supplier. At each stage there is a lag between when an order is placed and when it can be filled, and there are costs for storage and rush orders. Players are not allowed to share any information beyond what is conveyed by orders and shipments. All four enterprises in the supply chain have to decide what to order from their upstream supplier based on the orders they receive from their downstream customer and their inventory on hand. There is a two-week delay before an order placed by an enterprise reaches its upstream supplier. Similarly, there is a two-week manufacturing lead time from the time an enterprise receives an order until a shipment against this order reaches the downstream customer. In effect, there is at least a four-week lead time from the time an order is placed by an enterprise on its upstream supplier until the time it receives a shipment against this order.

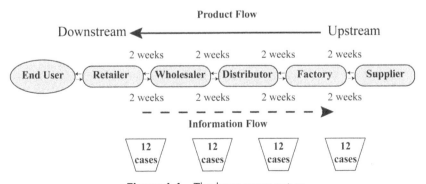

Figure 1.1   The beer game setup.

At the start of the simulation, the system is in a steady state with the consumer (end user) buying four cases of beer each week, whereas each enterprise is ordering and receiving four cases of beer each week. Each enterprise is holding an inventory of 12 cases of beer. The retailer's demand is revealed at the start of each week—for the first few weeks, this demand is steady at four cases per week. The demand on the other enterprises is determined by the orders working their way upstream—initially four cases per week. At the end of each week, each position in the supply chain decides the number of cases it wishes to order from its upstream supplier.

The steady state is disrupted in week 5 at which time the demand by the consumer increases to eight cases per week and is held steady thereafter. Even this one-time step change is enough to cause significant problems upstream. As the change in demand propagates upstream, shortages or surpluses accumulate at each stage in the supply chain. As indicated in Figure 1.2, orders and inventories spike wildly. These spikes become magnified as you move upstream.

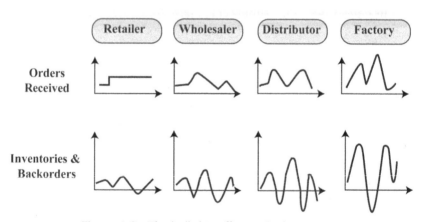

Figure 1.2 The bullwhip effect in the beer game.

Analysis of the Bullwhip Effect in the Beer Game*

A familiar theme in postgame discussions is that a major cause for the chaos in the supply chain is the lack of visibility. Participants work with limited

---

*This discussion is based on a paper by K. Gilbert (2003), "The Lean Enterprise," in *The Management of Strategy in the Marketplace*, E. R. Cadotte and H. J. Bruce (eds.), Thomson-Southwestern, Mason, OH.

information because no communication is permitted between the enterprises in the supply chain. In the absence of communication, each participant acts in his or her own self-interest and on the basis of his or her own forecasts. The one thing you know for sure about a forecast is that it's wrong; the one thing you never know is just *how* wrong. If participants have better visibility over the entire supply chain, chances are that they would do much better. Therefore, a commonly held belief that participants have after the beer game is that the bullwhip effect is mainly due to lack of point-of-sale (POS) data and/or good forecasts. In fact, obtaining POS data and good forecasts is often cited as the primary reasons why the enterprises in the supply chain should collaborate.

On the contrary, it turns out that the primary culprit for the bullwhip effect is *lead time*. Even when there are no breakdowns in communication, one still feels the bullwhip effect owing to procurement and manufacturing delays. This is not to say that POS information and improved forecasting have little impact. In fact, reducing lead time, in combination with improved visibility along the supply chain, can affect the bullwhip effect significantly and positively.

So what exactly is the impact each of these variables has on the bullwhip effect? It is instructive to analyze the beer game using a quantitative approach that identifies the impact of these variables more precisely. As discussed earlier, the beer game starts with each enterprise carrying 12 cases of beer and experiencing a demand of 4 cases of beer each week. The lead time for each enterprise to receive a shipment against an order is 4 weeks.

At the start of the simulation, the system is in steady state. The equilibrium then is disrupted, and the end-user demand increases to 8 cases in week 5. Consider the impact of the increased demand on the retailer. The retailer begins this week with 12 cases, receives 4 cases, but sells 8 cases, and ends the week with only 8 cases in inventory. The retailer now must decide how many cases to order.

Suppose that each player's ordering policy is based on two very simple but logical rules: one rule to provide the forecast and another rule to determine the order quantity.

1. *The forecast rule:* The forecast of the weekly demand for each of the next four weeks is the average of the weekly demand over the four most recent weeks.

2. *The order-quantity rule:* Based on this forecast, the amount ordered is just enough to replenish the ending inventory (four weeks from now when the order arrives) to a target of 12 cases.

Based on rule 1, the retailer forecasts his weekly demand to be 5 cases per week for each of the next four weeks: $(4 + 4 + 4 + 8) \div 4 = 5$.

Rule 2 requires that the retailer's inventory on hand plus the inventory on order be sufficient to cover the forecasted demand for the next four weeks and have 12 cases left in inventory. Therefore, the retailer must order the sum of the inventory target (12) plus the forecasted demand for the next four weeks minus the inventory that he already has on hand or on order:

Order = inventory target (12 cases) + forecasted demand for next four weeks (5 cases each) − current inventory (8 cases) − orders already placed for the next three weeks (4 cases each) = 12 + (5 + 5 + 5 + 5) − 8 − (4 + 4 + 4) = 12 + 20 − 8 − 12 = 12

The retailer thus will place an order for 12 cases on the wholesaler.

A fundamental insight: The consumer demand increased by 100 percent (from 4 cases per week to 8 cases per week), but the retailer's order to the wholesaler increased by 200 percent (from 4 cases per week to 12 cases for the following week). The retailer thus *doubled the variation in demand.* This increase in variation is due to the four-week lead time required to react to the forecasted increase in demand.

Next consider the wholesaler. Assume that the wholesaler behaves in an identical manner as the retailer except that the wholesaler's demand is created by the retailer's orders. Initially, the wholesaler receives 4 cases per week, sells 4 cases per week, and ends each week with 12 cases. Then the wholesaler unexpectedly receives an order from the retailer for 12 cases. The wholesaler will begin the week with 12 cases, receive 4 cases, sell 12 cases, and end with an inventory of 4 cases. The wholesaler uses the four-week average forecasting rule and the inventory target of 12 cases to arrive at the following demand forecast for each of the next four weeks: the wholesaler's forecast is $(4 + 4 + 4 + 12) \div 4 = 6$ cases per week. Hence the wholesaler's order will be:

Order = inventory target + forecasted demand for the next four weeks − current inventory − orders already placed for the next three weeks = 12 + (6 + 6 + 6 + 6) − 4 − (4 + 4 + 4) = 20

Thus the wholesaler's order on the distributor has increased from 4 cases per week to 20 cases the following week, an increase of 400 percent. Following the forecasting rule and order-quantity rule, the distributor reacts to the wholesaler's order of 20 cases by ordering 36 cases, an increase of 800 percent. The factory responds to this order by ordering enough raw materials from its supplier to make 68 cases, an increase of 1,600 percent.

The variation is thus doubled at each stage. Of the 64-case increase in the factory's orders, *only 4 cases* were directly attributable to a change in consumer demand. The lead times present in this value stream created *94 percent of the variation observed in the factory's orders.*

The results of this analysis are summarized as follows:

Lead times significantly exacerbate the bullwhip effect. For the beer game with a four-week lead time and orders placed using the forecasting rule described in this section, the variation in orders grows by a factor of 2 at each stage. In other words, the *increase in variation at each stage is multiplicative.* The computations presented earlier shows that the variation in orders grows by a factor of 1.25 at each stage.

The preceding discussion also shows that a moving-average forecast does not reduce the bullwhip effect. In fact *the bullwhip effect is present even when there is perfect information about the present and the future* and this information is *instantaneously available* to all enterprises in the supply chain, as discussed next.

The Impact of Forecasting and POS Data

Assume the same beer game scenario as before except that each stage is instantly made aware of the consumer's orders. Assume, too, that the consumer orders 4 cases in weeks 1 through 4 and 8 cases in week 5, as before. However, to enable a proper comparison with the analysis in the preceding section, we will assume that the perfect information scenario reveals that the consumer demand for the following weeks (week 6 onward) is 5 cases of beer. This assumption allows a fair comparison because the forecasting method used in the preceding section predicts a steady demand on the retailer for 5 cases of beer in the following weeks. We also assume that this demand information is conveyed instantaneously upstream. In order to keep the comparison fair, we assume that the lead time to react to an order is four weeks at each stage.

Following exactly the same approach as before, the retailer will order 12 cases of beer from the wholesaler in week 5 in order to bring the retailer's inventory back to the target level of 12 cases of beer. That is, the 100 percent increase in demand on the retailer translates to a 200 percent increase in demand on the wholesaler over the previous week, as before. Since the retailer sees the demand for the following weeks to be 5 cases of beer, the retailer tells the wholesaler to expect a demand of 5 cases for each of the following weeks. The wholesaler thus sees an order of 12 cases this week, is also aware that the retailer will order 5 cases each week thereafter, and is currently receiving 4 cases of beer from the distributor for the next four weeks. Thus, to bring up the target inventory to 12 cases, the wholesaler orders 16 cases of beer from the distributor. In other words, a 100 percent increase in the demand on the retailer translates to a 300 percent increase in demand on the distributor over the previous week. Similarly, the factory will receive an order for 20 cases, a 400 percent increase in demand over the previous week, whereas the raw materials supplier will receive an order for 24 cases, a 500 percent increase in demand over the previous week.

This example, which assumes perfect information about the present and the future, would require POS data to be available at all stages in the supply chain *and* a perfect forecasting mechanism. Admittedly, this is not a very likely scenario. The point of the example is to show that the bullwhip effect is still present even with such perfect information, albeit to a smaller extent. With such perfect information, the variation in the orders generated at successive stages does not grow multiplicatively. Instead, *it grows additively* by 100 percent at each successive stage.

A variant on the beer game, the *near-beer game*, demonstrates that POS data and good forecasting tools do not eliminate the bullwhip effect. In the near-beer game, the supply chain consists of three enterprises, a supplier, a brewery, and a customer. Participants manage the brewery, and only one type of beer is brewed. There is a delay of one week to receive raw materials from the supplier. It takes one week to brew the beer and one week to deliver it to the customer. The system is initially in steady state with the customer ordering 10 cases of beer each week. The brewery has 10 cases in inventory, 10 cases of beer brewing, and 10 cases of raw materials arriving from the supplier. In week 2, demand increases to 15 cases per week and remains at 15 cases thereafter. The game ends when the supply chain is back in equilibrium with 15 cases of beer. In the near-beer game, the brewery has perfect information about the demand for beer, but the bullwhip effect does not disappear.

The near-beer game imparts all the lessons conveyed by the beer game. It also teaches one additional lesson that the original game does not: the bullwhip effect is present even if there is perfect information about the future, information that is shared among all channel partners. Note that having perfect information about the future is even better than having POS data and excellent forecasting tools. The near-beer game thus demonstrates that the bullwhip effect is best addressed by reductions in the manufacturing and order lead times.

The Impact of Lead Times

The analysis provided so far indicates that lead times affect the variation in demand in a multiplicative manner. Hence the focus in the supply chain should be on reducing lead times. By minimizing lead times, we find that operating costs decline because less capacity is needed to handle demand fluctuations. Lead-time reduction also results in lower inventory. The well-known *Little's Law* provides a precise relationship between the lead time and inventory*:

> The lead time in the system is directly proportional to the inventory in the system. In particular, the average system lead time is equal to the average inventory in the system divided by the system throughput.

The implication of Little's Law is that when inventory in the supply chain is high, then lead times increase. Conversely, longer lead times in the supply chain result in more inventories in the pipeline. This problematic and cyclic relationship between lead times and inventory provides a powerful reason for reducing lead times.

---

*An intuitive explanation of Little's Law proceeds as follows: Suppose that each job requires an average of t time units of service. The throughput rate TH, which is the number of jobs processed per unit time, is $TH = 1/t$. Suppose that there are W units in the system, on average. The average lead time LT for a new order will be the time it takes to clear the W units in the system, so $LT = Wt$. This gives $W = TH \times LT$.

Ideally, if lead times were small and every enterprise in the supply chain could react to a *pull** signal, it would be possible to run the supply chain with near-zero inventory. Each enterprise in the supply chain would wait for its customer to place an order before it ordered parts from its suppliers and would begin production on the order only when the parts arrive. Thus they would not need to carry any raw materials, work-in-process, or finished goods inventory. In turn, the lower inventories in the pipeline usually result in lower lead times, generating a virtuous cycle. Needless to say, the ideal is unlikely to be realized in practice for most supply chains unless lead times are reduced.

Reducing lead times has an additional benefit. Suppose that the manufacturer in a supply chain operates in a build-to-stock (BTS) environment. If the manufacturer requires four weeks to build products, then the supply chain must maintain at least four weeks of inventory. The implication is that the manufacturer should build to a forecast four weeks out into the future. However, if the lead time is two weeks, then the manufacturer only needs to build to a forecast two weeks out into the future.

Consider the implications. The longer the time horizon for the forecast, the less reliable it is. Thus a forecast made for a demand that is two weeks out into the future is clearly more reliable than a forecast made for a demand that is four weeks out into the future.

Building to a forecast always carries an element of speculation. The enterprise that builds products based on forecasts typically pads the forecasted demand in order to buffer against the uncertainty in the forecast. Padding further distances the amount produced from true customer demand, adding to the variation in the supply chain. The longer the lead time, the more padding there is. Hence, as lead times decrease, the demands of elements in the supply chain converge more closely to a pure pull strategy with no variation added by the supply chain.

Lessons from the Beer Game

A key learning point from the beer game is that *structure drives behavior.* How the supply chain is constructed largely determines how it will perform.

---

*A pull signal is triggered by an actual demand from a customer. A pull system—a system that reacts to pull signals—waits for this demand signal before committing resources to production, instead of building products based on forecasts.

The structural framework for the beer game has the following components, all of which play a role in magnifying the bullwhip effect:

▲ *Lack of visibility along the supply chain*—no POS data and a lack of coordination or communication up and down the supply chain
▲ *Long lead times for material and information flow*
▲ *Many stages in the supply chain*
▲ *Lack of pull signals*
▲ *Order batching*
▲ *Price discounts and promotions*

The observation that structure determines behavior is not a novel concept. Deming alluded to this concept when he said that management must take the responsibility for poor performance and take steps to reduce process variation instead of blaming the workers for poor quality. However, certain behavioral phenomena, not necessarily driven by the structure, also contribute to the bullwhip effect:

▲ *Overreaction to backlogs*
▲ *Withholding orders in an attempt to reduce inventory*
▲ *Hoarding*—where customers order more than they need because they are anticipating a price increase or because the supplier has a promotional sale
▲ *Shortage gaming*—where customers order more than they need because they do not have faith in the supplier's ability to deliver quality products and/or because they do not expect the supplier to supply the entire order
▲ *Demand forecast inaccuracies*—where a customer adds a certain percentage to the demand estimates, resulting in reduced visibility of true customer demand
▲ *Attempting to meet end-of-month, -quarter, or -year metrics*

In the beer game, the bullwhip effect is observed even though the supply chain deals with a single product and there is just a one-time spike in demand. In the real world, enterprises usually deal with multiple products with demands that vary from period to period. Furthermore, in the real world, there are many other factors to consider. Quality problems and unplanned events such as strikes and accidents induce additional variation in the supply chain, exacerbating the bullwhip effect. It is easy to see why the bullwhip effect is present in almost any industry.

So how do we mitigate the bullwhip effect? The analysis of the bullwhip effect shows that long lead times and the lack of POS data exacerbate the bullwhip effect. A direct consequence of this observation is that since lead times increase with each additional stage in the supply chain, reducing the number of stages reduces the bullwhip effect. The analysis also shows how the variation at each stage is either additive or multiplicative depending on whether the system had perfect information about the future.

The use of POS data can also help reduce the bullwhip effect from a behavioral perspective. Managers of lean supply chains realize that end-user demand is more predictable than the demand experienced by factories. Hence they tend to ignore signal distortions sent through the supply chain and instead look at end-user demand. The implication is that they do not react to day-to-day fluctuations but instead run a level production schedule each day, which helps to mitigate the bullwhip effect.

It must be noted, though, that without perfect information about the future, sharing POS information does not give much leverage to the enterprises when lead times are high. Future consumer orders still need to be anticipated. Unless consumer orders are steady, the bullwhip effect will remain multiplicative. In summary:

▲ POS data can reduce the bullwhip effect.
▲ However, POS data does not eliminate the bullwhip effect. Lead-time reduction is also necessary.

Here are other ways to mitigate the bullwhip effect:

▲ Smaller order batches result in smaller fluctuations. This observation highlights the need for organizations to work with suppliers to get more frequent deliveries in smaller order increments.
▲ Keeping prices stable reduces the temptation to the customer to buy more than necessary when prices are low and cut back on orders when prices are high, resulting in a more level demand.
▲ Allocating products among customers based on past orders rather than based solely on their present orders will reduce hoarding behavior when there are shortages. Unrestricted ordering capability can be controlled by reducing the maximum order size and implementing capacity reservations. One option is to allow a customer to reserve a fixed quantity of each item for a given year and have the customer specify

the quantity to be sent with each order, shortly before the item is needed. Barilla SpA has adopted this approach in its distribution strategy.

In general, many enterprises are working with their upstream and downstream partners to try to mitigate the bullwhip effect. However, one of the lessons from the beer game is that structure drives behavior. So it is essential that enterprises first understand how to build the necessary structural framework within their own walls and then expand this framework to include their supply chain.

Structuring the Lean Supply Chain

It is often remarked that less than 10 percent of the total product budget is expended by the time a product design is complete, but in that same period of time, *80 percent of the cost of the product over its lifetime is committed.* A similar remark applies to the design and operation of a supply chain. The manner in which the supply chain is designed plays a very significant role in the cost of its operation over its lifetime.

Supply chain design did not receive much attention for the greater part of the twentieth century because most organizations operated in a production-centric mind-set. Scale economies drove supply chain operations, which worked well as long as demand outstripped supply and customers were willing to compromise their needs. However, such a mode of operation resulted in unwieldy behemoths—enterprises that produced their products in large lots.

These large batches of products were transported in full truckloads to regional warehouses and distribution centers, from which they were delivered to retail stores or to other manufacturing facilities. If a customer needed a more customized product, she had to place a special order and wait for a long time for the product to be manufactured and delivered. The lead time, namely, the elapsed time between order placement and product delivery, was usually measured in months. The suppliers to these manufacturing organizations, in turn, produced and delivered supplies in large lots. Manufacturers and suppliers were able to coexist, blissfully unaware of any perceived threats to their operation, lumbering along in true behemoth-like fashion.

As noted earlier, today's supply chain operates in a demand-driven, customer-centric world. Today, supply chains have to be designed to respond quickly to rapidly changing customer demands in an agile, gazelle-like manner.

Which organization in the supply chain should drive supply chain design? Consider first situations where this is a relatively straightforward question to answer.

Erecting the structural framework is no doubt a relatively easier task for an organization that has a dominant position in the supply chain. For example, consider the pasta maker Barilla SpA. Barilla implemented a just-in-time distribution (JITD) system that provides visibility on the demands that customers made on Barilla's distributors and retailers. With such a visibility, Barilla was able to specify where inventory should be held in the downstream distribution facilities.[7]

Barilla thus controls the flow of goods through the supply chain based on accurate demand information that is neither biased by the distribution/retail center's perception of customer demand nor by Barilla's ability to deliver on these biased demand estimates. In effect, Barilla has taken on the vital task of matching the supply from the production and distribution network with the demand from the end customer, which enables Barilla to mitigate the bullwhip effect significantly.

The reader should note that such a high degree of control of the supply chain is not always possible. Rather, Barilla is one of a relatively few organizations—organizations such as Apple, Walmart, Cisco, and Proctor & Gamble—that can dictate how the supply chain operates. Incidentally, even with this level of clout, it was not easy for Barilla to put through its JITD system.[8]

In a more general setting, where there is no dominant player in the supply chain, the organization driving the supply chain is often the one primarily responsible for the brand image of the end product. The brand owner could be:

▲ An upstream manufacturer such as Intel, which would have a significant influence on the supply chain because such manufacturers frequently introduce technology-driven changes

▲ A downstream manufacturer such as Proctor & Gamble, which could use its vast in-house and contract manufacturing network to position brands and provide market inputs to the rest of the supply chain

⏶ A retailer such as Walmart, which provides a large part of the final exposure to the marketplace

⏶ A trading company in commodities, which is often largely anonymous to the general business world but which wields considerable influence because of its volume of purchases

Enterprises that provide transportation, warehousing, or logistics services tend to diversify their business across many different products and services, and therefore, these enterprises are less likely to be brand owners. However, with international outsourcing, a number of these enterprises have vertically integrated into logistics-related businesses, such as global sourcing, quality certification, and transportation through different modes. Some of these enterprises also provide other key logistics services, such as tracking and insurance, customs, and commercial documentation. Consequently, these enterprises play an important role in the success of international supply chains.

In general, there are relatively few supply chains that have a dominant player. However, even when there is no clearly dominant player in the supply chain, it will benefit the supply chain members if they follow a process that will make their supply chain more competitive and less prone to the bullwhip effect. This book presents a roadmap that will help enterprises in their quest to build and manage their lean supply chain and to manage the bullwhip effect. A true, lasting competitive edge will be realized if all key members in the supply chain can agree to cooperate and jointly work with such a roadmap.

The Lean Supply Chain Roadmap

Figure 1.3 presents a seven-step roadmap that enterprises can use to build and manage their lean supply chain. In this roadmap, steps 1 through 5 relate more to the process of building (or structuring) the lean supply chain, whereas steps 6 and 7 relate more to the process of managing (or operating) the lean supply chain. These seven steps, briefly described next, are discussed in more detail in Chapters 2 through 8.

Step 1: Develop Systems Thinking Skills

The beer game demonstrates the importance of systems thinking and shows that a *locally managed* supply chain is *inherently unstable*. The systems

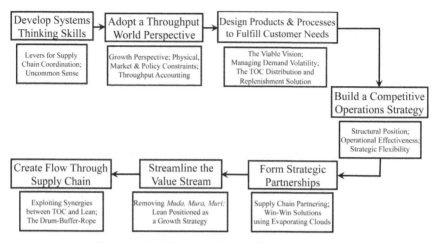

Figure 1.3 The Lean Supply Chain Roadmap.

perspective recognizes that if each element in the supply chain tries to optimize its own operations in isolation, everyone suffers in the long run. In the context of the beer game, each enterprise in the supply chain makes decision in isolation without input from its immediate upstream and downstream supply chain partners. Moving from a local optimization framework to a global optimization framework poses a tremendous challenge for enterprises because it is a radical shift from the traditional approach used to manage an enterprise. Even though systems thinking has been identified as strategically important, it is often not understood well enough to apply it in practice. Chapter 2 discusses systems thinking in more detail.

Step 2: Focus on Throughput

A stable, enduring lean supply chain has to focus on throughput. *Throughput*, as defined in this book, is the rate at which the enterprise fulfills its objective. If the enterprise is a for-profit entity, throughput will be the rate at which the enterprise makes profits. For a nonprofit enterprise, throughput can be viewed as the rate at which the enterprise accomplishes its mission with the available resources.

A focus on throughput, the *throughput world perspective*, is simply a focus on growth. A focus on growth results in decisions that are often quite different from decisions made with a cost world perspective, which focuses on containing or reducing costs. Arguably, a decision made with a *cost world perspective* is easier to achieve, but such a decision can lead to a less healthy outcome than a decision made with a throughput world perspective. Chapter 3 discusses the throughput world perspective. In particular, this chapter provides a detailed discussion on the Theory of Constraints, a philosophy introduced by Israeli physicist Dr. Eliyahu Goldratt in his book, *The Goal: Excellence in Manufacturing.*[9] This philosophy shows how enterprises can deliver excellent customer value and position themselves for unprecedented growth.

Step 3: Design Products and Services that Deliver Customer Needs

Nobody will question the statement that an organization focused on a growth strategy must design and deliver products that fulfill customer value. However, the desire to generate profits can result in the organization overlooking the rather obvious fact that it can exist only if it meets customer needs.

Many organizations look at customer needs and desires from their own perspective. An inward-looking perspective prevents these organizations from delivering the customer Value Proposition: a statement that conveys why the customer should buy the organization's product or service. The challenge is for organizations to continue delivering customer value in a customer-centric business environment. Getting the competitive edge in such a climate requires the organization to continually innovate and/or adapt to meet changing customer preferences.

The beer game shows how even a small change in demand at the end-user level can lead to large variations in demand for enterprises further upstream in the supply chain, especially when lead times are large. Hence a clear case can be made for the supply chain to design products and processes that can mitigate and/or cope with demand volatility. Managing demand volatility poses a number of challenges.

The first challenge is to develop policies that will reduce demand volatility as far as possible. Having mitigated demand volatility, the next challenge is to manage demand volatility with existing processes and equipment and yet achieve high levels of customer satisfaction and operational effectiveness. Chapter 4 expands on what is required for organizations to deliver a compelling offer to customers, an offer that the customer finds very hard to turn down. Chapter 4 also discusses the actions enterprises can undertake to deliver compelling customer value even while managing customer demand volatility.

Step 4: Develop a Competitive Operations Strategy

Sun Wu, better known as Sun Tzu, was a Chinese military general, a strategist, and a philosopher. He is acknowledged as the author of *The Art of War*, a book on military strategy, in which he said, "The good fighters of old first put themselves beyond the possibility of defeat, and then waited for an opportunity to defeat the enemy."

Sun Wu's statement captures the essence of why Operations strategy is an important step in the lean supply chain roadmap. A competitive Operations strategy is a natural follow-up to providing a compelling value proposition to the customer. However, that is often easier said than done. The Marketing function, which is primarily responsible for understanding customer needs and for presenting the value proposition, is often in conflict with the Operations function, which is responsible for delivering the value proposition. The challenge, therefore, is to carefully align Marketing and Operations strategies. Chapter 5 expands on how enterprises can develop strategic flexibility and coevolve Marketing and Operations strategies. Chapter 5 also presents a framework the Operations function can use to present a compelling argument for obtaining the investment needed to implement the Operations strategy.

Step 5: Form Strategic Alliances with Supply Chain Partners

A *strategic alliance* is a voluntary but formal agreement between two or more independent enterprises to pool their resources and work together toward a common set of objectives. Enterprises in a strategic alliance usually agree to collaborate while maintaining their status as distinct entities. In the context of a supply chain, such strategic alliances typically would be made between suppliers and customers, with the agreement that the supplier provides a smooth, uninterrupted supply of products or services to the customer.

However, strategic alliances also may involve sharing, exchanging, or codeveloping products, services, procedures, or processes. This step is discussed in Chapter 6.

Step 6: Streamline the Value Stream

The famous inventor Thomas Edison is reputed to have said that "vision without execution is a hallucination." A competitive Operations strategy requires a deft execution of the strategy. Chapter 7 discusses Lean, a philosophy that allows enterprises to visualize their overall value stream, streamline their operations, and remove wasteful activity at key steps along the value stream. In keeping with the systems perspective, this chapter emphasizes the importance of viewing Lean as a growth strategy rather than a methodology simply aimed at reducing waste.

Step 7: Create Flow Along the Supply Chain

The ability to react quickly to customer demand without carrying large amounts of inventory at various stages in the supply chain is better achieved if every enterprise in the supply chain works in harmony to build products at the rate demanded by the end user. This concept of *flow balance* essentially means that all the enterprises are "rowing the boat" at the same pace. Clearly, if some enterprises in the supply chain work faster than some others, the imbalance in flow will result in inventory piling up in front of the weaker links, namely, the enterprises that work at a slower pace.

Balancing flow across the supply chain requires a systems perspective. The idea is to focus on the product and identify all the steps that the product goes through in the process of moving from the raw material stage until it is delivered to the end user. Are there process steps that introduce unnecessary delays? Is the product subject to any unnecessary non-value-added activities? Where are the potential bottlenecks that delay the smooth flow of the product? Are some of these bottlenecks due to unnecessary processing steps? Have information-processing delays been eliminated? Such questions will bring to the surface problems with existing work practices that may hinder the smooth flow of the product. Creating a smooth flow of products along the supply chain is one of the most important steps in the lean supply chain roadmap. This topic is treated in more detail in Chapter 8.

Implementing the Lean Supply Chain Roadmap

Implementing the lean supply chain roadmap involves a carefully conceived project plan and an effective execution strategy. The Theory of Constraints provides a very useful, proven methodology, Critical Chain Project Management (CCPM), for managing projects. This technique, introduced by Goldratt in 1997,[10] has been applied very successfully in a wide number of project implementations.

The goal of project management is to complete projects using human and material resources in the most productive and timely manner. The most widely used project management methodology to date is PERT/CPM. PERT/CPM is the combination of two very similar approaches, *Program Review and Evaluation Techniques* (PERT) developed by the U.S. military in 1957, and *Critical Path Method* (CPM), developed by Du Pont in 1958 to help plan, schedule and control complex projects. PERT/CPM facilitates a graphic representation of the logical dependencies between the tasks in the project. However, it masks a number of inefficiencies that are specifically addressed by CCPM.

CCPM is based on a number of key principles:

▲ *Reduce the amount of work in execution.* This is achieved, to a large extent, by releasing new work based on the status of the most loaded resources because they limit the amount of work that can be completed.

▲ *Remove safety buffers from individual tasks, and aggregate these safety buffers into a project buffer that protects the overall project.*

▲ *Do not create precise schedules for resources at planning time.* Rather, set schedules during *execution* based on how much buffer is remaining. In a multiproject environment, tasks with the lowest buffer ahead of them get the highest priority.

▲ *Avoid multitasking resources to the extent possible.*

A number of CCPM principles go counter to traditional intuition. For example, the principle that specifies releasing work based on the availability of constraining resources, at first glance, may seem to go counter to an objective that aims to *complete work as soon as possible.* However, releasing work prematurely into the system results in overloading already constrained resources and thus at best serves only to distract the focus on completing projects in a timely manner. The key concepts and principles of CCPM are presented in more detail in Chapter 9.

Conclusions

Devolution is a term discussed in the context of biologic systems based on the notion that a species can undergo a backward evolution, changing from a relatively advanced form into a more primitive form. The term is used to convey the notion that while evolution makes a species more advanced, some modern species have lost functions or complexity and seem to be degenerate forms of their ancestors. While this notion is typically rejected by modern evolutionary theory, the concept may apply to how we build and manage supply chains. We live in a customer-centric era. The customer-centric era requires organizations to take a fresh look at the ways in which they manage their operations within the context of their supply chain and their business ecosystem.

The battleground has shifted—from competition between enterprises to competition between supply chains. The battle is no longer between Home Depot and Lowe's; it is Home Depot's supply chain competing against Lowe's supply chain. The manager of an organization can no longer afford to manage his or her business in isolation but needs to adopt a systems perspective.

The bullwhip effect underscores the need for organizations to understand the dynamics of the supply chain and the root causes of the bullwhip effect. The bullwhip effect occurs because of:

▲ Long lead times for material and information flow
▲ Lack of visibility along the supply chain
▲ Actions undertaken within the enterprise, such as order batching, price discounts and promotions, and so on

In particular, lead times significantly affect the performance of the supply chain:

▲ Longer lead times lead to increased inventory in the system. Conversely, increased inventory in the system causes lead times to increase, resulting in a vicious cycle.
▲ Similarly, flow is enhanced by reducing lead times. Reduced lead times and improved flow go hand in hand, creating a virtuous cycle.

Managers need to understand the root causes for these long lead times, lack of visibility, and so on. They should understand how local optimization decisions such as order batching can hurt their supply chain.

The lean supply chain roadmap presents an approach to structure the lean supply chain. The roadmap is a seven-step prescriptive guide for building and managing the lean supply chain that enterprises can use to:

▲ Develop systems thinking
▲ Understand customer value from a "big picture" perspective
▲ Focus on throughput
▲ Develop partnerships and operations strategies that effectively deliver products and services to satisfy customer needs
▲ Create a smooth flow of products along the value stream

As you continue to read this book, think about the following issues:

▲ Does the success of your organization depend on partnerships and collaborative relationships within the supply chain? How aggressively is your organization pursuing collaborative relationships across your supply chain?
▲ How can your organization become indispensable to the supply chain?
▲ What types of technology are you acquiring to advance your supply chain competencies? Are you a leader or a follower? If you are a follower, then what are the leaders doing?

I will address all these issues in subsequent chapters.

References

1. OpPrac (2008), "The Race for Supply Chain Advantage: Six Practices that Drive Supply Chain Performance," McKinsey Research Report on Operations Practice, 2008.
2. D. Gilmore (2010), "State of the Logistics Union—2010: Not Good," *Supply Chain Digest*, June 10, 2010.
3. M. L. Swink, R. Golecha, and T. Richardson (2010), "Does Supply Chain Excellence Really Pay Off?" *Supply Chain Management Review*, March–April 2010, pp. 14–21.
4. W. E. Deming (1982), *Out of the Crisis*, MIT Center for Advanced Engineering Study, Cambridge, MA.
5. T. Aeppel (2010), "Bullwhip Hits Firm as Growth Snaps Back," *Wall Street Journal*, January 27, 2010.
6. J. W. Forrester (1958), "Industrial Dynamics: A Major Breakthrough for Decision Makers," *Harvard Business Review* 36(4).

7. J. H. Hammond (1994), "Barilla SpA (A)," Harvard Business School Case 9-694-046, Cambridge, MA.
8. J. H. Hammond (1995), "Barilla SpA (D)," Harvard Business School Case 9-695-066, Cambridge, MA.
9. E. M. Goldratt and J. Cox (1984), *The Goal: Excellence in Manufacturing*, North River Press Publishing Company, Croton-on-Hudson, NY.
10. E. Goldratt (1997), *Critical Chain*, North River Press, Great Barrington, MA.

CHAPTER 2

Envisioning the Lean Supply Chain: Systems Thinking

The book *Streamlined*[1] presents a vision for the lean supply chain. In this lean supply chain, the consumer demands a product from its supplier (the *retailer*). The retailer fills this order immediately and places an order with its supplier (the *factory*) to replenish the product just sold. The factory immediately satisfies the retailer's demand from its inventory, places an order with its raw materials supplier to replenish the materials just consumed, and so on all the way up the supply chain.

Every member in this lean supply chain operates with a level production schedule, responds very quickly to customer demand, and delivers just what the customer wants, on time. It is a supply chain in which enterprises fill orders at a relatively low cost without carrying a lot of inventory, one in which the bullwhip effect is noticeably less pronounced. Is this a realistic vision?

The answer is yes. This chapter discusses how systems thinking, or "big picture" thinking, provides clarity to an organization and its supply chain partners on what their constraints are and where they should focus their efforts in order to gain a competitive edge.

The Traditional Approach to Managing Systems

The traditional approach to managing large, complex systems is to split up the system into individual components or processes. The individual processes are then studied in detail, with the intent of instituting efficient operations. This approach is often referred to in the literature as the *analytic method*. The word *analysis* means "to separate any material or abstract entity into its constituent parts." Proponents of the analytic method often recognize that this may not be the ideal way to manage these systems, but they persist with this method because they are either unwilling or unable to manage systems any other way.

Local Optimization

In a business context, the analytic method reduces the enterprise into smaller units and establishes financial goals for each of those units. The analytic method became entrenched in the minds of decision makers in the heyday of U.S. industry when it was more convenient to run large businesses as a collection of autonomous operating divisions coordinated by a strong central administration.

The core objective for such an organizational and control structure was to create a system in which managers of autonomous units could focus solely on their domain of authority. These units were charged with meeting or exceeding their targets. The logic was that if every unit improved, then, *ipso facto*, the entire enterprise would improve. The result was an enterprise structure in which each unit focused on improving its local performance.

This system of operating businesses was very successful—most post–World War II enterprises that organized themselves around this model experienced significant growth. Policies, procedures, performance metrics, and other elements that define organizational structure and function were based on this implied belief in local optima.

Such an approach, however, affects decision making in a negative way and produces a number of undesirable consequences. Promoting isolated efforts that focus on improving specific functions ignores the interactions between those functions. W. Edwards Deming[2] provides several examples of how a lack of systems thinking and poor cooperation can be destructive to an enterprise. In one of Deming's examples, an increase of $30 in the cost of an engine would have resulted in an $80 decrease in the cost of the transmission. However, the center in charge of producing the engine was reluctant to accept the idea because it adversely affected that particular center's profits.

The lack of a systems perspective invariably leads to metrics, policies, and procedures that promote local rather than global optimization. Local measures often can conflict with corporate goals, as the example provided by Deming illustrates. Most managers know intuitively that they must ignore traditional measures occasionally if they really want to grow their business. Unfortunately, consistent pressure and reinforcement that force managers to work with local measures can, over time, obfuscate their intuition.

Using Systems Thinking to Meet the Challenge

Systems thinking follows a fundamentally different approach from the analytic method. While the analytic method studies the different subsystems in relative isolation, systems thinking focuses on their synthesis. That is, systems thinking studies how the processes in the system interact with other processes within the system. Instead of optimizing a singular process in isolation, systems thinking works by considering all the significant interactions the particular process has with all other processes. Such an approach often results in a radically different decision than would be generated by traditional forms of analysis, especially if the processes in the system depend on each other.

For example, the purchasing department traditionally demands and receives discounts from suppliers for bulk purchases. While management may reward the purchasing department for controlling costs, the enterprise is now carrying more inventory than it actually requires. Although the purchasing department may be pleased with this transaction, the enterprise did not benefit from it. From the supplier's perspective, the transaction may have resulted in increased sales for her enterprise, but her production department now has to produce this bulk order, which generates a bullwhip effect upstream. From a systems perspective, a simple solution would entail the purchasing department placing a blanket purchase order on the supplier and then having the supplier deliver the order in small lot sizes on an as-needed basis.

In hindsight, systems thinking is so intuitive that one may wonder why it was not adopted earlier to manage supply chains. One reason is advocated by American scientist Peter Senge,[3] who claims that enterprises do not practice systems thinking because they focus on "detail complexity" rather than "dynamic complexity." A manager who deals only with detail complexity is obstructed from seeing how different types of interactions reach beyond his enterprise and how these interactions vary over time.

Additionally, systems thinking was not applied in the past because until a few years ago, requiring the members in a supply chain to work toward a unified supply chain plan would have been viewed as a dream at best. However, the Internet and the availability of technology that provides visibility on end-user demand to all supply chain partners have led to a perceptible change. Supply chains that provide visibility on customer demand are in a better position to ensure that small fluctuations in end-user demand do not amplify into huge swings in the demands placed on the manufacturer.

The key points to note about systems thinking are as follows:

▲ Each system component makes a contribution to the system as a whole, but only the system delivers the end result. As an analogy, the engine is essential for the car, as are the transmission, the tires, and all the other subsystems. However, only the system in its entirety—the automobile in this example—can provide transportation.
▲ Improving subsystem performance in isolation actually can have a negative impact on the system as a whole. This is often phrased as follows: "the sum of local optima does not equate to the global optimum."

These key points are summarized by the first Lean Supply Chain Principle:

Lean Supply Chain Principle 1

Improving the performance of every subsystem in isolation will not improve system performance. Improvements in subsystem performance must be gauged only through their impact on the whole system.

Applying Lean Supply Chain Principle 1

To illustrate Lean Supply Chain Principle 1, consider the sourcing of material from low-cost countries (LCCs). From the purchasing department's point of view, sourcing from LCCs can save the organization considerable sums of money if the department is able to acquire the material at a significantly lower price. In many organizations, the purchasing department is rewarded on a metric called the *purchase-price variance* (PPV). This metric, also referred to as the *purchase-order variance* or the *material-cost variance*, is the difference between the actual purchase cost and the planned purchase cost (based on the standard cost).

Here's an example of how this metric is used. If the standard cost for a product is $10 per unit and 10,000 units of the product are purchased every year, the annual standard (planned) purchase cost is $100,000. If the purchasing department sources this product from an LCC at $4 per unit, the actual annual purchase cost is $40,000, resulting in a PPV of –$60,000. A negative PPV is a favorable outcome for the purchasing department, and a decision may be made to source this product from the LCC.

This sourcing decision may improve the performance of the purchasing department, but it may not be very well received by the logistics department. While the purchasing department benefits from the LCC sourcing, its action imposes an additional burden on the logistics department that is usually measured by the total logistics cost as a percentage of revenue. The logistics and purchasing departments typically work at cross-purposes because of the way in which the actions of these departments are measured.

Purchase-Price Variance Versus Total Cost of Ownership

Assuming that such interdepartmental problems are resolved, this sourcing decision could well be the right decision for the organization as a whole if the purchasing department considers all the costs involved in sourcing the product from the LCC, namely, the *total cost of ownership* (TCO). This is easier said than done. In addition to the purchase price, which already may include transportation costs and custom/port charges and fees, the TCO calculations should consider the cost of additional pipeline inventory, the cost of quality and obsolescence, internal process costs, the cost of flexibility, and so on. It is possible to estimate some of these costs, but it is very difficult to quantify the *unknown* and *unknowable* costs, such as the cost of increased lead time, the cost of flexibility, the cost of the time and effort spent on sourcing from the LCC, and communication barrier costs.

In particular, the cost of lead time can be very high. It severely affects the performance of the supply chain and hurts the organization's competitive position. Unfortunately, because the cost of increased lead times generally is unknowable, many organizations simply choose to ignore it in their TCO calculation.

In 2007, I worked with the supply chain division of a Fortune 500 organization. This division was composed primarily of purchasing managers whose actions were driven by the PPV metric. The controller of this division and I developed a model for calculating the TCO. Figure 2.1 shows the spreadsheet we evolved to determine TCO for a structural steel item that could be obtained from multiple international sources. The data in this spreadsheet are modified to preserve confidentiality. The entries in the figure that have a question mark represent items that we were unable to quantify.

Unfortunately, few organizations go through a TCO exercise but instead opt for a simpler PPV approach that sometimes results in unfavorable outcomes. Many manufacturers who thought that offshoring manufacturing and supply chain activities would make them more competitive are now rethinking this strategy. An article in *Supply Chain Management Review* notes that "the same factors that made offshoring a sure-fire tactic for reducing costs have shifted dramatically and now are eroding many of those savings. As a result, on-shore and near-shore production is now viable and competitive in many cases."[4]

The examples provided so far illustrate why offshoring decisions made from a myopic perspective can lead to negative consequences. However, there are situations where organizations can benefit to some degree by offshoring manufacturing activity. For example, if an organization wants to establish a global presence, it might choose to move the manufacture of some components or modules of its products to a country in which the demand for these same products is high. The organization now can partner with a local enterprise to manufacture and sell those products, tailoring the products to address possibly unique customer preferences in that region of the world. In general, a broad global perspective is necessary when making sourcing decisions because many variables need to be considered.

Although the purchasing department was used to outline some problems that can occur with local optimization, it is easy to see how Lean Supply Chain Principle 1 applies in a variety of other settings. For instance, the sales department typically is measured on sales dollars. If a salesperson accepts a large order from a customer that requires a special, difficult-to-procure component, the order would benefit sales but may impose a huge burden on purchasing. Furthermore, the total cost involved in procuring this component ultimately may outweigh the sales price.

The Theory of Constraints (TOC) is a management philosophy based on systems thinking that shows how enterprises can overcome the local

Supplier	KOREA	U.S.A	CHINA	EMEA
1. Initial Inputs:				
Purchase Price (Per Metric Ton)	$1,800.00	$1,980.00	$1,600.00	$2,400.00
# Tons	750	750	750	750
Expected No. of Shipments (40,000 lbs/shipment)	41	41	41	41
2. Transportation Costs				
Freight Cost per Shipment (incl. duties & fees)	$6,000.00	$2,500.00	$6,000.00	$5,000.00
II: Product and Lifecycle Cost				
3. Cost of Additional Inventory				
Inventory Carrying Cost	9%	9%	9%	9%
Pipeline Inventory (= 1 Shipment)	$2,939	$0	$2,612	$3,918
Safety Stock Inv. (= 1 Shipment)	$2,939	$3,233	$2,612	$3,918
4. Cost of Quality and Obsolescence				
Factor for Warranty Claims (%)	5%	5%	5%	5%
Scrap and Obsolecence Risk (%)	0%	3%	0%	0%
Inspection Costs per Shipment	$500	$0	$500	$500
Disposal Costs per Shipment	$0	$0	$0	$0
5. Cost of Schedule Non-Compliance				
Expedite Cost (Air Freight)/Shipment	$10,000	$4,000	$10,000	$10,000
No. of Expedited Shipments per Year	3	1	3	3
Stockout and Lost Sales Costs	$0	$0	$0	$0
6. Risk Costs				
Currency Risk (assumes fixed-price contract)	0%	0%	0%	0%
Country Risk	5%	0%	5%	2%
Competition (IP) Risk Factor	8%	0%	20%	0%
Job Switching Risks	0%	0%	0%	0%
7. Payment Term Advantages				
Cash Discount	0%	0%	0%	0%
Payment Terms in Days (pre-pay outside U.S.)	(90.00)	30.00	(90.00)	(90.00)
III: Internal Process Costs				
8. Cost of Administration (Qualifying Suppliers, Visiting Site Overseas, etc.)				
Offshore Supplier Qualification Costs	$50,000	$0	$50,000	$10,000
Cost per Trip	$8,000	$2,000	$12,000	$2,000
Number of Trips	5	3	5	4
9. Cost of Communication				
Addl. Connectivity Expense/Year	$0	$0	$0	$0
IV: Other Hidden Costs (How to cost loss of responsiveness?)				
Cost of Lead Time & Flexibility	?	?	?	?
Communication Barrier Costs	?	?	?	?
Longer Quality Feedback Loop Cost	?	?	?	?
Port Congestion Costs	?	?	?	?

Figure 2.1 Total Cost of Ownership for a Sourced Part.

optimization mind-set. In combination with Lean, TOC presents an excellent opportunity to build and manage the lean supply chain.

Management Philosophies to Enhance Lean Supply Chain Performance

TOC and Lean have helped to improve the performance of organizations over the past 30 years. However, these philosophies typically have been applied to manage operations *within* an organization. Furthermore, these organizations typically apply TOC or Lean concepts on a stand-alone basis, drawing little synergy from the concepts. This section provides a broad overview of the concepts surrounding TOC and Lean and briefly indicates how these two philosophies can work together to facilitate the management of the lean supply chain. Subsequent chapters will present, in more detail, the concepts underlying TOC and Lean and the synergies that can be drawn from them.

The Theory of Constraints

TOC presents concepts and principles for improving the performance of enterprises by focusing on a few leverage points in the system. These leverage points are the system's constraints. The concepts and principles for TOC were first published in *The Goal: Excellence in Manufacturing*[5] by Goldratt in 1984. This book is a fictional account of a manufacturing organization facing closure. The first edition of the book focused on improving the operations within the organization with the stated goal of "making more money, now and in the future."

A subsequent edition of this book, *The Goal: A Process of Ongoing Improvement*,[6] expanded the scope of TOC, moving it from a focus on manufacturing to a focus on more strategic themes. The revised title underscored the notion that the real goal for enterprises is not necessarily to make more money. Rather, it is to ensure that the organization is pursuing a *process of ongoing improvement* (POOGI) with the goal of achieving sustainable growth and stability. The revised goal allowed for the concepts and principles of TOC to be applied to service and not-for-profit enterprises.

Regardless of what the organizational goal is, TOC notes that since the system's constraints determine the extent to which the goal is realized, the intent is to obtain the maximum productive output from the constraint(s) to ensure sustainable growth and stability. The implication is that not all changes will result in improvement toward the goal but may in fact jeopardize stability. The challenge therefore is to arrive at a reliable focusing mechanism that is able to tackle complex problems and identify the points of leverage that will have the maximum systemic impact.

Cost World Versus Throughput World

TOC attacks the assumptions of the *cost world* perspective prevalent in traditionally managed enterprises. In the cost world, decisions are driven by a desire to control costs. While the enterprise can make more money if it reduces costs, a focus on cost control usually results in suboptimal decisions. For instance, the cost world perspective could result in a decision to outsource a product that is currently produced in-house. Such a decision could have a number of negative repercussions that need to be weighed carefully. One such negative repercussion is that the products that are still manufactured in-house become more expensive to produce because they now have to bear the overhead costs previously absorbed by the newly outsourced product.

TOC avoids the pitfalls of such localized thinking by adopting a perspective that has the objective of maximizing the enterprise goals. TOC refers to this perspective as the *throughput world perspective*. To leverage the throughput world perspective, TOC prescribes three measures, Throughput (T), Investment (I), and Operating Expense (OE). These measures will be defined precisely and clarified with a number of examples in Chapter 3. For the moment, it will be sufficient to define *Throughput* as the sales revenue less the variable expenses. Note that this definition of Throughput is expressed in monetary terms. *Investment* is defined as the money invested in purchasing whatever is needed by the enterprise to sell its products. In the TOC definition, Investment includes fixed assets as well as working capital assets. *Operating Expense* is defined by TOC as all the money the system spends turning Investment into Throughput. OE includes all fixed costs incurred by the enterprise regardless of the level of output.

Since the goal of an enterprise is to improve performance to ensure growth and sustainability, the measure demanding the most attention in TOC is T. Costs that are relatively fixed (measured by OE) should be considered as a secondary measure, a measure subordinate to the goal of maximizing T.

Addressing Systems Thinking Using TOC

The TOC measures T, I, and OE facilitate decision making with a "big picture" perspective. Returning to the earlier reference to the book, *The Goal*, Alex Rogo, the plant manager, receives advice from Jonah, an Israeli physicist who had helped Alex with some mathematical models while Alex was a student working on a grant. Alex has a chance encounter with Jonah in an airport, at which time Alex tells Jonah that he has installed robots in his plant to increase productivity by 36 percent.

Jonah asks Alex whether his plant is making 36 percent more money after installing the robots. Alex reflects on this question and answers in the negative. Jonah next asks Alex whether his plant is shipping more products every day after installing robots. Alex again answers no. Jonah then asks Alex whether he reduced expenses (answer, "No") or whether inventories went down (again, answer, "No"). Jonah now questions Alex's decision on installing the robots in the first place.

The dialog between Alex and Jonah is an example of how to apply systems thinking to decision making. For any decision under consideration, ask whether it will:

▲ Increase T, which represents the rate at which the organization fulfills its goal
▲ Reduce I, the investment in working capital and/or fixed assets, or
▲ Reduce fixed expenses (OE) in the long-term

If the answer to all three of these questions is no, then the decision under consideration should be considered suspect as to its soundness. The manager must consider whether this decision is truly in the organization's best interest.

TOC often presents an *un-common sense* solution to a problem. An un-common sense solution is a solution that appears to be counterintuitive but makes perfect sense once it is explained—so much so that one wonders why the solution was not discovered before. Similarly, an un-common sense statement is a statement that usually confounds someone hearing it for the first time.

In general, un-common sense thinking is out-of-the-box thinking that results in seemingly counterintuitive statements or conclusions. These counterintuitive statements and conclusions, however, make perfect sense after they are explained. At the very least, these statements or conclusions result in greater awareness of some of the misconceptions that are present in traditional practice.

Theory of Constraints and Un-common Sense

Taiichi Ohno, widely acknowledged as the person responsible for the Toyota Production System, is reputed to have said, "The more inventory you have on hand, the less likely you are to have the one item your customer actually wants." This statement by Ohno is an un-common sense statement. Why would an organization not be able to satisfy customer demand if it carried a lot of inventory?

On further reflection, the real intent of Ohno's statement becomes clearer: he is warning managers that large inventories are a symptom of poor management practices that can hinder an enterprise's ability to deliver customer value effectively. For example, inventories could be high because they were built on speculation, anticipating a yet unrealized demand for this inventory from a downstream customer. However, building this inventory may have misallocated capacity and raw materials that could have been better applied to a real customer demand.

Many of the TOC concepts presented in the following chapters are common sense concepts that at first glance appear to be un-common sense because they challenge traditional management practices. The TOC concepts that reflect un-common sense thinking are highlighted and clarified when they are presented. For example, the statement, "If you want to get your projects done sooner, work on one project at a time instead of many at a time" implies that working on multiple projects will result in a phenomenon commonly referred to as *multitasking*. The statement therefore asserts that multitasking will delay all the projects in progress. This un-common sense statement will be further clarified when the problems associated with multitasking are discussed in Chapter 9.

On a side note, it was arguably un-common sense thinking that led the British band Radiohead to shock the recording industry in 2007 when it announced that fans could download the band's new album, *In Rainbows*, for free—or for as much as the fans were willing to pay. While this announcement may have seemed bizarre because Radiohead was a popular band in 2007 and easily could have sold its new album, this was a brilliant move. The announcement resulted in increased publicity for the band. The announcement also resulted in increased traffic to Radiohead's Web site by fans who wanted to download the music from the Web site rather than using a file-sharing network; the Radiohead Web site allowed a faster download with a guaranteed quality bit-rate encoding. The result of this seemingly questionable business decision eventually generated considerable profits for the band in the long run.

Lean

Lean is founded on the JIT principles conceived by Japanese automobile manufacturers in the 1930s and perfected in the 1970s. Unlike TOC, which owes its origin entirely to Goldratt, Lean consists of concepts and principles developed by a number of individuals over the years.

Henry Ford pioneered some of the concepts underlying Lean that are still practiced widely today. Taiichi Ohno built on Ford's concepts to develop the well-known Toyota Production System, a method that was applied with great success in the Japanese automobile manufacturing industry. In 1990, the book, *The Machine That Changed the World*,[7] kindled interest in JIT production and Lean in America. Subsequently, the book, *Lean Thinking*,[8] was published in 1996, in which the stated goal of Lean was to eliminate *muda* ("wastefulness"). This latter book prescribed a specific course of action to implement Lean concepts within an enterprise.

The principles surrounding Lean were applied initially to the automobile industry in the United States, a natural consequence of the fact that JIT principles were specifically developed for the automobile industry in Japan. However, Lean is now applied in a wide variety of industries. These concepts and principles have been applied successfully in industries as diverse as paints, furniture, electrical switchgears, aerospace, aircraft maintenance, electrical appliances, and office products.

As U.S. enterprises began to understand and embrace the principles of Lean, the body of knowledge naturally started to grow and become disseminated. It was observed that these principles, in particular, the concept of flow, could be extrapolated beyond internal operations to entire supply chains. Lean became a new way of making, distributing, and selling products that evolved from a marriage of new capabilities in manufacturing, IT, and logistics.

Lean focuses on eliminating wasteful activity at all levels in the enterprise (or the supply chain, for that matter). Eliminating wasteful activity achieves two purposes. First, it reduces lead times* and enables the enterprise to be more flexible and responsive. From the supply chain perspective, the enterprise is more responsive to the downstream customers and provides smoother, more predictable demand for the upstream suppliers. For example, the automotive supplier Denso has a starter motor and alternator plant in Maryville, Tennessee, with very short product cycles. Denso produces every product multiple times per shift. The short product cycles make it possible for both Denso and its upstream suppliers to produce virtually in lockstep with the automobile manufacturers that use their starters and alternators.

Only a day or two elapses between the time a casting or a coil of wire is made at the Denso facility and the time the casting or coil becomes part of a starter or an alternator on a completed car. The benefits of this short lead time—short quality feedback loop, responsiveness to the customer, and elimination of supply chain costs related to inventory tracking—are realized primarily outside the four walls of Denso's operation. In fact, if all elements of the supply chain in the automobile industry were as responsive as Denso, the automobile industry would be poised to adopt a true build-to-order (BTO) model such as the one popularized by Dell, Inc.

Second, the elimination of wasteful activities results in increased capacity that could be deployed to expand the business. Lean thus facilitates a *growth strategy*. Enterprises that implement Lean concepts respond to customer demands faster and more reliably than their competitors. In turn, the rapid, reliable response from these enterprises encourages customers to place orders that are more reflective of actual demand rather than orders that the customer has either inflated to build a safety cushion or deflated to reduce excess inventories.

The enterprise is now able to work with a smoother production schedule, which allows it to communicate a steadier material supply schedule to its suppliers. This mode of operation facilitates strong relationships with suppliers, providing Lean enterprises with another competitive advantage.

---

*The *lead time* is the elapsed time from the moment an order is received until the time the order is executed and delivered correctly to the customer.

Lean enterprises thus are able to build custom products for individual customers without carrying large amounts of inventory.

Synergies Between TOC and Lean

TOC and Lean are philosophies that combine to support organizational growth by addressing different aspects of a strategic plan. TOC, with its systems perspective, can identify the key process steps that provide the greatest leverage. Subsequently, the tools provided by Lean remove wasteful activities at these key process steps. The result is reduced lead times and increased *throughput velocity*, that is, the speed with which products are delivered to the customer.

Lower lead times result in lower inventory levels, and vice versa. That is, reduced lead times will result in a reduction in inventories across the supply chain. The reduction in inventories facilitates the smooth flow of products along the supply chain, allowing it to operate with reduced inventory levels. Correspondingly, product costs also are reduced, resulting in more profits for the enterprises in the supply chain or, alternately, making it more attractive to consumers if cost savings are passed on to them. The increased customer satisfaction, in turn, enhances the growth strategy by ultimately generating additional demand and improving market share.

An article published by Goldratt in 2009[9] succinctly captures the potential synergies that exist between TOC and Lean. In this article, Goldratt suggests that the successes of Henry Ford and Taiichi Ohno were largely due to the fact that they built their planning and execution systems around four concepts that apply to the planning and execution of lean supply chains in general:

1. Improving flow (or equivalently lead time) is a primary objective of operations.
2. This primary objective should be translated into a practical mechanism that guides the operation when not to produce (prevents over-production).
3. Local efficiencies must be abolished.
4. A focusing process to balance flow must be in place.

A major impediment to flow is caused by enterprises that produce products in anticipation of future demand using forecasts to drive their production schedules. When enterprises use forecasts to drive their production schedules, they exemplify *push* systems that push products out in the form of finished goods inventory, building an adequate buffer of inventory to accommodate demand variation. To put it another way, push systems schedule production and let inventory absorb demand variation. As a result, enterprises that work with push systems commit their resources to often-unneeded products and are unable to react to a firm customer order.

In contrast, a *pull* system waits for a demand signal from the customer before committing resources to make products. A pull system will have lower inventories than a comparable push system owing to the simple fact that pull systems place a limit on inventories and use capacity to absorb demand variation. Clearly, it is desirable for enterprises to use pull signals to trigger supplies from their upstream enterprises as well. Carrying this idea one step further, the intent is to:

▲ Start with the customer.
▲ Deliver what is demanded.
▲ Build what is sold.
▲ Supply what is consumed, and above all,
▲ Balance the flow.

Such a mode of operation effectively realizes the vision that was presented at the start of this chapter. Figure 2.2 presents this vision graphically, and Chapter 8 describes how to put the vision into practice. In particular, Chapter 8 shows how synergies between TOC and Lean will help to realize this vision.

The preceding discussion underscores some key themes that are emphasized throughout this book: *Systems Thinking, Lead-Time Reduction*, and the concept of *Flow*. The following quote by Fred Smith, the founder of Federal Express, succinctly summarizes this discussion:

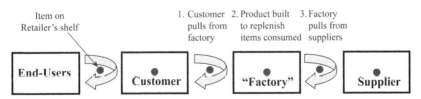

Figure 2.2   Use pull signals to create flow across the supply chain.

Find the essence of each situation, like a logger clearing a log jam. The pro climbs a tall tree, locates the key log, blows it, and lets the stream do the rest. An amateur would start at the edge of the jam and move all the logs, eventually moving the key log. Both approaches work, but the essence concept saves time and effort. Almost all problems have a key log if we learn to find it.

This quote also underscores the importance of systems thinking. From a local perspective, it would have been more intuitive to try to move the logs, one at a time, eventually reaching the key log. The global perspective allows the pro to quickly identify the bottleneck and move the key log first.

From a systems perspective, the term *supply chain* suggests a linear relationship among the various elements in the supply chain and therefore is a misnomer. This term, which is so ingrained in our vocabulary, is no longer an appropriate metaphor for describing the integration required to deliver goods and services competitively to consumers.

Consider the characteristics of a chain. It is bidirectional, with a single beginning and end, and has a fixed sequence connecting each link in a prescribed order. Furthermore, the links are made of steel, never to be broken. These characteristics do not, however, describe the emerging reality of today's supply chains. Rather, enterprises are forming *trading communities* to facilitate the coordination of people, assets, and information to deliver the right items, in the right quantities, to the right place, at the right time. Meeting these expectations requires coordination of multiple inputs and outputs among several enterprises. It is not simply a matter of passing orders upstream only to have upstream suppliers place orders, in turn, for their supplies further upstream. The time delays and distortions are too great for this type of fulfillment. Vendors, brokers, original equipment manufacturers (OEMs), transportation providers, warehouses, and customers need information to coordinate their activities to provide goods and services in timely and efficient ways.

Unlike a chain, links between enterprises are not made of steel but are fluid arrangements that can be disconnected, reconnected, weakened, or strengthened depending on customer needs. The term *supply web* better reflects this new paradigm. In fact, the reader may now have deduced that the supply chain is actually part of a larger system, a system that affects the operation of all the enterprises within the supply chain. An increasing number of enterprises are realizing that they are a part of a constantly adapting system of interrelationships and interdependencies—in reality, they are elements of a *business ecosystem*.

The Business Ecosystem

The business ecosystem includes the organization and its customers and suppliers, as well as the competitors, owners/stakeholders, complementors, government agencies, and other regulatory bodies that have an impact on the operations of the organization. Figure 2.3 illustrates a business ecosystem for a supply chain.

In Figure 2.3, *complementors* are business entities that facilitate the development and growth of an organization's supply chain, even though these entities do not participate directly in producing the product. To give a simple example, Microsoft and Intel are complementors to one another in the PC industry. Each new generation of Microsoft software creates demand

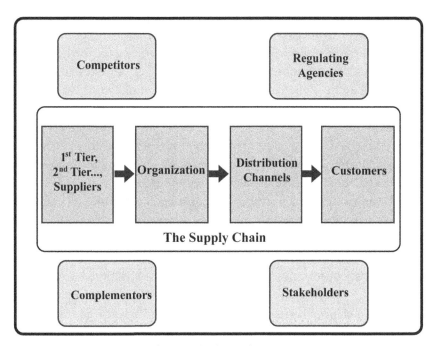

Figure 2.3 The supply chain's business ecosystem.

for computing power from Intel. Each new generation of Intel processors creates demand for Microsoft's latest software.

In a larger context, complementors should be viewed not just as business entities but rather as industries that nurture one another. For example, advances in silicon wafer manufacturing techniques have abetted recent advances in telecommunications.

Some organizations deliberately build, acquire, or merge with other enterprises that complement their products. Pepsi-Cola Company and Frito-Lay Company merged to form PepsiCo, Inc., in 1965. PepsiCo has leveraged sales of products from both divisions by advertising that a bag of Doritos chips tastes much better with a can of Pepsi. The salty snacks industry thus is a complementor to the soft-drink ecosystem.

An enterprise's awareness of the ecosystem in which it exists can highlight more effectively potential threats that the enterprise might encounter. To give a simple example, if a supplier of tape casings to a VHS video recorder manufacturer in the late 1990s had been more attuned to the entertainment media ecosystem, then it could have identified the threat posed to the overall VHS industry by the advent of the more efficient DVD player.

At the same time, astute knowledge of the ecosystem can illuminate a number of opportunities for creating synergies among the members of the ecosystem. Consider, for example, the recent and exciting developments in the field of additive manufacturing. *Additive manufacturing* is the process of creating a physical object through the selective fusion, sintering, or polymerization of a material. Unlike conventional manufacturing techniques, such as metal cutting (nowadays sometimes referred to as *subtractive manufacturing*), in which excess material is removed until the final product is achieved, most additive manufacturing processes do not yield excessive scrap. Additive manufacturing holds considerable promise for the future because it typically does not require large amounts of time to remove unwanted material, and thus time and costs are reduced. Additive manufacturing has the ability to create parts that could not have been produced by subtractive or forming manufacturing processes. Many enterprises with expertise in manufacturing and computer-aided design are now forming alliances to explore the tremendous potential offered by additive manufacturing. These partnerships are explored in Chapter 6, which discusses strategic partnering in the lean supply chain. Members in the additive manufacturing ecosystem conceivably could even partner with competitors to coevolve capabilities and launch a new product that they otherwise would have not been able to launch on their own.

To give another example of how a systems perspective and knowledge of the ecosystem can identify potential opportunities or threats, consider the air transport ecosystem and the impact of airline deregulation. It is widely recognized that airline deregulation, which began in 1978, has been a real blessing to travelers, providing them with lower fares and more frequent schedules. Within just a few years of deregulation, air transportation went from being a privilege available only to business travelers and the wealthy to a common, frequent mode of transportation.

Aside from benefiting passengers and generating a few startup airlines, did airline deregulation affect anyone else? Consider this: an enterprise in the automobile rental business at the beginning of 1978 could have anticipated the resulting increase in airline traffic and positioned itself for the accompanying increase in demand for car rentals at airports. The use of a systems perspective and knowledge of its ecosystem would have given this automobile company a distinct advantage over its competitors.

The customer benefited directly from airline deregulation because it allowed the transportation carriers to become more market-oriented and provided them with incentives to develop a better infrastructure for their business. The airline and trucking industries expanded service to smaller cities and to other countries. At the same time, deregulation resulted in a substantial decrease in the transportation rate, especially in the airline and trucking industries. Both shippers and carriers were free to innovate with respect to their products, services, routes, and prices. Better yet, they were able to pass on much of the resulting savings to their customers. Deregulation led to the rise of the air express industry and integrated *third-party logistics providers* (3PLs).

As enterprises continue to explore ways and means of building and managing lean supply chains, they should be aware of the extrinsic elements (i.e., the complementors, competitors, regulatory agencies, and stakeholders) in their supply chain's business ecosystem. The ecosystem perspective can bring tangible and intangible benefits to every member of the ecosystem. An organization competing for a contract may win the job partly as a result of the strengths of its partnerships. When the organization is awarded that contract, its partners reap the benefits as well. The organization's sales force is now able to sell a more complete package to the customer. Other enterprises in the ecosystem also benefit—they realize increased business without even directly promoting sales of their products. For example, an increase in the sale of putters and drivers by Callaway Golf Company is very likely to generate a corresponding increase in the sale of men's golf shoes. The golf shoes industry is a complementor to the golf club ecosystem.

In the long run, the greatest benefits of an ecosystem perspective are likely to be less tangible. Far greater benefits may derive from intangibles such as:

▲ The freedom to focus on core competencies
▲ The opportunities to connect with other supply networks and to tap into their knowledge base
▲ The ability to improve current product offerings and to create new ones
▲ The opportunity for sharing innovative solutions with ecosystem members
▲ The ability to remain agile in the marketplace

At this point the reader may be thinking: "I'm having enough trouble just trying to comprehend my own enterprise, let alone the whole supply chain. Why should I have to worry about a business ecosystem?" Hopefully, the answers to these questions are beginning to develop as well. Remember always that the business ecosystem plays a significant role in supply chain management. The key points to keep in mind are these:

▲ Too many managers devote their attention to immediate operational issues within their enterprise and ignore the supply chain in which the enterprise operates, let alone the extrinsic elements of the business ecosystem. In other words, these managers fail to see the big picture.
▲ The ecosystem perspective gives real meaning to the term *supply web* rather than *supply chain*. In a business ecosystem, a partnership is not a marriage; it is a mesh of interlocking relationships among customers, suppliers, and other supply chain partners. These relationships are fluid arrangements that can be disconnected, reconnected, weakened, or strengthened.
▲ A partnership with an enterprise in one ecosystem could open doors for potential partnerships with other supply chains or other ecosystems, enabling the enterprise to make contacts that otherwise would not have been available. Partnerships also facilitate joint relationships with

customers and benefit from the opportunity to pursue new alliances with them directly.

These key points are summarized by the second Lean Supply Chain Principle.

Lean Supply Chain Principle 2

Focus on improving the performance of the lean supply chain— but do not ignore the supply chain's business ecosystem.

One example of a business ecosystem that has brought the vision of the ideal lean supply chain one step closer to reality is the PC ecosystem. I will present the PC ecosystem and support this discussion with case studies on Dell and Apple, two organizations that have redefined the PC ecosystem.

Personal Computer Ecosystems

The PC industry presents a fascinating case of ecosystem development. In the late 1970s, Apple, Tandy Corporation, and other organizations introduced early versions of the PC. They began building ecosystems around their individual enterprises. When IBM entered the PC industry in 1981, it adopted an open-systems approach. IBM's strategy was to depend on suppliers to provide standardized components. It encouraged the suppliers to access its computer architecture by publishing technical literature.

IBM stimulated demand for its new machine through clever marketing and distribution channels. IBM's approach was a big success by any measure. Its PC business grew from $500 million in 1982 to $5.65 billion by 1986, and IBM computers dominated the market. Shortly after IBM entered the PC industry in 1981, it allowed other enterprises to manufacture PC clones. With IBM's open policy, most PC manufacturers simply copied the format of the IBM machine.

IBM soon found that demand outstripped capacity. Perhaps as a consequence, it continued to maintain high prices, which allowed manufacturers such as Compaq and others to enter the market. IBM tried to cope with the demand and invested directly in a number of key suppliers to nurture their businesses so that they could become better suppliers of components to IBM. Concerned that the regulators in the PC ecosystem could intervene with antitrust objections, IBM also informed its suppliers that the assistance came without any strings attached. The key suppliers, such as Intel and Microsoft, thus were able to diversify their risk portfolios by also supplying to computer makers such as Compaq. As a result, PC makers such as Compaq eventually threatened to erode IBM's market share. IBM did not object to its competitors using the same suppliers that it had nurtured in its supply chain because demand still was outstripping supply. By 1986, the combined revenue of the IBM PCs and the PC clones was approximately $12 billion.

On the other hand, Apple, the other market leader at that time, decided to adopt its own standards. These standards were not compatible with IBM's and were based on a closed operating system architecture. For instance, Apple refused to license its Macintosh software to the rest of the industry but instead held its patents very tightly, in complete contrast to IBM's open policy. In July 1980, IBM asked Bill Gates of Microsoft to write the operating system for its upcoming PC. In July 1981, Microsoft bought all rights to an operating system called DOS from its developer, Seattle Computer Products, and renamed it MS-DOS. When Gates tried to get Apple to license its operating system, Apple refused. Microsoft set to work creating its own copy of an operating system for the PC market.

Apple's closed-system architecture discouraged software developers from developing applications and games. These software developers favored writing software for the IBM PCs and the clone manufacturers. Despite a superior architecture, Apple started to lose market share, and its revenue of $2 billion in 1986 was completely dwarfed by the $12 billion generated by the PC makers.

Despite the entry of PC clone manufacturers such as Compaq, IBM felt secure in its position. It had built the PC ecosystem practically from the ground up and had about 50 percent of the market share for PCs around 1986. However, like all PC manufacturers, IBM relied on a long supply chain with a distribution channel and was pushing products out to the retail outlets. The stage thus was ripe for a new entrant into the PC business. That new entity was Dell. Dell redefined the PC ecosystem with its Dell-Direct model, a model that eliminated the "middleman" and thus greatly simplified and streamlined Dell's supply chain.

CASE STUDY

The Business Ecosystem for Dell

Dell's strategy and operations exemplified the benefits that can be gained from lean supply chains. Dell has ranked among the top five organizations in the AMR Supply Chain Top 25 list for most of the years AMR Research has been publishing this ranking. Even though the Dell-Direct model now has been adopted by some of Dell's competitors, and even though Dell is not using the Dell-Direct model exclusively, it nonetheless has maintained top ranking in this list. Dell was ranked second in 2009 and fifth in 2010.

The ecosystem played a significant role in Dell's rise to a dominant position in the PC marketplace in the 1990s through the early 2000s. When Michael Dell started operations in 1984, the PC ecosystem was perfectly positioned to enable his vision to become the market leader in PC manufacturing and assembly. IBM, the market leader at that time, had made large-scale investments in production, research and development, and marketing and distribution to exploit the PC market. In sum, IBM had established a PC business ecosystem centered on itself. The IBM business ecosystem included outside suppliers for its components and software. IBM's open policy allowed Dell to take advantage of the research and development on the PC. Dell also was able to reach out to IBM's key suppliers.

Dell began operations in Austin, Texas, with a startup capital of $1,000. Such a small investment meant that Dell was a small player in the game, compared with IBM and Apple. However, Dell was assisted by the fact that the PC industry was poised for a huge growth spurt; customers were starting to realize that the IBM PC and the Apple Macintosh could bring computing power into their homes.

Dell was the first manufacturer to sell computers directly to the end users in the PC industry with the Dell-Direct model, a BTO model that allowed consumers to configure their product within a limited range of options. Dell's supply chain thus was simpler than the supply chain for its competitors. The Dell-Direct model was almost serendipitous. Michael Dell was forced to adopt the direct distribution channel when

CASE STUDY

he began his business because his scale of operations was small and lacked distribution partners as well as the power to negotiate with retailers. So Dell bypassed the wholesalers and retailers and fashioned a telephone direct-sale model.

With the emergence of the Internet as a viable technology, Michael Dell seized on the opportunities provided by the Internet, opportunities that he could not have foreseen when he started operations in 1984. Dell fully exploited the Internet's ability to allow customers to view product specifications and to place orders for products online. In particular, corporate and governmental agencies found it very convenient to order products online. By December 1996, Dell's Internet sales were $1 million a day.

Dell increased customer satisfaction while increasing its sales and profits by capitalizing on its integrated supply channels and technology. For example, when a customer placed an order for a computer with a Sony 17-inch monitor, the Dell information system immediately knew whether or not this monitor was available at the Sony plant in Mexico from where the units were shipped. If that monitor was out of stock, Dell would offer the customer the option of buying another monitor that it had in stock (such as a 19-inch monitor) and would entice the customer to do so by offering a discount on the unit. This practice is referred to as *up-selling*. In all likelihood, the customer accepted the offer and walked away with a positive feeling of having purchased a superior product at a discount. At the same time, this positive customer experience enhanced Dell's reputation of being able to deliver what customers wanted when they wanted it. By February 2000, Dell's online sales generated $40 million in daily revenues, almost 50 percent of total sales.

To gain a competitive advantage, Dell first worked with its customers and its suppliers to determine the right levels of component inventory to maintain in its assembly facilities. As his business grew, Michael Dell *Lean*-ed out the supply chain. He did so by reducing the supply base, establishing long-term arrangements and partnership agreements with preferred suppliers. The number of suppliers was

CASE STUDY

reduced from 204 in 1992 to 47 in 1997. In the three years from 1999 to 2001, only two or three of the top suppliers had changed.

Being an incumbent in a stable ecosystem and having control of a dominant design, namely, the Dell-Direct model, certainly gave Dell a big advantage over its competitors. However, the advantage was not permanent. Despite having good products or services produced by well-run processes, organizations like Dell will survive the "natural selection" in businesses only if their processes and supply chains continue to function superbly. In his book, *The Death of Competition: Leadership and Strategy in the Age of Business Ecosystems*, author J. F. Moore indicates:

> Even excellent businesses can be destroyed by the conditions around them. They are like species in Hawaii. Through no fault of their own, they find themselves facing extinction because the ecosystem they call home is itself imploding. . . . Incumbency must be continually reinforced and restored. Even Intel and Microsoft, the current sovereigns of the computer chip and the PC operating software ecosystems, must be on guard for they are constantly being challenged. . . . The major challenge for many companies is to get others to co-evolve with their vision of the future. In a global market, you want to make use of the other players—for capacity, innovation, and capital.[10]

In the business world, there are many factors that favor organizations competing with the market leader. The dethroning of IBM through the entry of a large number of clone companies into the IBM-created PC ecosystem proves this point. The same outcome befell Dell. While Dell is still performing well, it is no longer the "darling of Wall Street." The new Wall Street darling in the computer industry is Apple.

Dell's strategies and tactics were driven by a mind-set that it was dealing with a commoditized product. Apple created a flourishing business ecosystem that was not built around the computer platform. Instead, it was built around the digital media ecosystem, an ecosystem that subsumes the PC ecosystem.

CASE STUDY

The Business Ecosystem for Apple

In December 2010, Apple became the second largest company in America based on its market value after oil giant Exxon Mobil. A number of research analysts covering the stock predicted an even higher stock price for Apple, and research firm Piper Jaffray raised its price target to $438, which would have given Apple a market capitalization that would eclipse Exxon Mobil's.

Apple now controls only a slim percentage of the PC market, but it has a commanding position in the digital media market. Its strategy to move its focus from the PC to the entertainment industry is producing huge dividends. Digital media soon may trump the sales of PCs as customers spend their money on Apple's "i-products," namely, iTunes, the iPod, the iPhone, and the iPad. In February 2011, Apple teamed up with newspaper mogul Rupert Murdoch to launch *The Daily*, a subscription option for paid news content on the iPad. Figure 2.4 depicts the current Apple product portfolio.

While Apple has a commanding position in the digital media industry, it has to contend with competition from a number of key

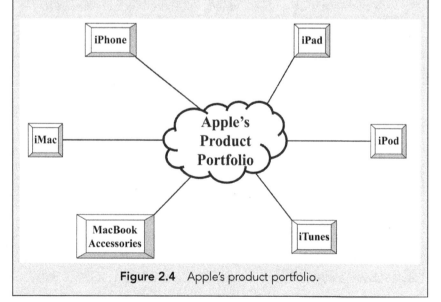

Figure 2.4 Apple's product portfolio.

CASE STUDY

players. Google is offering the Android operating system as a free and open platform, in contrast to Apple's strategy to continue to operate its products using a relatively closed system. While critics indicate the potential problems with Apple's closed system, the fact is that the closed system currently provides Apple with a significant advantage over its competitors in both hardware and software. For one thing, Apple is the only computer company that designs and creates all its hardware and software. Thus it controls the entire ecosystem in which it operates.

No doubt Apple creates and designs its own software. However, while Steve Jobs might suggest that Apple "manufactures everything it sells," the reality is that Apple runs on the same types of hardware as do PCs made by other PC manufacturers such as Dell and Hewlett-Packard. Apple uses Intel CPUs, Nvidia graphics processors, Seagate solid-state hard disk drives, LG or Toshiba liquid-crystal display (LCD) panels, Samsung memory chips, Broadcom Wi-Fi chips for both Wi-Fi and Bluetooth connectivity, and Infineon baseband chips. Even the Mac's OS X and subsequent operating systems are based on a variant of the Unix operating system. Furthermore, all these components are assembled by Foxconn in China. Even though Apple gets its components from different sources, just like its competitors, and even offshores its assembly operation to China, Apple still has some distinct advantages that make it the dominant player in the digital media ecosystem.

A major reason for Apple's dominance is its ability to standardize its products. Apple has one operating system, it has one store—the Apple Store—and it has clear user interface rules for its application software (apps). Apple's mode of operation is that the user entering the Apple ecosystem makes a pact with Apple. In return for a higher premium paid to Apple, the consumer will enjoy a seamless experience with Apple products, an experience where everything works and plays flawlessly together. Such an integrated experience is hard for Apple's competitors to match, making the Apple ecosystem even harder to breach.

Apple has the first-mover advantage in the digital media ecosystem. It has pioneered the à la carte music purchase system via

CASE STUDY

iTunes, which it has since extended to cover movie rentals, posing a direct challenge to an established player, Netflix. With the advent of cloud computing, which provides users with the ability to access content from anywhere in the world, Apple's seamless system gives it a tremendous advantage.

What Apple does best is to remember that technology should be exploited to make it easy to use by customers. Its software offerings focus on the creative market, a deliberate strategy to make the Mac an excellent platform for creation and organization of any media, entirely in line with its digital media ecosystem theme. Apple develops software to ensure that the Mac platform supports the workflow process and all the media involved in the process, from initial recording with the media to the final output of creative work. Its digital-hub strategy aims to ensure that the vast majority of digital input and output devices work within its ecosystem.

To maintain such a seamless ecosystem, Apple imposes a degree of control that occasionally can border on the excessive. Perhaps one day customers might rebel, for instance, against the copyright restrictions Apple places on its digital files, or they might rebel against the lack of variety in Apple's line of media players.

For the moment, however, the customers do not seem to mind. They seem to enjoy the seamless digital media ecosystem Apple has built, downloading music on their iPhones, or renting movies on their iMacs, or playing games on their iPads in a reliable, consistent, and predictable manner. Apple's suppliers are also happy to play along, even though some suppliers have reservations, because Apple is continuing to dominate the digital media market and is also gaining market share in the PC industry.

While the customers do not seem to mind the tight grip Apple maintains on almost every aspect of its iPad tablet, iPhone, and iPod music and video player, this control has drawn complaints from some suppliers and media enterprises. Buying magazine or other sub-scriptions through the iTunes Store requires just a few clicks, and the store will use customer billing information already on file. Since Apple

CASE STUDY

decides which applications can run on its media, it prohibits publishers that sell products through iTunes from linking to other stores outside its app store or from offering better terms to subscribers elsewhere.

According to a *Wall Street Journal* report,[11] legal experts indicate that some of Apple's rules and restrictions could pose antitrust problems. Regulatory bodies such as the European Commission, the European Union's executive arm, are monitoring the subscription service launched in February 2011 for digital media on the iPad carefully to ensure that digital subscription rules do not stifle competition.

Apple also has to cope with several other challenges to maintain the momentum it has built and to continue to maintain its status as a Wall Street darling. Apple must work continually on integrating all its platforms and services in a seamless manner. Maintaining its closed ecosystem also poses a potential risk for Apple. Critics of this closed ecosystem model maintain that Apple is repeating its past mistake of the 1980s, which caused it to lose market share in the PC industry to the IBM/Microsoft platform. They further point to the success of open-source software models. However, this may not be as valid a criticism under the current conditions. In the 1980s, there was no interoperability, and there were fewer software programs or apps. Today, it is possible to use a PDF or HTML document on any platform. In the current setting, the platform with the most user-friendly interface will succeed.

For the moment, Apple has a commanding lead over its competition, although it will no doubt continue to face competition from established organizations such as Google and Microsoft—two organizations that aspire to dominate the digital media ecosystem. However, with over 160 million iTunes accounts, Apple has built a strong user base that will be difficult to erode in the near term. To take market share from Apple, a competitor would have to do much more than build a better device. The competitor would have to create an entire ecosystem, perhaps starting from a very small base, and that system would have to equal or better Apple's "standardized" ecosystem.

Apple, like Dell, will survive the "natural selection" process that takes place in businesses if its efficient supply chain continues to

CASE STUDY

function superbly. Returning to Moore's thesis in *The Death of Competition*,[12] he favors the selection of partners to create something of value, achieve market coverage, and block alternative ecosystems, and Apple has been successful in these aspects to date. With the changing environment, however, Apple has to renew and reinforce its ecosystem continually.

In later stages of the business ecosystem, members must look beyond their community for new ideas and work to prevent partners and customers from defecting. Enterprises must reach out constantly to customers to gather information, allowing predictions as to how the marketplace will change. Similar to the plant and animal ecosystems that prevail in nature, in the corporate Galapagos, it is a coevolve or die kind of environment.

Conclusions

The systems perspective can result in a radically different decision than would be generated by a traditional form of analysis. The sum of local optima does not equate to the global optimum. As Lean Supply Chain Principle 1 states, improving subsystem performance in isolation will have a negative impact on the performance of the system as a whole. Improving subsystem performance in isolation can lead to unexpected consequences. For example, simply focusing on purchase-price variance instead of the total cost of ownership can result in increased lead times and promote the bullwhip effect.

A practical approach for applying systems thinking to business decisions is to evaluate every decision based on three questions:

▲ Will the decision increase the profit-making potential of the organization?
▲ Will the decision reduce working capital and/or fixed assets?
▲ Will the decision result in reduced fixed expenses in the long-term?

If the answer to all of these questions is in the negative, then the decision probably should not be undertaken.

The TOC and Lean are management philosophies that can work together to enhance the competitiveness of the supply chain.

▲ TOC promotes systems thinking.
▲ Some of the TOC concepts and principles can result in un-common sense solutions.

Adopting a systems perspective implicitly requires managers to evaluate their decisions in the context of the business ecosystem. Awareness of the ecosystem can alert managers to potential threats as well as potential opportunities that the enterprise can exploit. As Lean Supply Chain Principle 2 states, organizations should not ignore the supply chain's business ecosystem when they try to improve the performance of their supply chain.

As you continue to read this book, think about the following issues:

▲ What tools and techniques are you using to manage your enterprise and the supply chain? Are you applying systems thinking, focusing on lead-time reduction and building flexible response capabilities?
▲ Are you employing concepts and philosophies such as Theory of Constraints and Lean to reduce waste and adapt to changing customer preferences? Are you applying un-common sense thinking to your business decisions?
▲ Are you living in the throughput world, or are you stuck in the cost world? If you are in the cost world, how can you move to the throughput world?

References

1. M. M. Srinivasan (2004), *Streamlined: 14 Principles for Building and Managing the Lean Supply Chain*, Thompson, Mason, OH.
2. W. E. Deming (1993), *The New Economics for Industry, Government & Education*, Massachussetts Institute of Technology Center for Advanced Engineering Study, Cambridge, MA.
3. P. M. Senge (1994), *The Fifth Discipline: The Art and Practice of the Learning Organization*, Doubleday, New York.
4. J. Ferreira and L. Prokopets (2009), "Does Offshoring Still Make Sense?" *Supply Chain Management Review*, January–February 2009, pp. 20–27.
5. E. M. Goldratt and J. Cox (1984), *The Goal: Excellence in Manufacturing*, North River Press Publishing Company, Croton-on-Hudson, NY.

6. E. M. Goldratt and J. Cox (1992), *The Goal: A Process of Ongoing Improvement*, North River Press Publishing Company, Great Barrington, MA.
7. J. P. Womack, D. T. Jones, and D. Roos (1991), *The Machine That Changed the World*, Harper-Collins, New York.
8. J. P. Womack and D. T. Jones (1996), *Lean Thinking*, Simon & Schuster, New York.
9. E. M. Goldratt, (2009), "Standing on the Shoulders of Giants," *The Manufacturer*, available at www.themanufacturer.com/uk/content/9280/Standing_on_the_shoulders_of_giants; accessed June 2009.
10. J. F. Moore (1996), *The Death of Competition: Leadership and Strategy in the Age of Business Ecosystems*, Harper Business, New York.
11. T. Catan and N. Koppel (2011), "Regulators Eye Apple Anew," *Wall Street Journal*, February 18, 2011.
12. J. F. Moore (1996), *The Death of Competition: Leadership and Strategy in the Age of Business Ecosystems*, Harper Business, New York.

CHAPTER 3

Adopting a Throughput World Perspective

If you were asked to perform one of two tasks and you knew that task one was easier than task two, which task would you choose? In all probability, you would choose task one.

The cost world perspective presents a serious threat to the design and operation of the lean supply chain because it offers a relatively easy and quick option to an enterprise that presents financial reports to its shareholders each quarter. It is easier for these enterprises to improve gross margins and quarterly profits through a cost-reduction program rather than through a program that will increase sales throughput because the latter program requires more time to implement and bear fruit. Unfortunately, as observed in Chapter 1, cost-reduction programs often result in a more complex supply chain that can inadvertently reverse supply chain effectiveness, increasing costs and waste instead of increasing profitability.

The throughput world perspective often results in decisions that are very different from decisions made from a cost world perspective. Maintaining a throughput world perspective, however, requires a lot of courage and effort because decisions made from this perspective do not produce tangible results immediately. Albert Einstein said that "any intelligent fool can make things bigger, more complex, and more violent. It takes a touch of genius—and a lot of courage—to move in the opposite direction." The question is, "How can enterprises move to a throughput world perspective?" The Theory of Constraints (TOC) provides the answer. TOC offers the tools and techniques for tackling complexity and for identifying the points of leverage that have maximum systemic impact.

TOC and the Thinking Process

TOC is based on Goldratt's premise that complex solutions to complex problems will not work—the more complex a problem appears to be on the surface, the simpler the solution must be. This core principle of *inherent simplicity* drives the Thinking Process, an approach to problem solving that relies on systems thinking.

The notion that reality is complex presents a major obstacle to problem resolution. When a problem situation is approached with a preconceived notion that the situation is complex, there is an unconscious push to derive a sophisticated solution to the problem. (Note that the dictionary definition for *sophisticated* is "complex or intricate." Incidentally, an alternate dictionary definition for *sophisticated* is "deceptive or misleading.") Goldratt explains that the problem with a complicated solution is that it never works. People working toward complex solutions soon start believing that they do not know enough or that a lot of detailed knowledge is required to even understand the situation.[1] This feeling of inadequacy often derails the solution method very quickly.

To provide an example of how the perception that reality is complex obscures vision, ask someone how many constraints he has in his enterprise. The typical answer to this question is a shaking of the head and a mumbled answer that there are so many constraints in his business that it is difficult for him to even come close to providing an answer. However, if he were to stop and think about it, from a "big picture" perspective, the answer should be fairly obvious. At any point in time there can be only one or at most a handful of constraints in the system: the core problems that should be addressed first. When those constraints are overcome successfully, a new constraint(s) will surface.

The Thinking Process is designed to bring the core problem(s) to the surface and to identify the most effective way to make the problem go away. It begins with the premise that to improve the performance of any system, three questions must be answered: "What to change?" "What to change to?" and "How to cause the change?" To answer these questions, the Thinking Process uses a set of logic diagrams, based on cause-and-effect relationships, starting with the *undesirable effects* (UDEs) that are observed in the current mode of operation. These UDEs are not the real problems but rather are indicators of the causes that prevent the system from reaching its full potential. The logic diagrams uncover the core problems constraining the system from reaching its full potential and help to identify the "injections" or actions that will diffuse the core problems (make them go away).

A key premise underlying the Thinking Process is that diffusing the core problem effectively requires a win-win solution. Most of the time, managers content themselves with a compromise solution to the problems. Consider the ramifications. Typically, these problems manifest as conflicts involving two or more groups. When people develop a compromise solution, they invariably leave some parties feeling cheated. These parties will constantly strive to alter the solution so that they come out better.

An Un-common Sense Minute

Solutions to conflicts need not be a zero-sum game where one party's gain results in another party's loss. The *evaporating cloud* (a conflict-resolution technique) is a key tool in the Thinking Process that is designed to provide win-win solutions to conflicts. The evaporating cloud resolves conflicts by addressing the assumptions that lead to the conflict. Thus the evaporating cloud provides an un-common sense solution to conflict resolution: "in order to resolve conflicts, ignore the conflict." Instead of focusing on the conflict, the solution is to focus on the assumptions that lead to the conflict.

Pursuing a parallel train of un-common sense thought, Goldratt asks managers to reflect on why their employees are not performing up to their potential. Instead of getting rid of poorly performing employees, managers instead should focus on getting rid of the bad assumptions that resulted in the poor performance. A similar sentiment was echoed by Deming when he said that management must take the responsibility for poor performance and take steps to reduce process variation instead of blaming workers for poor quality.

To summarize the discussion so far:

- All systems operate in a cause-and-effect environment.
- Nearly all the undesirable effects that are observed are not the *problems* but *indicators* of some underlying causes.
- It does not make sense to treat the undesirable effect—that would be analogous to applying a bandage on an infected wound.
- It is necessary to identify and eliminate the critical root cause.

The rest of this chapter instead discusses how enterprises can move from the cost world to the throughput world by focusing on the system constraints. The evaporating cloud is discussed in greater detail in Chapter 6, but for a more detailed discussion on the Thinking Process refer to the *Theory of Constraints Handbook*.[2]

Focusing on the Constraint

From a systems perspective, the operation of an enterprise (or a supply chain, for that matter) may be viewed as a set of interdependent processes that transforms inputs into outputs. To describe the management and operation of these processes in a TOC context, an analogy is often drawn between a set of processes and a chain. Just as the interdependent processes within an enterprise work together to generate profit for the shareholders, the links in a chain work together to pull or lift objects. However, the ability of the chain to pull or lift objects is limited because the chain is only as strong as its weakest link. The strength of the chain is improved by strengthening the weakest link. Strengthening other links has no impact on the strength of the entire chain.

In an analogous manner, enterprises should focus on strengthening the constraint that prevents the enterprise from reaching or exceeding its goal because any loss of output at the constraint resource(s) results in a loss of progress towards the goal for the enterprise. Efforts aimed at improving the performance of other resources will not increase the throughput of the enterprise. These key points are summarized by the Third Lean Supply Chain Principle.

Lean Supply Chain Principle 3

Time lost at a bottleneck resource results in a loss of output for the whole enterprise (entire supply chain). Time saved at a nonbottleneck resource is a mirage.

There is very little disagreement on the core issue that constraints are extremely important and need extra managerial attention and focus. With the simple chain analogy presented earlier, it is fairly obvious how the performance of the system can be optimized. In practice, traditional management metrics can mask the true constraint. In the following discussion, the words *bottleneck* and *constraint* are used interchangeably.*

Let's first consider a situation where constraint identification is relatively easy. Consider a production system with two processes in which the upstream process moves products to the downstream process in large batches to save on transportation costs. Since the downstream process is idle while the batch is built, the upstream process is a temporary constraint during the time the batch is being built at the first process. The situation reverses when the downstream process starts to work on the large batch. For this two-stage process, a policy of batching resulted in both processes behaving like physical constraints at different points in time. In reality, both processes might have ample capacity to meet the demand, and the actual constraint might be market demand—not enough demand for the product.

No doubt, for this simple two-stage process, it is possible to deduce the real constraint—market demand—quite easily. In a more complex situation, it is harder to identify the real constraint. A perceived constraint may be the visible effect of an underlying root cause. In general, constraints appear in the form of *physical constraints, market constraints,* or *policy constraints.*

Physical Constraints

Physical constraints are the easiest to identify. Physical constraints include machine capacity, material availability, labor capacity and space availability. A resource constraint can be determined quite easily in a factory by identifying the resource where work-in-process (WIP) inventories usually accumulate. If a resource shuts down often owing to a lack of components, then there is a materials constraint. Similarly, if the output is not meeting customer demand because of operator availability, then there is a labor constraint.

---

*The TOC zealot will differentiate between a bottleneck and a constraint as follows: a *bottleneck* is a resource or process whose capacity is less than the demand placed on it. A *constraint* is a resource, method, measure, or mind-set that limits the performance of a system.

Market Constraints

Market constraints are a little harder to identify. A market constraint exists if the demand for the enterprise's products and services is less than installed capacity or if the enterprise is unable to offer its ideal product portfolio to the market. If the enterprise has excess capacity, it is a sure indication of a market constraint. However, a market constraint can arise even if an enterprise that produces a variety of products does not have enough capacity to satisfy the demand across all products. In such a situation, there could be a limited demand for the product(s) that the enterprise would really prefer to sell.

Policy Constraints

Most of the constraints to system performance result from poor policies. For example, the enterprise could create a *methods constraint** by never producing a batch of units below an *economic order quantity*. When resources are forced to produce in large quantities, there is a high probability of misallocating resource capacity and producing products for which there is no current demand.

A *measures constraint* occurs if the measurement system drives behavior incongruous with enterprise goals. Goldratt frequently states, "Tell me how you measure me, and I will tell you how I behave." For example, if the purchasing department is measured on purchase-price variances, it can aggressively seek quantity discounts, resulting in increased raw materials inventory. A poorly designed compensation scheme for the sales department often results in a measures constraint. If the salespeople are rewarded based on sales revenue, they will have a powerful incentive to sell the highest-priced products, even if those products are not the most profitable products.

A third type of policy constraint is a *mind-set constraint*. A mind-set constraint arises when the thought process or culture of the organization blocks the design and implementation of methods and measures required to achieve enterprise goals. An organization with which I recently worked

---

*TOC now characterizes the term *policy constraint* as a misnomer because bad policies are not constraints. Rather, bad policies hinder effective constraint management by inhibiting the ability to exploit the constraint fully. It is, however, convenient to continue referring to these bad policies as constraints in this book.

provides a good example of the mind-set constraint at work. The continuous improvement team in this organization frequently encounters resistance to its efforts from the other employees. The continuous improvement team refers to the mind-set constraints that generate such resistance as "The Trinity." The Trinity is (1) "You don't understand," (2) "We are different," and (3) "That won't work here!"

Policy Constraints and Cost Accounting Systems

Without question, cost accounting systems can provide valuable information to management on where costs are incurred while delivering a product or service to the customer. This information is used by management for resource allocation and other financial decisions. However, accounting systems can be double-edged swords, especially when they are used to drive future decisions on what products to offer the customer or what products to discontinue. These accounting systems can present a unique blend of method, measures, and mind-set constraints, as the next section shows.

Estimating Product Costs with Cost Accounting Systems

How does the sales department decide whether or not to accept a new customer order? How does Operations decide what products to schedule and what batch size to run? How does the controller decide whether or not to approve the purchase of new equipment? Such decisions are made based on a standard set of guidelines and operating procedures, typically using information prepared by the cost accounting department.

Modern cost accounting systems originated during the industrial revolution. Managers of large, complex businesses needed a system for recording and tracking costs to help them make critical business decisions. The early cost accounting systems were not very sophisticated. Fixed costs were relatively low, and only a few products were produced by the enterprise. Most of the costs in the early stages of the industrial revolution were variable costs—costs that varied directly with the output volume, such as the cost of labor, raw materials, and the power needed to run the business. Managers simply could add up the variable costs and use the total variable cost to guide them in decision making.

Cost accounting systems remained simple in the early part of the twentieth century. However, when factories started to produce a large variety of products, there was an expressed need to determine the cost of these products more precisely, and *standard cost accounting* systems gained prominence.

The Standard Cost Accounting System

The standard cost accounting system was the driving force behind management control and decision-making processes for manufacturing enterprises during the twentieth century. Managers of large, complex enterprises relied—and still rely—on this system to provide correct information to help them make critical operational decisions.

The standard cost accounting method uses a *cost driver* that drives, or allocates, the overhead costs to specific products. For example, a cost driver often used by standard cost accounting is direct labor cost, in which case the overhead is allocated among the various products in proportion to the labor cost incurred in building those products. In general, the choice of cost driver depends on the nature of the business.

Standard cost accounting is an *absorption costing* method that attempts to absorb all the costs of production into the product cost. Absorption accounting is a *generally accepted accounting principle* (GAAP) requirement in the United States for external financial reporting and for tax returns. A large majority of countries follow the *International Financial Reporting Standards* (IFRS) for external financial reporting and tax returns. The IFRS also encourages the use of absorption costing for external reporting.

When it was first introduced, standard cost accounting was a powerful tool because it provided managers with the ability to make decisions that improved the performance of their areas and plants dramatically. However, some of the basic assumptions of standard cost accounting became invalid in the middle part of the twentieth century when product variety increased and fixed costs as a proportion of the total cost started to rise. There is growing awareness, even within the accounting profession, that the standard cost accounting system has fundamental flaws that hamper effective decision making.

A potential flaw with the standard cost accounting system—and absorption costing in general—is that all manufacturing-related expenses, depreciation, indirect labor, and utilities are allocated to the product based on just a single cost driver. Hence these methods are unable to provide a true representation of the product cost.

Absorption costing also increases the value of an item every time the item undergoes a process step because the labor- and equipment-related costs associated with that process are absorbed into the product cost. Since absorption costing absorbs overhead and labor costs into the product cost every time the product is processed by a resource, the shop floor supervisor now has a powerful incentive to use the resources in the shop at close to 100 percent, pushing products through these resources as quickly as possible. These products may not be needed downstream, but that is not the supervisor's concern because she is measured based on how well she has absorbed her manufacturing overhead costs. The result is high levels of inventory accumulation when the output from these resources is not consistent with requirements downstream.

What is the *real* value of the WIP or finished goods inventory? Arguably, its value is zero dollars unless there was a customer demand for this product. If the item in inventory was not produced in response to an order, a unit of raw material was consumed that could have been used to produce a product that actually was needed. Furthermore, a critical resource may have been used to produce this inventory.

The following case study is based on an actual incident, reported in *The Haystack Syndrome*[3] and in *Synchronous Management,* Volume 1.[4]

CASE STUDY

Illinois Sound Machine

Illinois Sound Machine is a well-known enterprise that appointed a new CEO in the later 1970s. The CEO was eager to prove his ability to the shareholders. His first major initiative was to cut costs by outsourcing any component manufactured in his plant that could be procured at a lower cost from an outside supplier.

The CEO asked his cost accounting department to provide him with accurate product costs for every component manufactured in his plant. He also instructed his purchasing department to find the best purchase

CASE STUDY

price for these components. He next instructed an assistant to meticulously compare the product cost for each component with its corresponding purchase price. Components were outsourced if the product cost exceeded the purchase price. As components were outsourced, some production lines were shut down, and the direct laborers operating those lines were laid off.

After four months, the CEO asked for an updated list of the components that were still manufactured in the plant, comparing their product cost with their purchase price. The new list revealed a number of new components whose product cost exceeded their purchase price because these manufactured components had to bear the overhead burden that the outsourced components had shared previously.

The CEO was puzzled, but he explained this situation away as a residual effect of the previous administration. He asked his staff to repeat the outsourcing exercise all over again. More production lines were closed, and some more direct laborers were laid off. The fourth quarter arrived, and the financial statements presented a bleak picture. The CEO was still puzzled. He toured all the facilities in the enterprise and found lots of idle capacity. While the blue-collar employees had been laid off, the buildings, equipment, and infrastructure were still present, albeit without much work to do.

The CEO had to act fast. Perhaps he realized that absorption accounting principles could help him in this situation because he made a quick assessment and realized that the bulk of the enterprise's investment was in the final assembly plant.

The CEO obtained loans from more than 200 banks, used this money to buy raw materials, hired new operators, and ran his assembly plants round the clock, building up finished goods inventories. He persuaded his distributors to accept shipments of finished products with the option to return unsold products. These shipments were booked as sales.

Since finished goods inventories absorb all the overhead costs, and since many of these products were booked as sales, the enterprise showed a healthy profit at the end of the year. The CEO informed the

CASE STUDY

shareholders that he had achieved his goal of returning the enterprise to profitability and received a generous bonus. However, the enterprise was now operating with a very weak foundation. Dealers were returning unsold products, and bank loans were becoming overdue. The economy did not help much either. In order to survive, Illinois Sound Machine had to lay off tens of thousands of workers. It shrank to one-third its original size and completely restructured under a different name.

The Illinois Sound Machine case provides an interesting blend of method, mind-set, and measures policy constraints:

▲ *A methods constraint:* An arguably flawed method of absorption costing that adds value to a product as it moves through a series of process steps.

▲ *A measures constraint:* A measurement system that rewards managers if they use their resources to produce more output because a higher output better absorbs labor and overhead.

▲ *A mind-set constraint:* A notion that the enterprise can become profitable through make-buy decisions on select components without considering how these decisions affect the other components manufactured in the enterprise.

As noted earlier, cost accounting systems are unable to provide the true product cost owing to the way overhead costs are allocated. Consequently, these systems also distort the true profit-making potential of products. The following example demonstrates this point.

CSN, Inc.

Three home-maintenance specialists, Crossley, Steele, and Nice, have banded together to form CSN, Inc., based in New Orleans, Louisiana, where demand for home-maintenance services is high. CSN offers the following types of services: plumbing, window cleaning, gutter guard installation, and landscaping.

The total monthly wages for these three men is $18,000 including benefits. These wages are categorized as administrative overhead costs. The non-administrative overhead costs, including rental charges, truck fleet maintenance, marketing and advertising, and depreciation, amount to $9,000 per month.

CSN is seeing ample demand for all its products, but there is a shortage of qualified workers in the area. Adhering to a motto, "Teach Your Children Well," that they have preached ever since their younger days, Crossley, Steele, and Nice have employed their own children, five high-school graduates, to run their home-maintenance operations.

These five employees are each paid a competitive salary of $2,000 per month including benefits. In return, the employees are each expected to work 200 hours a month, giving CSN a total of 1,000 hours of available capacity. CSN thus has fixed its labor rate to be $2,000 ÷ 200 = $10 per labor hour. Table 3.1 presents the current demand, the average time per job, and some revenue/cost data for the services offered by CSN based on data gathered over the past six months. The table also shows the current number of jobs that CSN is completing each month for each type of service.

Table 3.1 Data for CSN, Inc.

	Plumbing	Window cleaning	Installing gutter guards	Landscaping
Monthly demand	250 jobs	160 jobs	145 jobs	120 jobs
Average time required per job	2 hours	4 hours	3 hours	5 hours
Current output	90 jobs	70 jobs	80 jobs	60 jobs
Average revenue per job	$130	$170	$200	$250
Material cost per job	$30	$10	$70	$75

Table 3.1 shows that CSN is currently completing an average of 90 plumbing, 70 window cleaning, 80 gutter guard, and 60 landscaping jobs per month. For this level of output, CSN uses up $(90 \times 2 + 70 \times 4 + 80 \times 3 + 60 \times 5) = 1,000$ hours of labor, and that effectively accounts for all the available capacity.

Based on these data, CSN assigns labor costs to the four products as follows: Plumbing takes 2 hours per job, so the labor cost for a plumbing job at a labor rate of $10 per hour is $10 $\times$ 2 = $20 per job. The labor costs for the other three products are window cleaning $40, gutter guards $30, and landscaping $50.

CSN is using standard cost accounting to spread the administrative and nonadministrative overhead costs. The cost driver chosen by CSN is the monthly production volume. Currently, CSN is completing (90 + 70 + 80 + 60) = 300 jobs per month. Hence each job is allocated an administrative overhead cost of $18,000 $\div$ 300 = $60 and a nonadministrative overhead cost of $9,000 $\div$ 300 = $30. Table 3.2 presents the allocation of the nonadministrative and administrative overhead as well as all the other costs. The resulting profit for each product is also presented in the table.

Table 3.2 Profit Computation for CSN, Inc., Using Standard Costing

	Plumbing	Window cleaning	Installing gutter guards	Landscaping
Average revenue per job	$130	$170	$200	$250
Material cost per job	$30	$10	$70	$75
Labor cost per job	$20	$40	$30	$50
Administrative overhead allocation	$60	$60	$60	$60
Nonadministrative overhead allocation	$30	$30	$30	$30
Profit per job	**–$10**	**$30**	**$10**	**$35**

Standard costing requires all the overhead and labor costs to be reconciled at the end of an accounting period based on actual usages. This is not currently an issue for CSN because it is using all its labor capacity, and all overheads are being absorbed, so there is no labor variance or overhead absorption variance to worry about. At the current levels of output, the profit for CSN is 90 $\times$ (–$10) + 70 $\times$ $30 + 80 $\times$ $10 + 60 $\times$ $35 = $4,100 per month.

The profit data provided in Table 3.2 suggest that landscaping is the most lucrative operation, followed by window cleaning. The general manager, Crossley, notices that CSN is nowhere close to meeting the demand for landscaping and window cleaning. He sets about maximizing the amount of landscaping and window cleaning jobs that can be completed with the available capacity of 1,000 hours. Fortunately for CSN, the demand for its services is so high that such a pursuit does not affect the demand for any of the services offered by CSN.

CSN first completes the demand for the most profitable job, landscaping. Since there are 120 landscaping jobs demanded each month, each requiring 5 hours of labor on average, CSN allocates 600 labor hours for landscaping. The remaining 400 hours are devoted to window cleaning, each job requiring an average of 4 hours to complete, which results in 400 ÷ 4 = 100 window cleaning jobs. At this stage, the available capacity is exhausted.

The resulting profit from this product mix appears to be 120 × $35 + 100 × $30 = $7,200. However, this is not the true profit. There are unabsorbed overheads and unabsorbed labor, resulting in overhead and labor variances.

These variances have to be reconciled by CSN as follows: The 120 landscaping and 100 window cleaning jobs each absorb, or recover, $60 of administrative and $30 of nonadministrative overhead, that is, $90 × 120 + $90 × 100 = $19,800. Since the total overhead cost is $18,000 + $9,000 = $27,000, the overhead variance is $27,000 − $19,800 = $7,200. Subtracting this variance from the apparent profit of $7,200 gives a net profit of $0! The "optimal" profit obtained with the standard cost accounting data is significantly less than the $4,100 profit obtained with the earlier arbitrary product mix.

What is the explanation for this unexpected result?

The answer is that if a product portfolio is "optimized" using standard cost accounting data (or any other technique that uses historical data to allocate fixed costs), historical data drive future plans and actions. If the optimization results in a different product portfolio from the current one, the allocated costs must be revised (or variances must be reconciled) to correctly account for the revised product portfolio. This may result in a different cost/profit picture that will drive the optimization process toward yet another product portfolio, and so on, *ad nauseam*.

Although the standard cost accounting system is used widely, its use is being questioned increasingly. The basic problem is how overhead is allocated across the products or services. Standard cost accounting collects all the fixed costs of manufacturing and places them into one overhead cost pool. Labor costs are not included in this cost pool because absorption accounting treats labor as a variable cost. Standard cost accounting allocates all the overhead costs based on some cost driver such as production volume, and so the resulting product costs are very approximate representations of the actual cost of producing these products.

Financial and nonfinancial managers have sought better ways to allocate overhead for many years, so they welcomed the activity-based costing (ABC) system when it was introduced in the 1980s. Although the basic elements of ABC were in existence for decades, it was developed and presented in a structured manner only in the 1980s.

Activity-Based Costing (ABC)

The ABC system provides an opportunity for obtaining a better approximation of the product cost than standard cost accounting systems are able to. The basic principle of the ABC system is that "activities consume costs, and products consume activities." The difference between standard cost accounting and ABC is that in standard cost accounting, products "consume" overhead costs, whereas the ABC system instead assumes that costs are consumed by activities (that may or may not add value to the product). ABC is a methodology that identifies costs associated with activities and links those costs to products based on how the products consume those activities. Rather than allocate the total cost of operating a resource directly to a range of products, ABC identifies the specific activities that go into making a specific product and attempts to figure out the cost of those activities.

With ABC, the accountant first enumerates all overhead activities and their costs. ABC focuses on using multiple cost drivers to guide allocations with greater accuracy than an allocation method that uses a single cost driver. ABC allocates activities and their costs into one of four categories: unit level, batch level, product level, and facility level.

Unit-level activities and their associated costs are the easiest to determine. *Unit-level activities* are activities performed for each unit of product. For example, a setup cost is a unit-level cost if the setup is made after a fixed number of units are produced at a resource because the total setup cost can be spread over these units to arrive at a per-unit product cost.

Batch-level activities are activities executed once for each batch of products. Batch-level costs are independent of the number of units in a batch and so are harder to allocate compared with unit-level costs. Examples of batch-level costs are supervisor salaries, machine setup costs not traceable to specific products, and material handling costs.

Product-level activities support the production of a product type or model. Product-level costs do not vary with the number of batches. Examples of such costs are engineering support costs and depreciation costs of equipment dedicated to a product line.

Facility-level costs include the costs of operating the accounting, human resources, general administration, sales, and plant maintenance functions.

The approach used to compute costs using ABC is conceptually simple. Using different cost drivers to allocate costs results in a less arbitrary allocation of overhead costs. Moreover, since ABC uses more meaningful cost drivers to drive the allocation of costs, it is arguably better than standard cost accounting for measuring performance.

However, the improved tracking accuracy comes with a cost. ABC requires more data to be gathered to monitor where costs are being expended, and a number of organizations find this task to be onerous.

The Tennessee Valley Authority (TVA) attempted to apply ABC in its organization and asked its engineers to track their activities so that they could be allocated more precisely into various cost pools. TVA decided to abandon ABC when the engineers asked the accounting department to provide them with a new cost driver that would accurately capture the costs for the time they spent tracking down their activities.

There are other problems with ABC. The choice of the cost drivers is still rather arbitrary. The choice of cost drivers has behavioral implications as well. Suppose that the purchasing department's expenses are allocated to different functional units in proportion to the number of purchase orders these units generate. If the functional units knew that the ABC system was allocating costs based on the number of purchase orders the functional units generated, they would tend to place fewer purchase orders. Fewer purchase orders would imply larger order quantities, which imply higher average inventory levels, an undesirable effect for the enterprise. If expenses instead were allocated on the basis of the number of stock-keeping units (SKUs), the allocation method would encourage development of products that use common parts, and that would result in a good practice.

The point to note is that cost drivers allocate cost or quantify some measure of past performance. Indeed, one can seriously question the validity of or logic behind trying to allocate *sunk* costs across products using historical data.

Let's revisit CSN and see if ABC is able to determine the optimal product mix and make more money than CSN's current monthly profit of $4,100.

Applying ABC to CSN, Inc.

Crossley is not happy with the standard costing system, especially when he finds that the "optimal" product portfolio using this method effectively would drive his profits from $4,100 down to $0. He thinks that the problem lies with the cost driver used to allocate the overheads. He wants to use ABC and allocate administrative overhead costs based on the actual time and effort spent by the managers on the various products. He also wants to allocate the nonadministrative overhead cost using labor hours as the cost driver instead of the old cost driver that was based on production volume.

Crossley gathers data on the actual time the three men spend on the various products. (This data-gathering process involves some effort on his part, and it also incurs some additional cost; the additional cost is ignored.) The data show that the administrators allocate their time to the four products as follows: plumbing 30 percent, window cleaning 35 percent, installing gutter guards 20 percent, and landscaping 15 percent.

Based on these data, Crossley calculates the administrative overhead cost to be allocated to plumbing as $18,000 × 0.30 = $5,400. Since 90 plumbing jobs are completed each month, the administrative overhead allocated to each plumbing job is $5,400 ÷ 90 = $60. The administrative overhead cost is allocated to each of the other types of services in a like manner, and Table 3.3 shows the resulting allocation.

Next, Crossley uses labor hours as the cost driver to allocate the nonadministrative overhead cost. The total nonadministrative overhead cost is $9,000, and the total available labor capacity is 1,000 hours, so nonadministrative overhead is charged at the rate of $9,000 ÷ 1,000 = $9 per labor hour. Since plumbing takes 2 hours, the nonadministrative overhead cost allocated to a plumbing job is = $9 × 2 = $18. The allocation for the other three types of services proceeds in a like manner. Table 3.4 shows the costs and profits using ABC. The table shows that landscaping is still the most profitable operation. Plumbing is no longer a losing proposition, but window cleaning is.

Table 3.3 Administrative Overhead Allocation for CSN, Inc., Using ABC

	Plumbing	Window cleaning	Installing gutter guards	Landscaping
Percentage effort	30%	35%	20%	15%
Administrative overhead allocated = $18,000 × percent effort	$5,400	$6,300	$3,600	$2,700
Number of jobs	90 jobs	70 jobs	80 jobs	60 jobs
Administrative overhead allocation per job	$60	$90	$45	$45

Table 3.4 Profit Computation for CSN, Inc., Using ABC

	Plumbing	Window cleaning	Installing gutter guards	Landscaping
Average revenue per job	$130	$170	$200	$250
Material cost per job	$30	$10	$70	$75
Labor cost per job	$20	$40	$30	$50
Administrative overhead allocation	$60	$90	$45	$45
Nonadministrative overhead allocation	$18	$36	$27	$45
Profit per job	**$2**	**–$6**	**$28**	**$35**

Suppose that CSN can choose its product offering as before. Based on the ABC data, the company first satisfies the demand for 120 landscaping jobs. The 120 landscaping jobs use $120 \times 5 = 600$ hours of capacity. The remaining 400 hours are applied to gutter guard installation to complete $400 \div 3 = 133$ gutter guards, leaving 1 hour of unused capacity.

The resulting profit from this product mix would appear to be $120 \times $35 + 133 \times $28 = $7,924$. However, this is once again not the true profit because there are unabsorbed overhead and labor costs resulting in overhead and labor variances. These variances are reconciled as follows: The 120 landscaping and 133 gutter guard installation jobs will each recover $45 of administrative overhead cost, that is, $45 \times 120 + $45 \times 133 = $11,385$.

Thus the administrative overhead variance is $18,000 − $11,385 = $6,615. The 1 hour of unused labor gives a labor usage variance of $10 and a nonadministrative overhead variance of $9. Thus the total of all the variances is $6,634. Subtracting this amount from the apparent profit of $7,924 results in a net profit of $1,290.

Once again, the "optimal" profit is actually much less than the $4,100 profit obtained earlier with an arbitrary product mix.

While ABC tried to allocate overhead costs among the products more equitably based on the activities involved, the allocation may drive behavior that runs counter to enterprise goals. In the case of CSN, ABC made plumbing and window cleaning more expensive simply because the managers devoted more of their time to these products.

To sum up the discussion on cost accounting systems, the problems they face with regard to determining product costs are as follows:

▲ The standard cost accounting system allocates all overhead costs to the products using a broad measure such as labor cost. This distorts the actual product cost.

▲ The CSN, Inc., example showed that if we "optimize" the product portfolio using standard cost accounting or ABC, the resulting profit can be *significantly less* than the profits obtained from an *arbitrary product mix.*

▲ A more equitable allocation of overhead costs using ABC helps to approximate product costs a little better, but ABC still suffers from some arbitrariness with regard to how the allocations are made. The choice of a cost driver is even more difficult when resources are shared by more than one product. For example, no single cost driver can reflect all the relevant activities that take place in the accounting department.

▲ The problem with ABC becomes worse when the analysis tries to allocate some costs that are unrelated to a particular product or to a particular customer. Examples of such costs include the CEO's salary and building and grounds maintenance costs. The fact that these are costs that cannot be allocated in any rational manner strengthens the belief that, in general, there is no such thing as a true product cost.

▲ ABC systems can be difficult to operate and expensive to maintain because the information requirements are significantly large.

▲ The CSN, Inc., example also showed that the allocation of sunk costs such as overhead can make a product that the enterprise wishes to promote prohibitively expensive to the customer, making it even harder to sell the product. Thus, while ABC is useful in determining where costs are incurred, its use to determine product costs and to identify which products are profitable becomes questionable.

The natural question to ask at this stage is how TOC will address some of the problems found with traditional cost accounting systems. TOC prescribes an alternate approach, *throughput accounting*, using the performance measures Throughput (T), Investment (I), and Operating Expense (OE). These three measures are designed to move enterprises to the throughput world and discourage the kind of manipulations that were made by the CEO of Illinois Sound Machine.

Throughput Accounting

TOC views a business as a profit-making machine. Throughput accounting focuses on improving the *rate* at which the enterprise makes profits through effective management of its constraints and prescribes three measures to support this focus.

Throughput Accounting Measures

The measures prescribed by throughput accounting are expressed in monetary units in line with the TOC view of a business as a profit-making machine*:

- ▲ *Throughput* (T). The rate at which the system generates money through sales.
- ▲ *Investment* (I). All the money the system invests in order to generate throughput.
- ▲ *Operating Expense* (OE). All the money the system spends turning Investment into Throughput.

The definition for T as the rate at which the system generates money through sales emphasizes the velocity of profit generation. The definition of T also deliberately differentiates between a unit produced and a unit *sold*. If a unit is produced but not sold, it remains on the books as inventory.

---

*For not-for-profit or nonprofit enterprises, Throughput is the rate at which the system meets its stated goal.

From a naive viewpoint, the definition for T resembles the definition for *contribution margin*, which is simply revenue less variable costs. But there are some differences. One difference is that contribution margin is expressed in monetary units, whereas T is the rate at which monetary units accumulate. Another difference is that contribution margin treats direct labor cost as a variable cost. With throughput accounting, direct labor cost is a part of OE, reflecting the fact that direct labor is a fixed cost for many enterprises today.

The TOC definition for Investment, I, is quite intuitive. In addition to raw materials, WIP, and finished goods inventory, I also includes money invested in equipment and the facilities.

Defining OE as the cost of turning I into T provides a simple way to categorize expenses and avoids making arbitrary distinctions. OE includes all costs that do not vary directly with output, such as salaries paid to managers. No attempt is made to categorize the salary of the CEO differently from the salaries of plant supervisors. Throughput accounting avoids these distinctions because allocating these indirect costs among the various products is very difficult, as observed earlier. Other items that would go into the OE bucket include depreciation and selling, general, and administrative (SG&A) expenses. These are fixed costs that typically do not vary with the production level.

Relating Throughput Accounting to Traditional Accounting

Figure 3.1 presents a model to relate T, I, and OE with sales revenue and with traditional accounting costs such as depreciation. The following discussion will clarify this model.

Defining I in monetary terms makes it possible to capture all the assets in one "bucket." Every time the enterprise purchases an assets—either a fixed assets or a liquid asset such as raw materials or components—the money invested in purchasing the asset goes into the Investment bucket, represented by I in Figure 3.1. In contrast to traditional cost accounting systems, throughput accounting does not add value to raw materials when they are converted to WIP and eventually to finished goods. Instead, WIP and finished goods inventory are valued at the same price as raw materials.

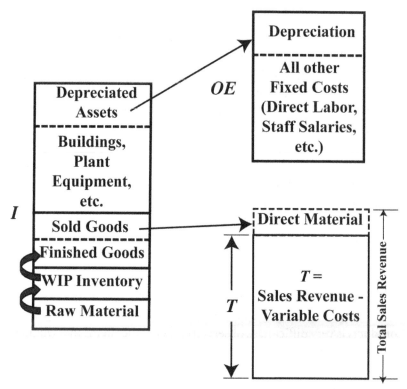

Figure 3.1 A model for relating *T, I,* and *OE.*

Since WIP and finished goods inventory are not burdened with direct labor or overhead cost allocations, the throughput accounting measures eliminate the kinds of manipulations observed in the Illinois Sound Machine case, in which the creation of finished goods capitalized all the expenses and artificially inflated profits. Traditional costing methods also make it possible to move expenses from one period to another by attaching them to inventory (as an investment), enhancing profit numbers when it is convenient to do so. With throughput accounting, it will not be possible to move expenses by such methods.

A numerical example will further clarify the discussion surrounding Figure 3.1 and also show how throughput accounting relates to traditional accounting.

Kings of Neon

Kings of Neon is an enterprise that manufactures lighting equipment for rock concerts. It has compiled the following information for fiscal year 2011:

Kings of Neon: Asset Base as of January 1, 2011

Fixed assets	$120,000
Raw materials inventory (units)	25,000
WIP inventory (units)	15,000
Finished goods inventory (units)	20,000

During 2011, Kings of Neon purchased fixed assets worth $25,000 and 40,000 units of raw materials. The raw materials purchase price is $10 per unit, so the value of the investment, I, at the start of 2011 is (fixed assets + raw materials inventory + WIP + finished goods inventory) = $120,000 + $10 × (25,000 + 15,000 + 20,000) = $720,000.

Kings of Neon sold 30,000 units in 2011 at a selling price of $30 per unit. Labor cost was $120,000, and salaries and other expenses accounted for $400,000 in 2011.

Kings of Neon depreciates its fixed assets using straight-line depreciation of 10 percent per annum on the asset base of $120,000. The implicit assumption is that these assets were acquired at the end of 2010 and will be depreciated over the next 10 years. Thus the depreciation in 2011 is $12,000. These activities are summarized as follows:

Kings of Neon: Activity in 2011

Raw materials purchases in 2011 (units)	40,000
Raw material purchase price per unit	$10
Number of units sold in 2011	30,000
Selling price per unit	$30
Direct labor wages	$120,000
Salaries and expenses	$400,000
Capital assets acquired in 2011	$25,000
Depreciation in 2011	$12,000

Using this information, Kings of Neon determines its fixed assets at the end of 2011 to be (fixed assets at start of 2011 + capital assets acquired in 2011 – depreciation in 2011) = $120,000 + $25,000 – $12,000 = $133,000.

Kings of Neon ended the year with 20,000 units of raw materials, 20,000 units of WIP inventory, and 30,000 units of finished goods inventory. The asset base at the end of the year is as follows:

Kings of Neon: Asset Base as of December 31, 2011

Fixed assets	$133,000
Raw materials inventory (units)	20,000
WIP inventory (units)	20,000
Finished goods inventory (units)	30,000

Operating expenses during 2011 = direct labor wages ($120,000) + salaries and expenses ($400,000) + depreciation ($12,000) = $532,000

The revenue from the sale of 30,000 units at $30 each is (30,000 × $30 = $900,000). The variable costs are the direct material costs involved in the sale, valued at the raw materials purchase price of $10 each: 30,000 × $10 = $300,000. Thus T = sales revenue − direct materials = $900,000 − $300,000 = $600,000. The profit is $T - OE = $68,000.

It should be noted that traditional accounting methods will arrive at the same profit. Traditional accounting methods, however, will capitalize all the expenses, adding value to the WIP and finished goods inventory, as discussed earlier.

At the end of 2011, there are 70,000 units of inventory, in the form of raw materials, WIP, or finished goods, each unit valued at $10. At the end of 2011, I = 70,000 × $10 + $133,000 = $833,000. The three throughput accounting measures have the following values:

I (start of 2011) = $720,000

T (in 2011) = $600,000

OE (in 2011) = $532,000

I (end of 2011) = $833,000

Even though Kings of Neon ended the year with more WIP and finished goods inventory, these excess units are neither capitalized nor included in

OE. Until such time as these units are sold, they will only contribute to *I*, in line with the definition of *I* as "the money the systems invests in order to generate throughput."

Relating Throughput Accounting Measures to Financial Measures

Although the throughput accounting measures are different from traditional cost accounting measures, they relate well to important financial measures: The primary financial measures of interest for an enterprise are net profit and return on assets (ROA). In terms of *T*, *I*, and *OE*, these financial measures are obtained as follows:

Net profit per year = $T - OE$

$$ROA = \frac{T - OE}{I}$$

The throughput accounting measures also provide other financial metrics of interest:

$$\text{Asset turns} = \frac{T}{I}$$

$$\text{Productivity} = \frac{T}{OE}$$

The traditional formula for inventory turns includes only the working capital inventory (i.e., raw materials inventory, WIP inventory, and finished goods inventory), whereas the throughput accounting formula for asset turns includes the capital assets. It is, however, a simple matter to split *I* into two components, I_{CA} and I_{WC}, where I_{CA} accounts for all the investments in capital assets and I_{WC} represents the working capital investment. The inventory turns now can be obtained as $T \div I_{WC}$.

The TOC view of business emphasizes a throughput world perspective—a focus on improving *T*. The cost world, with its emphasis on cutting costs, is more focused on reducing OE. As discussed in Chapter 2, where these two perspectives were first introduced, the difference in focus between the two perspectives can result in dramatically different decisions and outcomes. A simple numerical example will reinforce that discussion.

Cost World Versus Throughput World: Everclear, Inc.

Everclear, Inc., is in the business of manufacturing and selling Sunflowers detergent. This enterprise purchases liquid soap—the raw material—for $3 per bottle, adds washing soda and borax to the liquid soap, and sells this product as detergent for $10 per bottle. The cost of the additives—washing soda and borax—is $1 per bottle. Everclear currently sells 1 million bottles of this detergent every year for an annual sales revenue of $10 million. The annual procurement cost (liquid soap cost + cost of additive) is $4 million.

Everclear has 20 salespeople. These salespeople mix the additive into the detergent just before the product is sold to customers. The salespeople are each paid an average annual salary of $50,000 for a total labor cost of $1 million. The overhead expense (managers' salaries and other fixed expenses) is $5 million per year.

The only variable cost is the procurement cost. Labor and overhead are fixed costs. The throughput T = annual sales revenue – annual procurement cost = $10 million – $4 million = $6 million, and operating expense OE = labor + overhead = $1 million + $5 million = $6 million. The annual net profit is $T - OE$ = $0. Table 3.5 presents the data.

Table 3.5   Cost and Profit Data for Everclear

Item	Data
Sales revenue	$10,000,000
Raw materials cost	$3,000,000
Additive cost	$1,000,000
Wages to salespeople	$1,000,000
Overhead (including SG&A)	$5,000,000
Total cost	$10,000,000
Net profit	$0

Since Everclear is just breaking even, management is reviewing opportunities to improve profits. A study reveals that the salespeople are used only 80 percent of the time. To improve profitability, the enterprise fires four salesmen, 20 percent of the workforce. The layoff does not affect sales, but the remaining 16 salespeople are now working at full capacity. Since the wages paid to the salespeople is reduced by $200,000, the OE is now $800,000 + $5 million = $5.8 million, resulting in a net profit of $200,000. Table 3.6 presents the results of the cost-cutting initiative. Everclear is now making a profit, but the layoff has resulted in the remaining salespeople actively seeking other employment opportunities, and future throughput is in jeopardy.

Table 3.6 Leveraging Power of OE for Everclear

Item	Data	Leveraging power of OE
Sales revenue	$10,000,000	$10,000,000
Raw materials cost	$3,000,000	$3,000,000
Additive cost	$1,000,000	$1,000,000
Wages to salespeople	$1,000,000	$800,000
Overhead (including SG&A)	$5,000,000	$5,000,000
Total cost	$10,000,000	$9,800,000
Net profit	$0	$200,000

Consider an alternate scenario where the focus is on a growth strategy. Suppose that Everclear does not fire the four salespeople but instead uses them to launch a marketing campaign. At the same time, it drops the selling price of the detergent by 5 percent to $9.50 per bottle. The marketing campaign costs an additional $100,000 per year, but it increases sales by 20 percent, to 1.2 million bottles of detergent per year. The sales revenue is now $9.50 × 1.2 million = $11.40 million per year. The procurement costs have increased correspondingly to $4 × 1.2 million = $4.80 million per year, so the throughput $T = $11.40 million – $4.80 million = $6.60 million per year.

The labor cost is $1 million. The overhead cost has increased owing to the marketing campaign to $5 million + $0.1 million = $5.1 million. Thus the OE is $6.1 million, resulting in a net profit of $T - OE = $500,000. Table 3.7 presents the results from the growth strategy.

The net profit from the growth scenario represents a 250 percent increase over the net profit obtained from the cost-cutting initiative. The 20 salespeople are not stressed by the thought of any layoffs, and future throughput is better protected than with the cost-cutting initiative.

Table 3.7 Leveraging Power of *T* for Everclear

Item	Data	Leveraging power of *OE*	Leveraging power of *T*
Sales revenue	$10,000,000	$10,000,000	$11,400,000
Raw materials cost	$3,000,000	$3,000,000	$3,600,000
Additive cost	$1,000,000	$1,000,000	$1,200,000
Wages to salespeople	$1,000,000	$800,000	$1,000,000
Overhead (including SG&A)	$5,000,000	$5,000,000	$5,100,000
Total cost	$10,000,000	$9,800,000	$10,900,000
Net profit	$0	$200,000	$500,000

The Everclear example suggests that the leveraging power of *T* can significantly exceed the leveraging power of *OE*. The reason why *T* has more leverage is explained as follows: Since it is relatively harder to reduce fixed assets and infrastructure than to reduce labor, enterprises in the cost world often resort to cutting labor cost. But labor cost is only a small fraction of the total cost of operating the enterprise, so reducing labor cost does not provide much leverage. The throughput world, however, focuses on leveraging the fixed asset and infrastructure costs, which represent a large percentage of the total product cost.

The analogy drawn earlier, between a set of processes and a chain, can be used to underscore the difference between the cost world and the throughput world perspectives. Suppose that instead of strengthening the weakest link (improving *T*), the enterprise adopts a cost world perspective and focuses on improving efficiency at the current level of performance (improving *OE*).* Assume as before that the chain consists of 10 links, where each link has a load-carrying capacity of 100 pounds except for one of them, which has a load-carrying capacity of only 50 pounds. Management is unhappy with the cost of maintaining the nine strong links, so it "right-sizes" the chain by selling the nine heavy links, replacing them with nine links that each have a load-carrying capacity of 50 pounds. On first glance, this is a truly efficient chain because every link is capable of carrying exactly the same load. What is the problem here?

The problem is that the enterprise is now locked into the current level of performance. Before undertaking the cost-reduction program, there was one

---

*This analogy is attributed to Tony Rizzo, CEO of the Product Development Institute.

weak link that limited the load-carrying capacity of the chain to 50 pounds. Now there are 10 links, any one of which can break if the chain lifts more than 50 pounds. If the enterprise desires to improve its performance in the future, it will have to work on *all 10 links* in the chain. The same is true with enterprises that try to eliminate overcapacity. In addition to the vulnerable position in which the enterprise has placed itself, when business picks up, it also may find it harder to recruit employees fearful of getting axed in the next downsizing wave. The fourth Lean Supply Chain Principle summarizes this discussion.

Lean Supply Chain Principle 4

Decisions should be based on a throughput world perspective. While enterprises should try to increase throughput, decrease investment, and decrease operating expenses, the focus must be on improving throughput.

The fact that T theoretically can be increased without limit, whereas I and OE can be reduced by only a finite amount presents a powerful argument for why enterprises should focus on throughput. Given a choice between reducing I and OE, TOC gives priority to inventory reduction for all the reasons provided earlier, the most powerful reason being the relationship between inventory and lead time. TOC gives a third priority to reducing OE. Figure 3.2 depicts the priority rankings for the cost world and the throughput world.

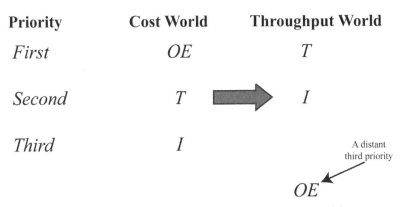

Priority	Cost World	Throughput World
First	*OE*	*T*
Second	*T*	*I*
Third	*I*	A distant third priority *OE*

Figure 3.2 Priorities in the cost and throughput worlds.

The cost world's focus on reducing operating expense could well be viewed by some managers as an effort to enhance the operational effectiveness of an enterprise. However, there is a big difference: Reducing operating expense actually can decrease operational effectiveness. The main problem with the cost world is that a focus on reducing operating expenses will sacrifice long-term throughput increases for short-term gains.

For Everclear, Inc., it was relatively straightforward to see why a focus on throughput delivered better results than a focus on cost reduction. To help organizations stay focused on throughput in more complex situations, TOC presents a systematic approach, called the *Five-Step Focusing Process*, to improve the bottom line by identifying the root cause of a problem and effectively dealing with it.

The Five-Step Focusing Process of TOC

The Five-Step Focusing Process is based on a *process of ongoing improvement* (POOGI). The first step in the process identifies the system's constraints.

Step 1: Identify the System's Constraint(s)

TOC asserts that any enterprise has very few real constraints, at most a handful. The constraint is a physical constraint, a market constraint, or a policy constraint. In turn, a policy constraint could be the result of the measures in place, the methods used, or the mind-set that governs the strategic and tactical decisions of the enterprise.

Step 2: Decide How to Exploit the System's Constraint(s)

Exploiting the constraint means to use the constraint as effectively as possible. Although the word *exploit* has a negative connotation, this word is chosen very carefully. For example, when the constraint is identified, it is tempting to consider a decision that simply does away with the constraint. Thus, if the constraint is a physical resource, the enterprise can consider acquiring additional resources. However, the enterprise may not be in a position to acquire those resources immediately. Similarly, if there are policy constraints, it also could take time to address these policies. What should the enterprise do in the meantime? Until the constraints are overcome, the enterprise should work the constraints as effectively (profitably) as possible; this is the real meaning of the word *exploit*.

If the constraint is a physical resource, the implication is that every minute the constraint is idle causes the enterprise to lose money. *Exploit* here means ensuring that the resource is never idle and waiting for parts or that it never has to work on a defective component. On the other hand, if the market is the constraint, in the sense that there is not enough demand for the products, *exploit* means making sure that not a single sale is lost as a result of poor actions or inaction.

A market constraint also implies that there is extra capacity, so the enterprise can try to grow market share by promising and delivering products more quickly to the customer. The enterprise can make this promise because the internal resources are not overloaded and so products do not wait a long time before they are processed by the different resources. *Exploit* the (market) constraint means guaranteeing 100 percent on-time deliveries to the customer. The market constraint also can be exploited by producing a mix of products that maximizes profits, as the CSN example demonstrated.

Step 3: Subordinate Everything Else to that Decision

Once the decision is made on how the constraint will be exploited, the third step in the Five-Step Focusing Process is to subordinate every aspect of system operation to this decision. Every part of the system must be actively managed, even though the nonconstraint resources need not be managed as diligently as the constraint resource.

The third step is often the most difficult step in the focusing process. How should the enterprise manage the vast majority of its resources that are not constraints by definition? If these resources are ignored, they may stop functioning correctly, they may become constraints themselves, or they even may function counter to enterprise goals.

In many instances, subordination deals with the process of scheduling. Typically, the work must be started and sequenced in such a way that the constraint either can always work or simply can work smarter. For example, the heat-treatment furnace is a constraint in many manufacturing operations. It is possible to increase throughput without increasing batch sizes if the scheduler schedules several different products into the furnace in one setup.

Chapter 8 presents a subordination technique known as the *Drum-Buffer-Rope* (DBR). This technique is also known as the *Pull-from-the-Bottleneck Model.*

Step 4: Elevate the System's Constraints

The fourth step tries to lift the restriction that prevents the enterprise from making more money. Elevating the constraint means identifying ways in which the performance of the system can be improved. If there is a physical resource constraint, then another identical resource may be purchased. If the market is the constraint, the constraint can be elevated in a variety of ways. One approach is to advertise more effectively or simply to advertise more. The enterprise also can try to find new markets for its products.

However, as the Five-Step Focusing Process indicates, this step should be performed only *after* the exploit step. The enterprise may think that it is necessary to elevate a perceived constraint and either buy more equipment or subcontract component manufacture without properly exploiting the real constraint. Thus, before considering actions such as subcontracting, launching an advertising campaign, and so on, the enterprise must execute the second and third steps. If the constraint still exists or another constraint emerges, then it is time to execute the fourth step.

Step 5: If a Constraint Was Broken in a Previous Step, Go Back to Step 1

If the constraint is elevated, it probably will not remain a constraint. The performance is now dictated by another element that has become the weakest link. To find the new weakest link, all the steps have to be revisited. But this is not the entire fifth step. Goldratt adds a big warning: *Do not allow inertia to cause a system's constraints.* For instance, the enterprise may have a policy of relocating workers to a constraint process. If this constraint is elevated (e.g., by replacing it with a faster process) and inertia causes the policy to remain in place, then workers will continue to get redirected to the old constraint even if they are no longer needed there, resulting in other resources needlessly becoming constraints. Step 5 therefore is a crucial step because it prevents inertia from derailing a continuous improvement process.

An Example of the Five-Step Focusing Process

The Five-Step Focusing Process is illustrated with an example of a small production system manufacturing two products, *P* and *Q*. This system is shown in Figure 3.3. The goal of this system is to maximize profit. The weekly demand for *P* and *Q* are 110 units and 60 units, respectively. There are four resources, *A*, *B*, *C*, and *D*, used by the production system to meet demand. These resources are shared among the various operations, as shown in the figure.

In the figure, resource *A* takes 15 minutes to process one unit of raw material *RM1*. That unit is next processed by resource *C* for 10 minutes before its material is ultimately used to make one unit of product *P*. Resource *A* also processes raw material *RM3*, and this material ultimately is used to make one unit of product *Q*.

Resource *D* is an assembly operation that does the final operation for both products. To produce a unit of product *Q*, resource *D* uses a unit of

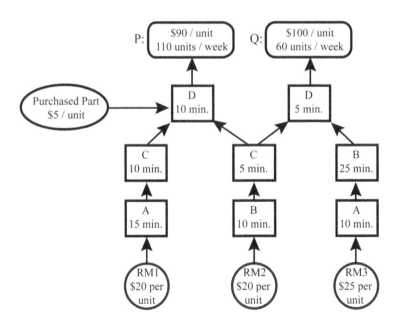

Time available at each work center: 2,400 minutes per week
Operating expenses per week: $6,000

Figure 3.3 A production system manufacturing two products.

WIP from resource C and a unit of WIP from resource B and takes 5 minutes to perform the assembly operation. When resource D assembles one unit of product P, it also uses a purchased part costing $5 to complete the assembly operation. Other pertinent data are presented in the figure. In particular, it should be noted that each resource operates independently for 2,400 minutes each week and that operating expenses, totaling $6,000, are incurred at the end of each week.

The profit contribution for a product is the selling price less the price of materials. Thus the contribution from product P is $90 – $5 – $20 – $20 = $45. Similarly, the contribution from product Q is $100 – $20 – $25 = $55. Step 1 is now executed to determine whether a constraint prevents the production system from meeting market demand.

Step 1: Identify the System's Constraints. A capacity analysis reveals that work center B is overloaded. Table 3.8 shows the workload on each work center.

Table 3.8 Capacity Analysis for the Production System

Work center	Load from P (@110 units)	Load from Q (@ 60 units)	Total time required	Time available
A	1,650	600	2,250	2,400
B	1,100	2,100	3,200	2,400
C	1,650	300	1,950	2,400
D	1,100	300	1,400	2,400

Step 2: Decide How to Exploit the System's Constraints. Since the entire demand cannot be met because of a capacity constraint at resource B, the enterprise must decide which product to produce first. Since product Q has a higher profit margin ($55 per unit) than product P ($45 per unit), the enterprise may choose to use the constraint resource to produce as much as possible of Q and then use the remaining capacity to produce P. Based on this choice, the enterprise will meet the 60-unit demand for product Q using 2,100 minutes from resource B. The remaining 300 minutes can be used to produce 30 units of product P. This product mix gives a net profit of $45(30) + $55(60) – $6,000 = – $1,350.

The preceding analysis worked with product costs and product profits. From a systems perspective (the throughput world), product costs and product profits do not have much meaning because the real intent is to make a profit for the enterprise. The constraint must be exploited to get the maximum throughput (dollars per unit time) from the constraint.

Analysis of the data reveals that product Q requires 35 minutes from resource B per unit, whereas product P requires only 10 minutes from resource B per unit. Each unit of product Q brings in a profit margin of $55. Thus the rate at which the constraint generates profit when it is processing product Q is $55 ÷ 35 = $1.57 per minute. Similarly, when product P is being processed, the profit-generation rate is $45 ÷ 10 = $4.50 per minute.

Thus the choice is to produce as many units of P as the market demands using the remaining constraint capacity to produce Q. The 110 units of P consume 110 × 10 = 1,100 minutes from the 2,400 minutes available for resource B, leaving 2,400 − 1,100 = 1,300 available minutes to produce Q. Resource B uses the 1,300 minutes to produce 1,300 ÷ 35 = 37 units of Q for a total marginal profit of $45 × 110 + $55 × 37 = $6,985.

After factoring out the operating expense of $6,000, the net profit is $985—a significant difference from the previous net loss of $1,350.

Step 3: Subordinate Everything Else to This Decision. For this example, step 3 requires the other resources to work on keeping resource B busy all the time. So the approach is to first allocate B to work on raw material *RM2* and have resource A process 36 units of raw material *RM3* for product Q while B is processing *RM2*.

Step 4: Elevate the Constraint. The constraint was exploited in step 2. Now it is time to elevate it. At this stage, recognize that in addition to resource B being a constraint, there is another constraint—the demand mix. Ideally, the enterprise would like to have more demand for product P because it results in more throughput (dollars per unit time) from the constraint. Thus the enterprise really has two choices—either to generate more demand for product P or to buy another resource B.

Either of these choices could elevate the constraint. If the latter option is considered, B is no longer a constraint because it now has capacity to produce the entire weekly demand. In such a case, the enterprise has to generate more demand. If there is additional demand, the internal constraint is not resource B. In all likelihood, it is resource A. In any case, since the constraint has been elevated, steps 1 through 5 have to be repeated all over again. This is why the Five-Step Focusing Process is also referred to as a Process of Ongoing Improvement.

Interpreting T

In the P-Q example just discussed, the second step, "decide how to exploit the system's constraints," provides insight on the interpretation of T as a rate. If the enterprise is a for-profit enterprise, the goal is to make profits, in which case the interpretation of T is the rate at which the system generates profits. By definition, the constraint determines the extent to which the enterprise fulfills its objective. Hence an alternate interpretation for T is the *throughput per unit of constraint*.

The revised definition of T means that if the constraint is available hours of capacity, then T is measured in dollars per constraint hour. If the constraint is floor space, then T is measured in dollars per square foot.

Interpreting T for a Digital Media Enterprise

In 2006, I was discussing TOC and its wide range of applications with the sales team for a large digital media enterprise. The sales team members were keen on applying TOC concepts, but they felt that the concepts were applicable only to manufacturing. I asked them to draw their supply chain, and we spent about 30 minutes trying to identify the constraint. The sales team ultimately identified the constraint as the available shelf space at the big-box retailers for displaying their products.

As soon as the team identified the constraint, the direction of the solution became clearer to the team. The goal for the team was to maximize the throughput per square foot of shelf space. The team identified some of the high-margin items as being space-intensive and started to think about how many units of these items should be displayed on the scarce shelf space. The idea was to allocate any space that was freed up to display lower-margin items that could generate more throughput dollars per square foot because they occupied much less space. The sales team also identified new stock-keeping units (SKUs) for display based on their throughput potential.

An Un-common Sense Minute

The *P-Q* example discussed earlier also provides an un-common sense statement opportunity: "in order to make more money, sell at or below cost." This statement, which, characteristically, does not make sense at first, begins to make much more sense if the cost is interpreted as the fully burdened cost.

The fully burdened cost for a product includes the labor and overhead costs that were allocated to the product using some cost drivers. The labor and overhead costs are sunk costs—costs that would be incurred regardless of whether an additional product is sold or not. The only real incremental cost incurred when the product is sold is the cost of the material used in the product. Therefore, unless the product used the constraint, the enterprise will make money if it sold the product for a price higher than material cost (but at a price that was less than the product cost, as determined by the standard cost accounting system or by ABC).

If the product used the constraint, then it still may make sense to sell the product at a price lower than the fully burdened cost if the product generates more profit per unit of constraint than do existing products in the enterprise's product portfolio. Pursuing this line of thought, it may make sense to outsource a product currently produced in-house if this product uses up valuable capacity at the constraint and there is an unmet demand for other products that can generate more throughput dollars per unit of constraint.

Applying Throughput Accounting to CSN, Inc.

Using the interpretation for *T* as the profit per unit of constraint, throughput accounting is applied to the CSN example as follows: the constraint for CSN is the total labor capacity of 1,000 hours. Table 3.9 shows the marginal profits for each of the four services and the number of hours required at the constraint to complete each type of service. Given these two sets of numbers, the value of *T* for each type of service is determined.

Table 3.9 Data for CSN, Inc., Using Throughput Accounting

Product	Plumbing	Window cleaning	Installing gutter guards	Landscaping
Demand for product	250 jobs	160 jobs	145 jobs	120 jobs
Marginal profit (revenue – variable cost)	$130 – $30 = $100	$170 – $10 = $160	$200 – $70 = $130	$250 – $75 = $175
Number of hours needed per job	2 hours	4 hours	3 hours	5 hours
Profit-generation rate (T)	$50.00 per hour	$40.00 per hour	$43.33 per hour	$35.00 per hour

For example, plumbing brings $100 in marginal profits to CSN and demands 2 hours of capacity from the constraint. Thus, when the enterprise works on plumbing jobs, T is $100 ÷ 2 = $50 per hour. When the enterprise works on window cleaning, the marginal profit is $160, and each window cleaning requires 4 hours per job, so T = $160 ÷ 4 = $40 per hour. Proceeding in this manner, the best product from a throughput standpoint is plumbing, with landscaping coming in last.

Allocating the constraint capacity first to plumbing, followed by gutter guard installations and then window cleaning, the optimal product portfolio is 250 plumbing jobs, 145 gutter guard jobs, and 16 window cleaning jobs. This portfolio uses 999 hours of labor capacity and results in a total marginal profit of 250 × $100 + 145 × $130 + 16 × $160 = $46,410. The fixed costs (i.e., labor cost, administrative cost, and nonadministrative cost) add up to $10,000 + $18,000 + $9,000 = $37,000. Subtracting the fixed costs from the marginal profit gives CSN a net profit of $9,410. (The portfolio may be fine-tuned to use the 1 hour of available labor capacity by substituting one gutter guard installation for a window cleaning job to get another $30 in revenue.) The profit resulting from throughput accounting represents a significant increase over the profit resulting from a product portfolio optimization using standard cost accounting and activity-based costing profits.

Conclusions

This chapter presented a number of key concepts and principles.

▲ Systems are analogous to chains. Every system has a weakest link, the constraint, that ultimately limits the success of the entire system.
▲ Many enterprises try to improve performance by attempting to improve all their processes at the same time. While it is a good idea to remove waste in any form, a potential downside is that the enterprise's focus may become diffused. Besides, time saved at nonconstraint resources can be a *mirage*. Strengthening links other than the weakest link does not improve the strength of the chain.
▲ At the same time, many enterprises try to reduce costs and trim resources so that the capacity of these resources matches the capacity of the weakest link. Enterprises following this approach are adopting a cost world perspective. The cost world perspective promotes local thinking and encourages behavior that runs counter to enterprise goals.
▲ The focus should be on *growth*—improving Throughput. TOC prescribes a throughput world perspective. Enterprises that adopt the throughput world perspective have an immediate advantage because most of the competition is still stuck in the cost world.
▲ Cost accounting systems can provide valuable information for identifying where costs are being incurred. However, care should be taken when using accounting systems that try to allocate fixed costs to products. TOC avoids making such allocations and instead presents a set of three simple measures to gauge the financial impact of any decision.
▲ The Five-Step Focusing Process provides a systematic way to identify constraints and to exploit/elevate them. The focusing process works particularly well with physical constraints.

References

1. E. Goldratt (2008), *The Choice*, North River Press, Great Barrington, MA.
2. J. F. Cox and J. G. Schleier, eds. (2010), *Theory of Constraints Handbook*, McGraw-Hill, New York.
3. E. M. Goldratt (1990), *The Haystack Syndrome*, North River Press, Great Barrington, MA.
4. M. L. Srikanth and M. Umble (1997), *Synchronous Management*, Vol. 1, Spectrum Publishing Company, Guilford, CT.

CHAPTER 4

Designing Products and Processes to Fulfill Customer Needs

Understanding customer value—this phrase is invoked so often that it may sound like a cliché, but no matter how clichéd the phrase, it conveys the essence of a business. It is the customer who drives the success or the failure of a business. The goal of any for-profit enterprise is to generate profits from the sales of its products or services, and it is the customer who provides the sales revenue.

Unfortunately, instead of looking outward to identify customer needs, many enterprises tend to look inward, focusing on how well their products and services perform relative to their competition. These enterprises become so absorbed with their product or service offerings that they are unable to view those products or services from any perspective other than their own. Their value proposition* touts the benefits customers can gain from these products or services, often forgetting that the customer wants a solution to his or her specific problem, not simply yet another product or service.

The Viable Vision

A relatively new concept, the *Viable Vision*, provides a whole new dimension to the phrase *understanding customer value*. The Viable Vision is a concept Goldratt shared with company owners and senior executives around the world in 2003. In its original format, the Viable Vision was a blueprint for

---

*A value proposition is a business or marketing statement that summarizes why a customer should buy the enterprise's product or service.

an organization to grow its business at a rate that would allow the organization's current revenue to become its net profit in four years. The Viable Vision subsequently evolved into a process that analyzes organizations and specifies the (few) key changes that will make them ever-flourishing organizations.[1] Goldratt defines an *ever-flourishing organization* as an organization that is able to achieve exponential financial growth without degrading its stability.

Note that exponential financial growth cannot be achieved simply by cutting costs because there is a limit to which costs can be reduced. The implication is that an organization aspiring to become an ever-flourishing organization must focus on growing the business at a significant rate. Growing the business at a rate such that current revenue becomes net profits in four years might, at first glance, seem fanciful. However, the Viable Vision is achievable for most organizations.

Assume that a $100 million organization currently makes $5 million in profits. To make a profit of $100 million in four years, it is not necessary for this organization to grow its business to 20 times its current size. Rather, the organization can realize the Viable Vision even with a growth that equals two or three times its current output, and this is a growth rate that is achievable in four years by any organization that adopts a throughput-focused perspective.

The idea is to have the organization sell its *high-octane products*. An example of a high-octane product is a product that generates the highest throughput per unit of constraint capacity, as discussed in Chapter 3. Selling high-octane products requires the organization to apply the Five-Step Focusing Process to identify the market (or policy) constraint that prevents the organization from selling more of the high-octane products and to exploit the constraint to achieve a higher market share for those products.

While organizations that adopt a throughput world perspective are in a good position to realize the Viable Vision, traditional organizations may find it harder to grow their business at a significant rate. These organizations typically focus on increasing profits through cost-reduction efforts. Organizations focused on cost reduction typically attempt to gain market share by passing on to customers a percentage of the reduced costs in the form of price reductions. An inevitable consequence is that these organizations are constantly engaged in a price war, struggling to increase market share incrementally by cutting costs and lowering their prices.

An implicit assumption behind a strategy that aims to gain market share through price wars is the belief that the market for the products is limited. Traditional organizations thus operate under a self-imposed mind-set constraint that restricts their thoughts and actions. The assumption that there is a limited market for their products constrains these organizations from seeking opportunities for expanding or opening the market dramatically.*

There are a number of ways to open or expand a market. One approach is to capitalize on the organization's competitive advantage—the organization's ability to address a specific customer need, which could take the form of guaranteed on-time delivery, quick response, product customization, or simply personal attention. It should be noted that while price may influence the customer's choice of suppliers for some commodity products, it is not the primary product attribute that drives the supplier selection process for non-commodity products.

It also should be noted that it is not necessary that an organization's competitive advantage should satisfy the needs of every potential customer. It is enough if a small percentage of the customer population finds this organization's competitive advantage compelling enough to make this customer segment buy the product or service from the organization.

It is possible that the organization might have to adapt its competitive strengths to better respond to specific customer needs. The important point for the organization is to ensure that its ability to deliver on the customer need is markedly higher than what the competitor can provide.

The next step is to convince the market that it will benefit from this ability. This step, in turn, requires the organization to present a proposition to potential customers that is so persuasive that the customer is unable to turn it down.† For example, the organization could guarantee on-time delivery with the promise of paying a sizable penalty if it fails to meet a delivery commitment.

Presenting such a compelling proposition requires an in-depth understanding of customer needs. In particular, organizations must carefully address the key question: "What do your customers do, and how do they accomplish what they have set out to do?" In other words, in what business is the customer engaged, and how does the customer excel in delivering the

---

*Note that expanding or opening the market corresponds to the Elevate step in the Five-Step Focusing Process.
† Goldratt terms such a proposition a "Mafia offer."

product or service in which he or she is engaged? The unstated implication is that the organization must be capable of delivering these needs better than its competitors are able to. It requires the organization to address some key questions aimed at understanding and solving the customer's pressing concerns. What are the customer's pain points? How can the organization help the customer to address his or her problems? These questions provide an opportunity for the organization to challenge the way in which it is currently producing and delivering its products to its customers.

The preceding discussion on the Viable Vision technique is summarized as follows*:

▲ Identify a significant additional market for the products offered by the organization.
▲ Find the assumptions that block the organization from moving into the additional market, and question the assumptions for their validity.
▲ Identify the actions needed to deliver to the new market demands.
▲ Devise a viable plan to exploit the organization's capability to deliver to the market.

The preceding discussion on the Viable Vision technique should illustrate why this concept provides a whole new dimension to the phrase understanding customer value. For further discussion on the Viable Vision technique, refer to the *Theory of Constraints Handbook*,[2] which provides numerous articles and references on this concept.

Understanding customer value requires the organization to identify the key features or attributes those customers are looking for, which the organization can provide through its products. These key attributes can vary depending on the different *market segments*. So a key step toward understanding customer value is to identify the market segments served by the organization.

Defining the Market Segments

Market segmentation is the division of a market into distinct groups of customers that might require different products or marketing mixes. The

---

* This summary is based on ideas presented by Dr. James Holt, Professor in Engineering & Technology Management at Washington State University.

intent is to classify members of a heterogeneous market—customers with different needs—into homogeneous segments of customers with similar needs and wants. Dividing the market into relatively homogeneous subgroups or target markets makes both strategy formulation and tactical decision making more effective. If the segmentation is done effectively, the enterprise can design a marketing mix that precisely matches the expectations of customers in the targeted segment.

Markets can be segmented in a variety of ways, but four factors typically used to segment markets are geographic (e.g., country or region, rural or metropolitan), demographic (e.g., age, sex, marital status, income, education), behavioral (e.g., intensity of product use, brand loyalty), and psychographic (e.g., individual or group traits, lifestyle). The segmentation also depends on whether the market relates to individual customers or enterprise customers. The graph in Figure 4.1 presents the distribution of customer orders for an organization that mainly services three market segments: retail customers, original equipment manufacturers, and governmental agencies.

Enterprises can use other factors for market segmentation. For instance, the Walmart distribution centers used to classify customers into two categories: "staple stock" and "direct freight" customers.[3] Staple-stock items are products customers would expect to find in the same place every day, such as toothpaste and shampoo. These products typically are replenished

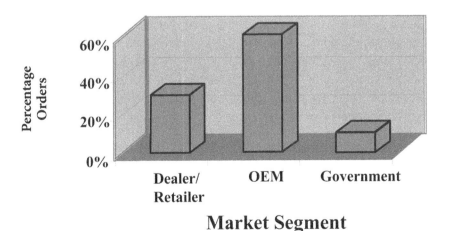

Market Segment

Figure 4.1 Defining market segments.

based on a pull signal from the retail stores. Direct-freight items are products that the buyers in the centralized office at Bentonville, Arkansas, procure in large quantities, usually at bargain rates, and push out to the retail stores. Direct-freight items are products that the customer at a retail store might find "here today, gone tomorrow."

Market Segmentation at Hindustan Unilever Limited

Hindustan Unilever Limited (HUL) is India's largest fast-moving consumer goods organization. This is an organization that displays all the characteristics of an ever-flourishing organization. Founded in 1933 as Levers Brothers (India), Ltd., HUL is a $4 billion organization with over 400 brands spanning 14 product categories in home, personal care, and food products. HUL has a wide outreach in India through a network of 7,000 redistribution centers covering more than 1 million retail outlets.

To understand why HUL represents an ever-flourishing organization, consider how it has grown its personal-products business. This business, which accounts for 26 percent of HUL's business, grew revenues from 750 million rupees in 1991 (US$28.4 million at the prevailing exchange rate of $1 = 26.40 rupees) to about 18 billion rupees in the year 2000 (US$400 million at an exchange rate of $1 = 45 rupees). For the year ended March 31, 2010, the revenue for the personal-products business was 50.48 billion rupees (US$1.12 billion at an exchange rate of $1 = 45 rupees).

HUL has grown its business at a very impressive rate through a combination of excellent marketing, supply chain management and operations, and service. HUL strives to maintain a competitive advantage by continuously reengineering its supply chain. HUL has segmented its market based on the size and location of its retail outlets and provides tailor-made services through teams dedicated to each one of these segments. HUL's market segments are:

▲ The *modern trade* segment (the organized retail sector)
▲ The *general trade* segment (the "mom and pop shops")
▲ The *rural market* segment

The modern trade segment is operated by large retailers and is focused on the urban market. Customers in this segment are serviced through HUL warehouses that supply nonperishable items to retail stores. This approach minimizes direct delivery to retail stores, allowing the retailers to devote more effort to customer-focused operations. Back-office and warehouse-related operations such as receipts, sorting, and repackaging are done at the warehouse. The general trade segment is serviced by wholesalers, grocery stores, pharmacists, kiosks, and general stores. HUL has developed customer-management and supply chain capabilities for partnering with supermarkets in the modern trade segment and emerging self-service stores in the general trade segment.

The rural market segment is specifically targeted as a growth opportunity for HUL. The HUL strategy is to "create consumers out of non-users," which presented a challenge because HUL had to find an innovative way to reach the millions of potential consumers in small, remote villages in India, where there was no retail distribution network, no advertising coverage, poor roads, and limited transportation. The solution was project *Shakti*,* a project launched in the year 2000 in partnership with nongovernmental organizations, banks, and government.

The goal of project Shakti is to penetrate rural markets by empowering underprivileged rural women to sell soaps, shampoos, and other personal-care products. HUL has enlisted over 45,000 Shakti entrepreneurs to cover more than 135,000 villages across 15 Indian states. These women are appointed as Vanis, or communicators, and are trained to communicate in social forums such as schools and village meetings. The Vanis act as direct-to-home sales distributors for HUL products. These women access remote village locations, traveling from door to door on bicycles. HUL provides these women training in selling, commercial knowledge, and bookkeeping to help them become micro-entrepreneurs.

Project Shakti has emerged as a successful low-cost business model and has enhanced HUL's direct rural reach in the so-called media-dark regions. About 50 percent of HUL's revenues come from the rural markets in India. Unilever (HUL's parent organization) is adapting the Shakti project for other markets such as Sri Lanka, Vietnam, and Bangladesh. Unilever is also considering a similar model tailored to Latin American and African markets.

In general, defining the market segments helps the enterprise to identify the particular attributes of its products that appeal to different market segments—the attributes that drive customer value. The customer values

---

*A Sanskrit word meaning "sacred force or empowerment."

are determined by the order qualifiers and order winners for the products in each segment.

Order Qualifiers and Order Winners

Order qualifiers[4] are attributes that a product must have for the customer to even consider purchasing it from an organization. *Order winners* are the product attributes that the organization can offer, which will make the customer place his or her order for that product with the organization. By definition, an order winner is also an order qualifier. Order qualifiers and order winners determine the competitive priorities on which the supply chain should focus. Should it be speed to market, product design, product quality, on-time delivery, or a combination of these factors? The answer to this question depends on what the customer would like this product to accomplish.

Order qualifiers and order winners no doubt will be different for different market segments. For instance, if the airline industry wishes to attract family vacationers who are traveling relatively short distances, then low-price tickets could be order winners. On the other hand, for business travelers traveling coast to coast in the United States, travel on wide-body jets may be the preferred alternative. Comfort and on-time travel could be order winners for business travelers.

Enterprises could decide to further segment the market to arrive at more targeted order qualifiers and order winners. A PC manufacturer/assembler may consider segmenting the market into desktop users, laptop users, and servers. Within the laptop segment, there could be a further segmentation into business laptop users and home laptop users. The business laptop user would have a different set of order winners, such as weight and size, than the home laptop user, who might find that cost is the order winner. Needless to say, order qualifiers and order winners must be determined carefully through market analysis.

Order qualifiers and order winners are dynamic attributes that change over time. Changes in the marketplace and changes in technology can change the order qualifiers and order winners. Many perennial order winners have become order qualifiers as a result of advances in manufacturing technology, planning systems, and IT. Consider laptop computers for business users. While weight and size may still be the current order winners, in the future they may just serve as order qualifiers. A new order winner already appears to be the ease with which the laptop can synchronize with digital media devices. A key function of the marketing department is to stay abreast of these changes so that the enterprise can remain proactive in meeting customer expectations and continuing to grow revenues.

Identifying order qualifiers and order winners for a product helps the enterprise to decide whether or not to market that product. If the decision is to enter the market for a product, the enterprise may choose to evolve marketing and operations strategies for fulfilling demand for this product. This decision involves the operations function because that function is responsible for delivering the order winners. HUL's decision to enter the rural market was influenced in part by the availability of rural women and local people who were able to travel door to door on bicycles to market HUL products.

For a Walmart retail store, availability very likely would be an order qualifier for staple stock items such as toothpaste, whereas cost would be an order winner, in which case the operations department may be responsible for ensuring availability of the toothpaste. For a retail store that sells office furniture, price would be an order qualifier, whereas ease of assembly likely would be an order winner. The marketing and operations departments in this store can work with the procurement department to ensure that the supplier of the office furniture designs the product for ease of assembly. For HUL, an order winner in the modern trade segment is lead time, and therefore, HUL is focused on cutting down lead times for the products in this segment.

In addition to understanding what the order qualifiers and order winners are, the enterprise must understand how it is currently delivering on these attributes. It may be necessary to evolve different product-delivery strategies for the different market segments. To evolve these delivery strategies, the enterprise should undertake a comprehensive review of the business practices, strategies, and operating tactics of world-class organizations that lead to superior economic performance. The enterprise can then decide whether and how these practices can be applied or adapted to deliver its own services and processes.

Benchmarking Best Practices

Benchmarking is a continuous, systematic procedure aimed at measuring an enterprise's services and processes against best-in-class practices.

Benchmarking is not aimed at imitation. Instead, benchmarking studies and learns from other businesses and adapts practices that best suit the enterprise. Benchmarking also helps organizations to identify their order winners.

Enterprises can choose to perform either *competitive* or *functional* benchmarking. In competitive benchmarking, enterprises compare themselves with other enterprises in the same industry, usually the leader in that industry. Competitive benchmarking allows the enterprise to avoid making the mistakes the leader may have already made in its journey to become the best in the industry. The obvious disadvantage of this type of benchmarking is that the enterprise becomes a follower. Typically, the leader will stay one step ahead of the competition.

Functional benchmarking, on the other hand, compares processes and activities such as customer service, the design process, and the product delivery system against outstanding practices by the best-in-class enterprises in any industry. This is a more ambitious form of benchmarking because it attempts to match up to selected enterprises that are recognized as world leaders in some processes. Enterprises might, for example, choose to benchmark Disney for customer service, Dell for rapid customization, Toyota for process execution, and American Express for its ability to get customers to pay quickly.

The advantage of functional benchmarking is twofold. First, the enterprise doing the benchmarking does not need to worry about lagging behind the leader in its own industry. Second, and more importantly, it offers opportunities for the enterprise to identify innovative ways of fulfilling customer demand. Taiichi Ohno credits his contributions to the Toyota Production System to two concepts: (1) the moving assembly line pioneered by Henry Ford and (2) the supermarket.[5] In a visit to the United States in 1956, Ohno observed how the supermarket operation provided stores with a continuous supply of merchandise, inspiring him to set up a pull system in which each production process became a "supermarket" for the succeeding process. Each process would produce to replenish only the items that the downstream process selected. When Ohno adopted the supermarket concept for Toyota, he gave the enterprise a competitive edge because no other automobile manufacturer was using the concept at that time.

Motorola provides another example of functional benchmarking. In 1994, Motorola looked outside the electronics and telecommunications industry for process innovations that would help it to build an efficient process for processing and shipping satellites to multiple cities and countries. Motorola wanted to ensure that these processes were repeatable, reliable and efficient so that it could ship the satellites on schedule. Furthermore, Motorola wanted to simplify the process to an extent where anyone could successfully complete the required tasks as quickly as possible and with minimal training.

Motorola benchmarked the operations of a freight forwarding organization specializing in big music events and concerts, to understand how it handled complex and high-dollar equipment on tight schedules. Motorola also studied how this organization was able to simplify its operations to the extent where it was able to hire roadies to build the stages in any city.

The fifth Lean Supply Chain Principle summarizes the preceding discussion.

Lean Supply Chain Principle 5

Focus on customer needs and process considerations when designing the product. Enterprises can gain tremendous competitive advantage through best-in-class practices that cut across industries.

The analyst conducting the benchmarking study should also investigate how the benchmarked enterprises manage customer demands. Customer demand volatility is often accepted as a necessary evil with such statements as "The customer always changes his mind." Enterprises usually do not account for the fact that a significant component of the variation observed in customer demand for their products is a result of their own actions. The analyst should therefore focus on the processes that the best-in-class enterprises follow to mitigate demand volatility.

Managing Customer Demand Volatility

It is a remarkable fact that demand volatility is often self-induced. A classic example of self-induced demand volatility is the instability created by sales promotions or rebates, which usually generate a sharp surge in end-user demand and result in the inevitable bullwhip effect upstream. Managers generally fail to recognize that demand volatility can be influenced significantly by an enterprise's sales or marketing activities. Conversely, sales and marketing often fail to use tools and techniques that can mitigate demand volatility.

Self-induced volatility is not initiated through sales and marketing actions alone. The end-of-quarter or end-of-year "channel stuffing*" actions that enterprises undertake, either to present higher operating margins or to show higher utilizations and overhead absorption, creates increased demand volatility. Channel-stuffing activities produce significant perturbations in the production operations within an enterprise and generate the bullwhip effect upstream. The result of these actions is inventory somewhere in the pipeline that probably will be disposed of through a sale, exacerbating the bullwhip effect.

Ignoring noisy data from promotional activity or end-of-the-quarter channel stuffing will help to prevent the bullwhip effect from propagating upstream in such situations. A simple approach to reduce volatility from promotional activities is to adopt an every-day-low-price policy, as practiced by enterprises such as Walmart.

Batching is another example of self-induced volatility. While end-user demand for a product may be fairly level, enterprises often deliver the product in large lots to achieve economies of scale. The manufacturer who chooses to wait until cumulative demand reaches an "economic lot size" before beginning production is resorting to batching. The beer game showed that a single spike in demand created large ripple effects upstream. Batching a steady end-user demand immediately generates a bullwhip effect on upstream suppliers. The solution here is to work with small batches and level production schedules.

---

* Channel stuffing takes place when an organization attempts to improve its performance by forcing more products through a distribution channel than the channel is capable of selling.

Customer demand volatility increases if the supplier takes a long time to respond or if the reliability of the supply is poor. The solution here is to devise a strategy for meeting customer demands in a quick and reliable manner, as discussed in the following section.

Quick and Reliable Response

A quick and reliable response reduces demand volatility in different ways depending on whether the supply chain is a build-to-stock (BTS) or a build-to-order (BTO) supply chain. For the BTO supply chain, long lead times and poor delivery reliability will generate demand volatility as follows: if the enterprise does not respond to customer demand in a timely manner, then the customer is more likely to hedge his or her actual requirements to compensate for the delays in fulfilling the order. The customer also will hedge his or her orders if the lead time to fulfill orders is highly variable, asking for the orders to be delivered earlier than necessary. The customer may now find that he or she has too much inventory, and that would result in either a dramatically reduced order quantity during the next order cycle or, perhaps, the cancellation of a scheduled delivery.

On the flip side, if the enterprise responds quickly and reliably to customer demands, the customer now will have more faith in the delivery process and therefore will be less likely to pad his or her actual requirements or hedge the desired delivery date. One way to reduce lead times in BTO supply chains is to adopt the *principle of postponement*. This principle is discussed in a following section.

For the BTS supply chain, the problem with long lead times was discussed in Chapter 1. If the lead time to respond to a customer demand is four weeks, then the supply chain must maintain at least four weeks of inventory. The implication is that the manufacturer will build to a forecast four weeks out into the future. The longer the time horizon for the forecast, the less reliable the forecast is, and so the manufacturer has to pad the forecasted demand to buffer against the uncertainty in the forecast. Padding further increases the variation in the amount produced from the true customer demand, adding to the volatility in the supply chain. One way to reduce the volatility for a BTS supply chain is to structure a *build-to-replenish* mode of operation, as the following case demonstrates.

CASE STUDY

Reliant, Inc.

In the year 2000, I worked with Reliant, a manufacturer in the medical products industry, on a project aimed at improving Reliant's market share in the custom procedural tray (CPT) product family. Reliant supplied these products to several Fortune 500 organizations, and these organizations distributed Reliant's products to end users using a BTS mode of operation. Each of the distributors had a warehouse on Reliant's production site. The end users all were located within 30 miles of the distributors.

Figure 4.2 shows the supply chain for the CPT product family. The distributors were an integral part of the supply chain, providing critical services such as consolidating shipments from multiple suppliers like Reliant and delivering the consolidated shipment to the end users. The implication was that the distributors could not be ignored or removed from the solution.

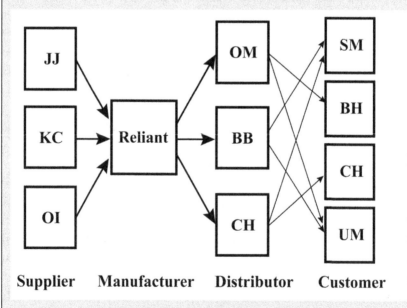

Figure 4.2   The supply chain for Reliant, Inc.

CASE STUDY

The CPT product family had about 10 different products with distinct applications. Reliant maintained multiple stock-keeping units (SKUs) for each one of these products to accommodate individual customer preferences. These SKUs were stored in the distributors' warehouses and in Reliant's plant warehouse. The customer demands for products were unpredictable and Reliant found it difficult to predict when a demand would occur and what the order quantity would be.

The demand variation resulted in large inventories stored in the distributors' warehouses and in the plant warehouse. Despite stocking large inventories, the distributor often would not have the SKU demanded by the end user in stock, a situation that evoked Taiichi Ohno's statement: "The more inventory you have on hand, the less likely you are to have the one item your customer actually wants."

A pilot study analyzed the demand and fulfillment for CPT_A, one of the products from the CPT product family. This product had two SKUs. A typical order quantity for this product was for 30 to 100 units of a given SKU. Reliant would build these units against production orders generated internally by production control using a forecasting system that employed demand history to predict future demand. Each unit went through an assembly operation that took about 15 minutes to complete. The assembled units went through a subsequent processing step—a batch operation that could process as many as 100 units in one batch and took two hours to complete, irrespective of the batch size.

Even though the work content for producing one CPT_A was only two hours and 15 minutes, the lead time for the order was two weeks because of numerous delays and non-value-added steps in the overall process. There was a delay is transmitting an order to the department that picked all the necessary assembly components from the parts warehouse. After the parts were picked, the order queued up in the assembly shop and waited until the orders ahead of it were assembled. There was a delay in transporting the assembled product to the next processing step, which was done at another location 15 miles away. The completed order was returned to the original site, where it was packaged for delivery to the distributor.

CASE STUDY

The pilot study selected one of the end users for CPT_A and identified the distributor that delivered the product to the end user. The study discarded one of the two SKUs because it had not been used by the end user for a very long time. The study next determined the number of CPT_A units consumed by the end user to be between two and four units a day, which translated to a maximum demand of 20 units per week. This was a much steadier demand than Reliant faced based on the distributors' orders.

The study concluded that the unpredictability in the demand for CPT_A was mainly a result of the two-week lead time to respond to the distributor's order and that the distributor was inflating its order to Reliant to accommodate the two-week lead time. In turn, the end user was inflating his order to account for the uncertainty surrounding the delivery of his requirements from the distributor. The bullwhip effect was clearly present.

Based on this information, the solution developed for Reliant was to partner with the end user and the distributor as follows: The end user would start each week with 20 units of CPT_A, the maximum weekly consumption. Reliant would build enough units of this product each week to raise the inventory level at its plant warehouse to 20 units by the end of the week. At the end of each week, the end user would provide Reliant with information on the number of units of CPT_A actually consumed that week. In return, Reliant would replenish these units from its inventory over the weekend and produce the same number of units the following week.

The build-to-replenish mode of operation implemented in the pilot study was a success. The end user and the distributor gained confidence in Reliant's ability to deliver, and neither of them had to hedge orders any more. The bullwhip effect was noticeably absent. While the pilot study was successful, Reliant still faced some initial resistance from its own salespeople and from the end user in its attempts to rationalize the number of SKUs for the other products. Reliant had to proceed more slowly to deploy this practice across the rest of the CPT product family.

An Un-common Sense Minute

The Reliant case study provides support to an un-common sense statement: "If you want your products to be immediately available to your customer, move them away from your customer." When Reliant's supply chain maintained finished goods inventory at the distributor warehouses, there was opportunity for misallocation. Consider the distributors shown in Figure 4.2. Distributor BB may be stocked out of product CPT_A, but distributor OM may have a large inventory of this product. However, if the entire finished goods inventory of CPT_A is held at the plant warehouse, thereby moving these products even further away from the customer, Reliant can be assured that there will be no such misallocations.

Maintaining the inventory at the plant warehouse instead of allocating—or misallocating—the inventory to the distributor warehouses carries another benefit. The inventory in the entire system can be reduced without jeopardizing sales. This phenomenon, usually referred to as *risk pooling* or *aggregation*, is discussed next.

Risk Pooling

When demand for a product is fulfilled from multiple locations, each location must carry an inventory equal to the average demand at the location plus a safety stock to accommodate any demand variation. The exact amount of safety stock to be carried will depend on the desired service level. The total inventory across all locations is the sum of the average demands plus the safety stocks maintained at each location. If those demands were instead satisfied from a centralized location, then the amount of inventory required for meeting a desired level of service typically would be less than the total inventory that would be maintained across all locations to get this same level of service. An intuitive explanation for this phenomenon, often referred to as *risk pooling*, is that if demands at the individual locations are independent of each other, a higher-than-average demand at one location likely will be offset by a lower-than-average demand at some other location during the same time period.

Risk pooling is explained with a numerical example using some concepts drawn from statistical theory. Suppose that the product, CPT_A, is demanded at four locations and that the average demand at each location is 24 units per week. Let's assume that the demands at the four locations are independent of each other and that the standard deviation of the demand at each location is 10 units.

Statistical theory tells us that if demand follows a normal distribution, an inventory level equal to the average plus 3 standard deviations of the demand is adequate to satisfy the demand 99.87 percent of the time. Therefore, to reach a 99.87 percent service level, each location must carry 24 + 3 × 10 = 54 units of CPT_A, and so the total inventory carried across all four locations is 4 × 54 = 216 units.

If instead the entire demand is satisfied from a central location, the average aggregate demand at the central location is the sum of the average demand at each location, namely, 4 × 24 = 96 units. However, the standard deviation of the aggregate demand will be less than the sum of the standard deviations at individual locations owing to risk pooling. The standard deviation of aggregate demand is obtained as follows:

Statistical theory tells us that the variance of an aggregate demand is the sum of the variances of individual demands when these demands are independent. The variance of a demand is simply the square of the standard deviation of the demand. Thus the variance of the demand at each location is 100, and the variance of the aggregate demand is 400. Working backwards, the standard deviation of the aggregate demand, which is the square root of the aggregate demand variance, is 20 units. Therefore, to satisfy the demand 99.87 percent of the time, the central location should have to carry only 96 + 3 × 20 = 156 units.

Risk pooling can reduce inventory levels by a significant amount. The higher the variation in demand, the greater the benefit will be from risk pooling. However, the benefits derived from risk pooling decrease if demands at the individual locations are positively correlated.

Risk pooling averts inventory misallocation. Risk pooling also will avoid any capacity misallocations that otherwise may occur during the delivery of a product or service, as explained in the following section that discusses the RAP Principle.

The RAP Principle

A very useful approach to managing demand volatility is to *maximize external variety with minimal internal variety*. This approach succinctly captures the basic principle that should be followed, especially when designing supply chains that deal with high product variety and demand volatility. Enterprises can execute according to this principle by structuring their product offerings so that commitment of materials and resources is postponed for as long as possible. In other words, it is best to work with a relatively small number of standard products (*modules*) internally in semifinished or finished form to configure a large variety of end products. It will be convenient to refer to this above principle as the RAP (keep the in-process inventory as *raw as possible*) principle. Figure 4.3 illustrates the RAP principle.*

The RAP principle should drive the design of new products and services. It provides a very convenient way to meet customer demand quickly without storing a lot of finished goods inventory. At the same time, it delays committing raw materials, labor, and fixed assets to make products based on forecasts in anticipation of future demand. As shown in the "After" portion of Figure 4.3, differentiation of the product is postponed to the final assembly stage. By postponing differentiation to the final assembly stage, it is possible to maintain an inventory of the products in an undifferentiated form that is ready for conversion into one of three possible

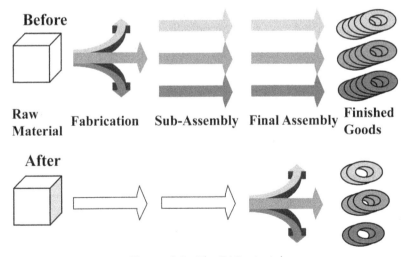

Before

Raw Material   Fabrication   Sub-Assembly   Final Assembly   Finished Goods

After

Figure 4.3 The RAP principle.

*This principle is often referred to in the literature as the *principle of postponement.*

finished products relatively quickly. The sixth Lean Supply Chain Principle captures this idea:

Lean Supply Chain Principle 6

Maximize external variety with minimal internal variety. It is desirable to maintain inventories in an undifferentiated form for as long as it is economically feasible to do so.

The RAP principle is particularly valuable for managing products that have a short life span. Postponement increases service levels while reducing costs and order-fulfillment risk, so it is especially useful when there are many derivative products and forecast error is high. The RAP principle also benefits from risk pooling. When a number of independent demands are aggregated, the risk-pooling discussion presented earlier shows that the aggregate demand has significantly less variation than the individual demands. When the RAP principle is adopted, the same standard modules go into a wide variety of end products. If modules rather than end products are stored, demand volatility can be managed with less inventory because the variation in the demand for modules is less than the variation in the demand for end products.

Benetton and Zara

Two apparel manufacturers/retailers that have exploited the RAP principle very successfully are Benetton and Zara. Benetton is an Italian clothing manufacturer that serves a global market. The textile and apparel industry has to deal with short product cycles for fashion articles, long production lead time, and forecasting errors for fashion items.

Every season, Benetton made sweaters and hosiery the traditional way by dyeing the yarn (fixing the garment color) and then knitting the fabric (fixing the style). However, it was never clear until well into the season which colors would be the best-sellers, and that led to a buildup of unwanted inventory. This inventory had to be cleared through huge markdown sales—a chronic problem that plagues many organizations in the textile and apparel industry. Such markdowns also promoted the bullwhip effect.

Benetton decided on a novel way to mitigate markdowns by understanding customer value. A systematic study of customer behavior showed that it was easier to predict style choices than color choices. Benetton evolved a new process that changed the production sequence for their single-color fabrics to do the knitting first followed by the dyeing operation. Such a simple application of the RAP principle resulted in a huge return for Benetton. By delaying the point of product differentiation until better demand patterns could be established, Benetton was able to align its supply chain with true customer demand.

Zara is a Spanish clothing manufacturer/retailer whose supply chain strategy is to set the industry standard for time to market, cost, order fulfillment, and customer satisfaction. At the heart of this organization's success is a vertically integrated business model that spans design, JIT production, marketing, and sales. This model gives Zara more flexibility than its rivals to respond to fickle fashion trends. Unlike other international clothing chains, Zara makes more than half its clothes in-house instead of relying on a network of suppliers.

Zara has adopted a number of lean supply chain techniques. For instance, it acquires fabrics in only four colors and delays committing these fabrics to the dyeing and printing operations until the last stage of production. By delaying commitment of the fabric to special colors, Zara substantially reduces the markdowns plaguing the textile and apparel industry. Zara keeps its designers attuned to changing customer preferences. Zara's sales managers send timely customer feedback from its 450 retail stores to in-house designers. As a result of better-managed inventories, reduced obsolescence, and tight linkages between demand and supply, Zara is well positioned to gain market share.

Despite best efforts to mitigate demand volatility using one or a combination of the approaches just discussed, suppose that demand variation is still present in the supply chain. How can the enterprise cope with this variation? The classic, traditional approach is to resort to finished goods inventory to buffer the variation. A potential drawback of this approach is that this inventory will result in slower responsiveness and longer lead times in the supply chain. The next section shows how the customer-time-based demand profile can help to minimize the amount of finished goods inventory required to manage such customer demand volatility.

Customer-Time-Based Demand Profile

From the enterprise's viewpoint, it is preferable to wait for a customer order so that the product can be built to customer needs. However, customers have differing delivery expectations. Some customers are prepared to wait for a product built exactly according to their specifications. Others are willing to compromise on product features if they can get the product immediately. For the latter type of customer, unavailability of a product could result in a lost sale, so the enterprise may have to carry finished goods inventory to meet demand from these customers.

Finished goods inventories do not always solve the problem. The fact that there is a lot of inventory of a certain product can simply mean that the enterprise has built and/or stocked the wrong kind of finished goods inventory. Deciding on the right kind of finished goods inventory is always a challenge. Enterprises would like to maintain as little finished goods inventory as possible, especially if they are operating in an industry such as the electronics industry, where some products depreciate almost as fast as groceries do.

What is needed is a *customer-time-based demand profile* that identifies customer expectations in terms of lead time and facilitates the development of finished goods inventory strategies accordingly. To understand how the customer-time-based demand profile could be used, consider a big-box retailer like Home Depot, which sells under-the-counter dishwashers. Customers for this dishwasher are individual home owners, retail stores, or building contractors. The home owner is either one who is in need of a dishwasher right now to replace a dishwasher that is broken and not repairable or is shopping around to replace a functioning dishwasher. For the former, the lead-time expectation on the order is zero. For the latter, shopping around with no sense of urgency, the lead time could be a month until a really good deal turns up. The retail store owner probably can wait for one or two days, whereas the building contractor probably can wait one week.

Clearly, different types of customers have their own lead-time expectations. Clearly, too, the dishwasher manufacturer does not have to carry finished goods inventory for all customer types. If the manufacturer can build and deliver dishwashers to order in three days, the big-box retailer only needs to carry finished goods inventory for retail store owners and customers seeking to replace a broken dishwasher. Figure 4.4 shows a customer-time-based demand profile.

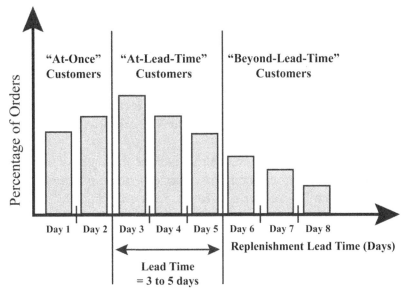

Figure 4.4 The customer-time-based demand profile.

The profile in the figure identifies the percentage of customers who demand products with a lead-time expectation of one day (they want their order filled right away) and the percentages of customers who are prepared to wait for two days, three days, and so on. To arrive at this profile, the enterprise has to gather data on customer orders received (not customer orders filled) and the delivery-time expectations associated with each order. Ideally, the organization should also gather data on potential customers who decided not to place an order simply because the lead time was too high, although this may be a difficult exercise. Ideally, too, it is advisable to develop one such time-based demand profile for each product rather than a generic profile for each market segment.

The time-based demand profile is a very useful tool to match customer expectations with operations capabilities. Suppose that the lead time for the enterprise to fulfill demand is between two and four weeks. All orders requiring delivery in less than two weeks would have to be met with finished goods inventory. Customers placing such orders are classified as "at once" customers. Customers placing orders that fall within the lead-time window are classified as "at-lead-time" customers. Customers prepared to wait for more than four weeks would be "beyond-lead-time" customers. Ideally, the enterprise would like to have more at-lead-time and beyond-lead-time customers and no at-once customers so that all orders could be built to demand, and the enterprise can operate in a pure BTO mode. At-once customers, on the other hand, require a BTS delivery strategy.

The time-based demand profile highlights the importance of lead-time reduction because the at-once customer base becomes smaller as the lead time to process an order decreases. To enable lead-time reduction, the enterprise could pursue strategies such as the RAP principle (postponement strategy) discussed earlier.

The time-based demand profile also may be used as the basis for pricing strategies. At-once customers might be charged a premium; beyond-lead-time customers might receive a discount. Such a pricing strategy could influence the demand profile itself so that there are more at-lead-time or beyond-lead-time customers.

The preceding discussion on the different ways to mitigate and cope with demand volatility is summarized as follows:

▲ Avoid using sales promotions/rebates and metrics that promote the end-of-the-quarter syndrome to the extent possible. If possible, use an "every-day-low-price" approach.

▲ Avoid batching. Try to work with small batches and a level production schedule.

▲ Improving the responsiveness and reliability of the delivery system will significantly reduce demand volatility.

▲ Maximize external variety with minimal internal variety. Be aware of the power of the RAP principle.

▲ It is desirable to maintain finished goods inventory as low as possible because that will help to decrease lead times and increase responsiveness in the supply chain. Finished goods inventory can be reduced significantly by using the customer-time-based demand profile.

▲ Where inventory is necessary, it should be placed at strategic locations in the supply chain to meet customer lead-time expectations.

The last bullet point—the strategic location of inventory in the supply chain—is discussed next. Strategic location of inventory has to be accompanied by delivery strategies that result in better availability of products to end users, even while maintaining lower inventories along the supply chain. TOC provides a methodology, usually referred to as the *TOC Distribution Solution*, to help enterprises effectively resolve the two key issues of strategic location and effective replenishment strategies.

The TOC Distribution and Replenishment Solution

The TOC Distribution Solution achieves significant reduction in inventories across the supply chain, accompanied by increased service levels. These improvements are achieved in a short time frame and with relatively little effort. The essential ideas underlying the TOC Distribution Solution are presented in this section. The interested reader can find more details on the solution from Goldratt's book, *The Choice*,[6] and from the downloadable program, "TOC Insights into Distribution and Supply Chain."* The book, *Isn't It Obvious?*[7] by Goldratt, shows how these concepts apply in the retail industry.

The TOC Distribution Solution first addresses the strategic location of inventory in the supply chain. Inventory essentially acts as a buffer that decouples the production location from the point of consumption (POC), and its management presents a classic conflict. On the one hand, a compelling argument can be made for using inventory to protect throughput. At the same time, inventory results in capital investments and provides increased opportunities for obsolescence, resulting in an equally strong argument for reducing inventory. The two opposing viewpoints present a concern that any inventory level chosen will represent an unsatisfactory compromise.

The TOC Thinking Process provides an approach to resolve the conflict. One of the Thinking Process constructs, discussed briefly in Chapter 3, is the *evaporating cloud*. The evaporating cloud is essentially a conflict-resolution diagram that provides an un-common sense resolution to conflicts: "in order to resolve conflicts, ignore the conflict." Instead of focusing on the conflict, the solution is to focus on the assumptions that lead to the conflict.

One of the assumptions that lead to the conflict is that inventory protects throughput in the face of long replenishment times, uncertain or unpredictable demand, unreliable suppliers, and so on. A possible *injection*, or resolution, is to consider placing inventory at the one or two strategic locations where it is needed. If this injection is acceptable, then where

---

*"TOC Insights into Distribution and Supply Chain"; available at www.toc-goldratt.com/category/TOC-Insights.

should this inventory be located? A related question is: how much inventory should be held at these locations?

The Five-Step Focusing Process described in Chapter 3 provides the direction of the solution. Consider step one of the Five-Step Focusing Process. Where is the constraint? The fact that an inventory buffer separates the production location from the end user implies that the system has adequate capacity to meet customer demand. If the demand rate exceeds the production rate, then there generally will be no inventory to stock. Therefore, the constraint is the market—there is not enough demand for the product.

The second step is to exploit the constraint. When the constraint is the market, *exploit* means to try to generate more demand for the products. The implication is that the system ensures that customers are always able to get the right product at the right time from the supply chain.

The third step of the Five-Step Focusing Process, subordinate, poses the real challenge. What should the system do to ensure that customers get the right product at the right time from the supply chain? In particular, this step repeats the questions posed by the Thinking Process: how much inventory should the system hold, and where should this inventory be located?

The Plant Warehouse

Consider first the question on where the inventory should be located. Should the inventory be located close to the POC, at the production location, or at some intermediate location? The discussion on risk pooling and the Reliant case study presented earlier in this chapter provide the answer. Unless the distance between the production location and the POC is so large that it will result in long replenishment times or excessive transportation costs, the inventory should be held at the *plant warehouse* (PWH). If it is expensive to operate with a PWH, then a *central warehouse* (CWH) can be used to store the inventory.

Storing inventory at the PWH (or the CWH) will eliminate inventory misallocation. Furthermore, the aggregated demand typically will have less variation than individual demands at the individual POCs. Hence, if the demands at the POCs are independent of each other, the PWH can achieve a desired service level with significantly less inventory than what otherwise would be needed if demand were met only with inventory stored at the various POCs. An additional benefit is that the production facility does not have to deal with urgent production orders that could come from any one of the stocking locations, each of which could throw the production facility in disarray. Any urgent production orders can now come only from the PWH!

The second question is: how much inventory should the system hold? The customer-time-based profile provides the answer: the individual POCs have to carry inventory to satisfy the at-once customers during the time it takes the PWH to replenish inventory consumed by the end users.

Setting Target Inventory Levels at the Points of Consumption

To set the inventory levels at the POCs, the TOC Distribution Solution first defines the *replenishment lead time* (*RLT*) as the elapsed time from the moment a product is sold until a replacement for that product is available at the point of consumption. *RLT* is the sum of three components—the order lead time, the production lead time, and the transportation lead time. The order lead time is the time from the moment a unit is consumed until an order is issued to replace it. The production lead time is the time it takes the plant to produce the order from the moment the order is issued. The transportation lead time is the time it takes to actually ship the finished product from the PWH to the POC.

It is instructive to relate the *RLT* to Lean systems that use containers to move products between the PWH and the POC. Lean systems generate orders as follows: as soon as a container of parts delivered to the POC becomes empty, the production location receives a *kanban** signal to replenish this container with a new set of parts. The time required for the system, measured from the instant the container became empty until the instant this container is returned to the POC with a new consignment of products, is referred to as the *kanban cycle time* (*KCT*). Note that the *KCT* is not the same as the *RLT*. This subtle distinction is clarified by the following example.

Kids Are Alright, Inc.

Kids Are Alright, Inc., is a game store started by Thomas Walker, affectionately known to his employees as Tommy. The most popular item

---

Kanban is a Japanese word that literally means "card signal."

in this store is the pinball machine. Tommy, a wizard at pinball during his teenage years, decided to sell this item in his game store when he found that pinball machines were still very much in vogue among teenagers these days.

The average demand for pinball machines is four units per day. This product is delivered to Kids Are Alright, Inc., in truckload containers by an upstream supplier, with each container carrying eight pinball machines. Each truck thus carries a two-day demand quantity of pinball machines.

Kids Are Alright, Inc., places an order on the supplier for a full container load of eight pinball machines every time a container becomes empty. This order is transmitted instantaneously to the supplier. The supplier takes an average of five days to produce this order and load it on a truck, and it takes the transportation system one day to deliver this order to Kids Are Alright, Inc.

Assume for now that there is very little variation in the system so that the actual customer demand rate, the production times, and transportation times are represented quite well by their averages. The average daily demand for pinball machines is $\bar{D}_{PM}$ = four per day. The average KCT for the pinball machines is KCT_{PM} = production time + transportation time = six days. Since every container carries eight parts, with a four-unit daily demand, an order is placed every two days. These two days represent the TOC definition of the order lead time.

Since it takes six days to return a full container of pinball machines, the time to replenish a pinball machine sold from this container, per the TOC definition of RLT, is six days plus the order lead time of two days $\bar{D}_{PM}$ = eight days. The data for Kids Are Alright, Inc., are summarized as follows:

▲ Average daily demand $\bar{D}_{PM}$ = four pinball machines per day.
▲ Average order lead time = two days.
▲ Average production lead time = five days.
▲ Average transportation lead time = one day.
▲ Average *kanban* cycle time KCT_{PM} = six days.
▲ Average number of units shipped against each order = eight units.

The average demand during a *kanban* cycle time is $\bar{D}_{PM} \times KCT_{PM} = 24$ units. The implication is that a total of 24 pinball machines are in the system, either at the production stage or in transit. Since each truck carries eight pinball machines, there are three trucks in operation at any point in time, delivering the machines to Kids Are Alright, Inc. Since the demand is assumed to be deterministic, every truck is replenishing exactly what the customers have demanded during the time period between two orders.

So far the analysis for Kids Are Alright, Inc., has proceeded assuming a deterministic scenario. Let's now consider the variations in the demand, production, and delivery.

Safety Buffers to Accommodate Variation

A *safety stock* or *safety buffer* is used to accommodate variation in the demand, variation in the replenishment lead time, and variation in the quality of the products delivered. The safety buffer is usually located at the POC, and the exact amount of safety buffer will depend on the desired service level, as described in the earlier section on risk pooling.

The TOC Distribution Solution suggests that it is probably a good idea to be a little paranoid when setting safety buffers. If it is reasonable to assume that the demand during a *kanban* cycle time is independent of previous demands and is normally distributed, the safety buffers can be set a little more precisely initially using the following approach:

Consider the Kids Are Alright, Inc., example. If Kids Are Alright, Inc., keeps track of the demands during *kanban* cycle times for a number of past deliveries, it can compute the average of these demands. This average will simply equate to which $\bar{D}_{PM} \times KCT_{PM}$ is 24 units for Kids Are Alright, Inc. The standard deviation of the demand during a *kanban* cycle time $\sigma_{\bar{D}KCT}$ now can be determined from this data.

Suppose that it is desired to meet the customer demand—that is, have no stock-outs—95 percent of the time. The normal distribution table provides Z-values for different service levels. For the 95 percent service level, the right tail of the probability distribution has a Z-value of 1.645. Thus the safety buffer to be maintained at Kids Are Alright, Inc., is $1.645 \times \sigma_{\bar{D}KCT}$. In general, the supply chain should consider building a safety buffer for each SKU. The service levels for the different SKUs could be different depending on how much the demand for these SKUs is affected by stock-outs. The more significant the impact of stock-outs is on demand, the higher the Z-value should be.

Looking for Opportunities to Reduce Safety Buffers

The TOC Distribution Solution recommends that the supply chain should examine opportunities for reducing the safety buffers at the outset, before operating the solution with these safety buffers. Let's revisit the reasons for having safety buffers—long replenishment lead times, variation in the demand from customers during the replenishment lead time (or during the *kanban* cycle time), quality problems, and so on.

The first question is whether the order lead time can be reduced by placing orders at more frequent intervals. In the Kids Are Alright, Inc., example, is it possible to order pinball machines every day instead of once every two days? If so, the average order quantity per shipment is the daily demand of four units rather than the current order quantity of eight units per shipment. While the *kanban* cycle time is still six days, the supply chain is a little more responsive. Furthermore, if the production delays are reduced to, say, three days, then the *kanban* cycle time is also reduced to four days. Let's see how these reductions affect the safety stock.

Consider first $\sigma_{\bar{D}_{KCT}}$, the standard deviation of the demand during the *kanban* cycle time. Since the *kanban* cycle time is reduced, the variation in the demand during the *kanban* cycle time will reduce, implying that Kids Are Alright, Inc., now works with a smaller safety buffer.

The Make-to-Availability Replenishment Mechanism

When orders are replenished more frequently by reducing the order lead time, it is easier to consider ordering *what was consumed the previous day* instead of a fixed order quantity every day. The TOC Distribution Solution recommends a *make-to-availability* (MTA) mode of operation at the plant that supplies the POCs. MTA represents a commitment to the customer that the system will maintain enough availability of products at a specific warehouse to be able to deliver a desired product immediately on request at any time. The definition of MTA differs from the BT definition—with BTS, no firm commitment is given to anyone.

In its ideal form, the MTA mode of operations works as follows: each POC lets the PWH know how many units of each SKU it sold the previous day, and the PWH dispatches these quantities to the POC the next day. The plant, in turn, starts producing the items that were sold. This mode of operation is very reminiscent of the method suggested for Reliant, Inc.

Increasing the Frequency of Replenishment

While the safety buffers will reduce with more frequent replenishment, a move to increase the frequency of replenishment typically will generate resistance for a variety of reasons, some of which could be valid reasons. Let's consider two possible objections that may arise.

▲ More time and effort are required when the order frequency increases.
▲ Some SKUs benefit from economies of scale—especially when they are shipped from remote locations. It is not economical to send smaller shipments because of increased transportation costs.

The first objection on time and effort is valid up to a point. Without question, more frequent ordering will involve more frequent reviews of the stock levels and possibly more paperwork, handling, and storage. However, the extra cost of managing these orders can be quite small, especially if the ordering and stocking processes are automated. The second objection may be valid, especially when shipping products from overseas, but it is possible to pack multiple different items into the transportation facility instead of a few larger-sized shipments.

Monitoring Safety Buffers Based on Buffer Penetration

If the enterprise has considered all possible opportunities to reduce the safety buffers, the next step is to implement the distribution system with these safety inventory levels and monitor the levels over time. The safety buffers are adjusted periodically based on the buffer penetration.

Buffer penetration is defined as the number of missing units from the safety buffer divided by the buffer size, expressed as a percentage. For example, if Kids Are Alright, Inc., determines that the safety buffer should be four pinball machines, then if the inventory at the store at some point in time drops to three pinball machines and there are no orders on the way, the buffer penetration is $(4 - 3) \div 4 = 25$ percent.

The TOC Distribution Solution recommends that each SKU being monitored should be reviewed periodically—say, every day or every order cycle—and is assigned a color code of green, yellow, or red depending on how much the buffer has been penetrated. If the buffer penetration is less than 33 percent, the color code assigned to that SKU is green. If the buffer penetration is between 33 and 67 percent, the SKU is color-coded yellow. If the buffer penetration is between 67 and 100 percent, the SKU is color-coded red. If the buffer penetration is greater than or equal to 100 percent—that is, if the item is stocked out or on backorder—the SKU is color-coded black.

The color code for an SKU indicates the urgency of replenishing the SKU inventory. An SKU with a red or black color code requires immediate attention to replenishment, possibly followed by a review of whether the safety buffer should be increased for that SKU. The safety buffer for the SKU should be increased if the SKU frequently receives a red or black color code. On the other hand, if the color code for the SKU remains green most of the time, then the safety buffer for that SKU very likely should be reduced.

Applying the TOC Distribution Solution at the POC

After the inventory targets at the PWH and the safety buffers at the POC are established, the focus should be on improving throughput at the POC through effective execution. Effective execution at the POC requires:

▲ A visual display that presents the right portfolio of products to the customers.
▲ A system to categorize the SKUs into *high runners* and *slow movers.*
▲ A stocking and replenishment mechanism to ensure availability of high runners at all times.

Displaying the Right Portfolio of Products to Customers

Consider how products are typically displayed in many retail stores. These POCs set aside a large space for items marked down in price—the clearance items. Such a practice could arise because the POC displays the products it receives from its suppliers. These are usually products that the POC is selling, but in many cases the POC may not have identified these products as fast- or slow-moving products. If the supplier pushes large quantities of a slow-moving product to the POC, the POC is forced to find ways to sell the product regardless of whether it is a fast- or slow-moving product.

The practice of setting aside a display space for products marked down in price is based on conventional wisdom that when the shopper encounters a large number of a product on display, he or she is more likely to perceive this product as a desirable product, especially if the product is marked down in price. This practice produces some undesirable effects for the POC, leading to a paradoxical situation in which holding high inventories actually jeopardizes sales:

▲ The POC has blocked some valuable shelf space for marked-down products that could have relatively low profit per unit of shelf space.
▲ The products on display are probably slow-moving products. These may not be the products that the customer really wants. Perhaps this is why these products had to be marked down and sold, possibly at a loss.
▲ The slow-moving products may have a short market life—especially if they are electronic goods—or these products may have a short shelf life.
▲ The inventory has tied up cash that the POC could have used to buy fast-moving products.

Are these the products that the stores really want to sell? If so, what profit potential do these products have, especially when they are sold at a discounted price?

To the supplier, the practice of pushing large quantities of a possibly slow-moving product to the POC has a twofold advantage: the supplier incurs reduced production and transportation costs by shipping a larger quantity, and this shipment potentially will reduce the ability of the POC to buy similar products from the supplier's competitors. However, this practice also has a down side for the supplier. Since these are slow-moving products, the demand for these products will be very uneven, and therefore, it will be a long time before the POC places the next order on the supplier for this product, assuming that the POC wishes to continue selling these products. If so, the supplier unwittingly has set itself up for the inevitable bullwhip effect. In any event, the practice of pushing large quantities ultimately results in a deteriorating relationship between the supplier and the POC.

The POC often does not devote adequate attention to the slow-moving items because it is working with an aggregate inventory budget. The typical approach is to set an order-up-to level for each SKU, adjusting the level as necessary, to operate within the total inventory budget. Such a practice often results in such statements as, "We have $5 million in inventory" or "We have six weeks of inventory." But these statements refer to aggregate numbers, which do not identify severe shortages for some fast-moving items and huge stocks for slow-moving items.

Categorizing SKUs as High Runners and Slow Movers

It is therefore advantageous, from both the POC's and the supplier's perspectives, to identify the slow movers. It is probably even more important for the POC to identify the fast-moving products—the high runners. The POC is quite likely to be stocked out of high runners because these products are so much in demand.

The potential loss in profits from stock-outs of the high runners is often vastly underestimated. Do customers always complain to the seller if they do not find the product they are seeking? Even if a customer places a complaint with the seller, does the salesperson register in the system that a customer did not find what he or she was looking for? Assuming that the unavailability of the high runner is registered in the POC's system, how often does the POC tell the supplier about this problem?

While it is important to categorize the items held at the POC as high runners, regular items, and slow movers, such a categorization should be done only after the TOC Distribution Solution is put in place. It is much easier to identify the high runners and slow movers after determining initial buffer sizes for these products.

The Stocking and Replenishment Mechanism

The typical mode of operation for a POC is based on an assumption that the customer will not purchase a product if it is not in stock—a mind-set constraint that forces POCs to store and display as many SKUs as possible within a limited shelf space. What is even worse is that the POC usually displays the slow movers in its valuable display space. The slow movers are not the products that the POC needs to display. Rather, the POC needs to display the high runners. However, quite often the high runners—the products that the POC really needs to sell—are stocked out.

The mind-set constraint that forces POCs to store and display as many SKUs as possible also overlooks the possibility that the customer-time-based demand profile may be dramatically different for slow movers and high runners. The solution is to get a deeper understanding of customer tolerance time.

For customers, it is very likely that their expectations of availability for the high runners are much higher than their expectations of availability for the slow movers. Once the TOC Distribution Solution is in place and replenishment of SKUs takes place more frequently, customers will be more assured that slow movers will be delivered more quickly even if they are not stocked by the POC. The assurance that a product that is not currently in stock will be delivered shortly even allows the POC to offer the slow movers without even holding inventory of these products. The POC can consider accepting orders for the slow movers with just one display model for each slow-moving product.

When a system for obtaining data on daily sales at the POC is in place, with replenishment taking place at frequent intervals, the POC can move to a system that operates the high runners on a BTS mode of operation and the slow movers on a BTO mode of operation. If the POC can establish such differing modes of operation with the suppliers, it can, in return, guarantee shelf space for the suppliers even while dramatically reducing the overall inventory at the POC. An additional benefit is that the POC is now able to offer and sell a larger portfolio of products.

The supplier benefits because it is guaranteed a price that is not based on the quantity purchased in one order but is instead guaranteed a price based on the quantity purchased during a given period. The salespeople at the POC, who constantly push to have a larger portfolio of products on display, will also be pleased with this arrangement, as will be the operations people, who do not now need to worry about storing and displaying the slow movers.

The TOC Distribution Solution described up to this point is summarized as follows:

▲ Instead of pushing products out to the POCs, it is better to maintain these items at a centralized location such as a plant warehouse or a central warehouse and replenish the stocks at the POCs based on the actual demand at these locations. The variation in the aggregate demand at the plant or central warehouse will be much less than the variation in demand at the individual POCs, so the plant warehouse needs less inventory to meet customer demands.

▲ Each POC should maintain a safety buffer of inventory to buffer against any demand variation. The safety buffer should be determined based on the desired service level.

▲ The enterprise should try to move toward an order-daily-replenish-periodically mode of operation. When the frequency of ordering and replenishment is increased, the safety buffers maintained at the POC should be reduced.

▲ The safety buffers should be monitored periodically and adjusted based on the buffer penetration.

▲ The POC should consider stocking and displaying the high runners rather than the slow movers. The POC also should consider using a BTS mode of operation for the high runners and a BTO mode of operation for the slow movers.

Measures for Sustaining the Solution

The TOC measures T, I, and OE help the enterprise to arrive at the right policies and decisions. These measures have to be translated in order to guide the execution of these policies and decisions. Metrics for judging execution should let the enterprise know if the execution was carried out reliably and effectively. At the same time, these metrics also should provide guidance to the enterprise on what corrective actions need to be undertaken when the execution is not carried out reliably or effectively.

TOC prescribes three measures to gauge the reliability, effectiveness, and efficiency of execution. These three measures are *throughput-dollar-days* (TDD), *inventory-dollar-days* (IDD), and *local operating expense* (LOE).

The TDD metric is motivated by the need to measure the degree to which a delivery commitment to the customer is satisfied. This metric evaluates the dollar value of the degree to which the delivery commitment was satisfied based on the rationale that if a delivery commitment is missed, then missing the delivery by one day is not the same as missing the delivery by one month. TDD is calculated as the sum of all the dollar values of missed commitments multiplied by the number of days the commitment was late. For example, if the enterprise delivered 15 units of a $20 item two days late, then the TDD for that missed delivery is $15 \times 20 \times 2 = \$600$. The goal is to have *zero* throughput-dollar-days.

The TDD metric helps the enterprise to prioritize orders that have to be expedited when they are missing committed delivery dates. For example, if an enterprise is late on two different products, each valued at $1,000, what additional information does the enterprise need to guide the efforts to expedite these products? If one of these products is a BTS item and the other is a component that is holding up the assembly of a million-dollar system, clearly the latter product gets the higher priority. No doubt, to properly use the TDD metric, the enterprise needs to know where these products will be used by its customers.

The IDD metric helps the enterprise to measure the effectiveness of execution by computing the value of excess inventory. It is evaluated as the dollar value of inventory on hand multiplied by the number of days the inventory has been stored. The goal is to have the minimum inventory-dollar-days needed to ensure that the enterprise is meeting delivery commitments reliably.

The LOE metric helps the enterprise to measure the efficiency of operation of departments or functions. The intent is to identify all the expenses incurred by the department or function, such as salaries, utilities, indirect material, scrap, and so on. In keeping with the TOC philosophy of not allocating sunk costs, LOE will only include expenses that are under the control of the department or function. More specifically, LOE will not include any allocation of expenses—such as corporate overhead—over which the department or function has no control. As with the IDD metric, the goal is to reduce LOE, but not at the cost of compromising the enterprise's ability to meet delivery commitments reliably.

Conclusions

▲ Understanding customer value is the first step toward nurturing an enterprise into an ever-flourishing organization.

▲ Order winners and order qualifiers allow the enterprise to translate customer needs to specific attributes on which the enterprise can focus to secure orders.

▲ The phrase *maximize external variety with minimal internal variety* captures the best approach to designing the production and delivery process. The RAP principle ("Keep the material as *raw as possible*") is a convenient way to meet customer demand quickly without storing a large finished goods inventory.

▲ Adopting the RAP principle also results in reduced variation in the system because aggregated demand has significantly less variation than individual demands.

▲ It is not enough to benchmark against the competition; this will result in the enterprise adopting the same practices (good and bad) as the lead competitor and promote a follower mentality. Instead, there is a tremendous competitive advantage in adopting best-in-class practices that cut across industries.

▲ If an enterprise has to hold inventory, it should be located strategically in the supply chain. Use the RAP principle to determine how far upstream in the supply chain it can be located and still meet customer lead-time expectations.

Creating a smooth flow of products in the supply chain provides multiple benefits. In particular, it helps to reduce lead times.

▲ Reduced lead times and improved flow go hand in hand, creating a virtuous cycle.

▲ Lead times are also influenced considerably by the variation in the system, and therefore, the manager of the enterprise should focus on reducing variation.

▲ It is therefore even more important that products and processes are designed so as to mitigate demand volatility.

The TOC Distribution Solution provides a systematic approach to enable better deliveries even while storing lower inventory levels in the supply chain:

▲ The TOC Distribution Solution reduces the variation in demand by setting up a PWH or CWH that delivers the products to the POC based on the items actually sold by the POC.

▲ With this solution, each POC maintains a safety buffer of inventory to buffer against any demand variation, with the safety buffer determined based on the desired level of service.

▲ The solution tries to move toward a more frequent replenishment mode of operation. When the frequency of ordering and replenishment is increased, the safety buffers maintained at the POC should reduce.

▲ The TOC Distribution Solution works with an MTA mode of operation. MTA represents a commitment to the customer that the system will maintain enough availability of products at a specific warehouse to be able to deliver the desired product immediately on request at all times. MTA is a little different from BTS—with BTS, no firm commitment is given to anyone

▲ The solution asks the POC to consider stocking and displaying the high runners rather than the slow movers. The POC also should consider using a BTS mode of operation for the high runners and a BTO mode of operation for the slow movers.

References

1. E. M. Goldratt (2010), "Introduction to TOC—My Perspective," in *Theory of Constraints Handbook*, J. F. Cox and J. G. Schleier (eds.), McGraw-Hill, New York.
2. J. F. Cox and J. G. Schleier, eds. (2010), *Theory of Constraints Handbook*, McGraw-Hill, New York.
3. K. R. Gue (2001), "Warehouse Tours"; available at http://web.nps.navy.mil/~krgue/Teaching/teaching.html.
4. T. Hill (2000), *Manufacturing Strategy*, Irwin McGraw-Hill, Boston.
5. T. Ohno (1988), *Toyota Production System: Beyond Large-Scale Production*, Productivity Press, Cambridge, MA; translated from the Japanese book, Toyota seisan hoshiki, Daiyamondo, Tokyo, 1978.
6. E. Goldratt (2008), *The Choice*, North-River Press, Great Barrington, MA.
7. E. Goldratt (2009), *Isn't It Obvious?* North-River Press, Great Barrington, MA.

CHAPTER 5

Building a Competitive Operations Strategy

"We all have ability. The difference is how we use it." This statement is attributed to Stevie Wonder, a musical legend who has won multiple Grammy Awards and a Grammy Lifetime Achievement Award, and was one of the first inductees into the Rock and Roll Hall of Fame. Wonder overcame many obstacles in his career, capitalizing on them instead of being overwhelmed by them. As a premature infant he was placed in an incubator and accidentally given too much oxygen, resulting in his blindness. The ever-optimistic Wonder said his blindness allowed him to concentrate on his sense of hearing. He thus found a way to use his abilities most effectively.

I was reminded of Stevie Wonder's statement when I read a report Andersen Consulting (now known as Accenture) produced in 1994. The Andersen Consulting report compared management practices and manufacturing performance of 71 enterprises that supplied car seats, exhausts, and brakes to automobile assembly plants.[1] The enterprises included in the study were located in nine countries: Canada, France, Germany, Italy, Japan, Mexico, Spain, the United Kingdom, and the United States.

Andersen Consulting identified 13 of these enterprises as "world class" with regard to their performance on key metrics such as productivity, quality, inventories, deliveries, and schedule variation. The study found, on average, a 2:1 difference in performance on these key metrics between world-class enterprises and the rest. The world-class enterprises experienced less variability in both the delivery schedules received from customers and the deliveries made by major suppliers. The quality gap was even more significant. For every defective exhaust system produced by a world-class enterprise, non-world-class enterprises had 170 defects. The world-class enterprises also were able to achieve higher quality, higher productivity, lower space requirements, and lower supply chain inventories *simultaneously*.

Andersen Consulting's findings evoked Stevie Wonder's statement because the enterprises included in the study were making the same products, but some enterprises were using their resources much more effectively than the others. The study also raised two questions: What factors accounted for the observed differences in ability between the world-class and the non-world-class enterprises? A more intriguing question to me was: How were the enterprises identified as world class able to improve performance *simultaneously* along multiple dimensions?

Before attempting to address these questions, let's examine how enterprises compete to leverage positions in the marketplace.

Gaining a Competitive Advantage

Figure 5.1 presents a framework that captures the different ways in which enterprises can gain a competitive advantage in the marketplace. The framework suggests that competitive advantage can result in one of two possible ways: Either the enterprise enjoys a strong *structural position* that allows it to dominate the marketplace, or the enterprise competes on the basis of superior *process execution*. The figure also indicates that *operational effectiveness* and *strategic flexibility* are vital for superior process execution.

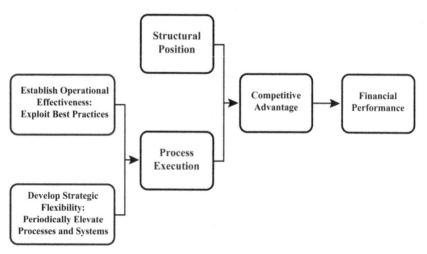

Figure 5.1 A framework for gaining a competitive advantage.

Structural position relates to the position the enterprise occupies within its competitive environment and to the structure of that environment. Enterprises that try to improve their structural position work to achieve a favorable competitive advantage by changing and controlling the structure of their industry. These enterprises achieve a dominant structural position mainly by erecting barriers that dissuade other enterprises from competing with them.

Process execution relates to how well the enterprise executes its core processes. Broadly speaking, core processes include product development, demand management, and order fulfillment. Enterprises compete through process execution in two ways:

▲ By managing these core processes as effectively as the best-in-class enterprises in their industry are able to (operational effectiveness)
▲ By constantly reevaluating and reinventing these processes and the systems that support these processes (strategic flexibility)

Some enterprises, such as Apple, successfully exploit their structural position and achieve excellent process execution simultaneously, which places these enterprises in an excellent position to dominate their business ecosystem.

Building a Structural Position

Arguably, most enterprises have some form of structural position, but only a very small percentage of all enterprises have a *dominant* structural position. Enterprises with a dominant structural position enjoy limited rivalry either because they are a pure monopoly or because they operate in an industry in which few enterprises would attempt to enter owing to high entry costs. An enterprise that typifies a dominant structural position is Microsoft. Despite the threats posed by the increasing market share of Apple computers, the Microsoft Windows operating system has a commanding share of the operating systems market in the PC ecosystem. Microsoft also enjoys a very large market share for Microsoft Office software products used in PCs, such as Microsoft Word, PowerPoint, and Excel.

Microsoft maintains its structural position by encouraging other independent software developers to create compatible products. In pursuing this strategy, Microsoft, itself a software developer, cooperates with thousands of other enterprises that otherwise could be considered its competitors. Microsoft thus has built its own software ecosystem within the context of the PC ecosystem.

Thousands of software developers are trying every day to come up with the next operating system and the next office software product that will replace Microsoft's system. However, users of Windows operating systems and Microsoft Office products will not consider other software unless these developers can assure full compatibility with Microsoft products. These developers also have to be able to provide the kind of technical support that Microsoft gives its users and be able to upgrade their software products like Microsoft often does. The entry barriers are simply too great.

Enterprises such as the Coca-Cola Company have leveraged structural position through brand identity and by cementing a carefully executed distribution strategy that provides easy access to Coca-Cola products at practically any place in the world. Other enterprises such as utilities and power-generation enterprises enjoy structural position because they are in industries that put pressure on other potential suppliers to *not* compete. These are industries where overall customer value is maximized by having a single supplier. Regulations typically are in place to keep such enterprises from abusing their monopoly status, but they nevertheless face very limited competition.

The discussion to this point makes it clear why it is more common to find enterprises competing through process execution.

Competing Through Process Execution

As Figure 5.1 indicates, an enterprise tries to compete through process execution in two ways: operational effectiveness and strategic flexibility. Let's examine each one of these alternatives.

Operational Effectiveness and the Productivity Frontier

The Andersen Consulting study mentioned earlier raised two questions:

▲ What were the factors that accounted for the observed differences between the world-class and non-world-class enterprises, even though the enterprises compared in the study were making the same products?

▲ How were the enterprises identified as world class able to improve performance along multiple dimensions simultaneously?

If it really is possible for enterprises to improve performance along multiple dimensions simultaneously, this would contradict the findings of a number of researchers who found that tradeoffs had to be made among the elements that deliver customer value. The tradeoff concept was formally introduced by Skinner,[2] who said

> The variables of cost, time, quality, technological constraints, and customer satisfaction place limits on what management can do, force compromises, and demand an explicit recognition of a multitude of tradeoffs and choices.

This line of reasoning would decree, for example, that an effort to obtain better quality would decrease productivity because building a high-quality product would require more effort. Similarly, it could be expected that improved service would not be possible without maintaining high inventory levels.

The notion of tradeoffs remained entrenched in the corporate world until concepts and programs such as Theory of Constraints (TOC), Just-In-Time (JIT), and Total Quality Management (TQM) challenged this notion in the early 1980s. These programs changed the way activities were performed. They eliminated inefficiencies, improved customer satisfaction, and forced managers to think about best practices. Managers found that improvements in quality led to improvements in areas such as cost and flexibility—findings that were apparently paradoxical yet in agreement with the Andersen Consulting study. What explains the apparent paradox?

The paradox can be explained by a *productivity frontier* that, at any given time, represents the sum of all existing best practices.[3] It represents the maximum value that an enterprise can create in the delivery of a product or service using the best available technologies, skills, and management techniques. Figure 5.2 illustrates this concept. An enterprise that wants to compete through operational effectiveness would strive to position itself somewhere along the productivity frontier.

The productivity frontier shown in the figure presents a plausible explanation for the two questions raised by the Andersen Consulting study. World-class enterprises were positioned above non-world-class enterprises

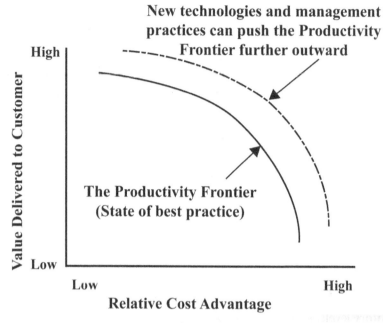

Figure 5.2 The productivity frontier.

in the figure and therefore performed better. Moreover, if a world-class enterprise was positioned below the frontier, improving its operational effectiveness would allow it to move outward toward the frontier, improving along multiple dimensions such as quality and productivity simultaneously.

Such simultaneity was indeed experienced by U.S. manufacturers when they adopted Japanese principles in the 1980s to reduce setup times for the dies in their press shops. These manufacturers were able to lower cost and at the same time better differentiate their products. In doing so, they dispelled notions that tradeoffs were *always* necessary.

Once an enterprise is positioned on the frontier, then the productivity frontier concept asserts that the enterprise is doing as well as it can along multiple dimensions. At this stage, if the enterprise wishes to improve yet further on a metric such as quality, it has to find another position along the frontier, implying that it has to trade off another metric such as productivity. New technologies and more innovative management practices, however, can push the productivity frontier outward, as indicated in Figure 5.2, further improving performance along a number of dimensions simultaneously.

Operational Effectiveness and Competitiveness

An enterprise competing by exploiting operational effectiveness in effect raises the bar for every other enterprise in the industry. While enterprises can exploit operational effectiveness and attempt to discourage competition, it often does not lead to sustained competitive advantage for the enterprises. These enterprises, in fact, may begin to suffer from persistently low profits. For instance, time-based competition provided a significant competitive edge for many Japanese enterprises in the mid-1980s. However, when there were no breakthrough innovations, Japanese manufacturers were forced to cut prices in an everlasting struggle to maintain market share. While the customer ultimately benefited, the price wars did not help the profitability or the commercial viability of the enterprises.

The struggles of the Japanese manufacturers convey another message. Although the goal of many enterprises is to compete by imitating best practices within their industry, this goal may not be a long-term growth strategy. *It is unwise for an enterprise to expect to achieve any sort of sustained competitive advantage if its only goal is to be as good as its toughest competitors.* Besides, even as the follower is trying to emulate its toughest competitor, the leader is very likely to be innovating and continuing to increase its lead. In summary:

▲ When enterprises compete by exploiting operational effectiveness, they tend to benchmark themselves against best-in-class competitors. Unfortunately, the more benchmarking enterprises do with each other, the more they look alike.

▲ As competitors imitate one another's improvements in quality, cycle times, or supplier partnerships, strategies begin to converge, and eventually, this results in no enduring winners.

Operational Effectiveness: Necessary but Not Sufficient

The preceding discussion reveals that while operational effectiveness is a necessary condition for competitiveness, it is not sufficient. What else can enterprises do to gain a sustained competitive advantage?

In a customer-centric era that continues to see ever-increasing levels of competition across all industries, mere adoption of better practices and techniques does not create a sustainable competitive advantage. The practices and techniques may be based on breakthrough ideas, but breakthrough practices and techniques can rapidly become the industry's standard operating procedure.

To draw an analogy from sports, the "Fosbury flop" pioneered by Dick Fosbury in the 1968 Olympiad was a breakthrough technique. However, it rapidly became the standard, and in fact, practically every athlete competing for the high jump event in the 1972 Olympiad was practicing the Fosbury flop.

Thus what was once a competitive advantage soon becomes the "ante required to play the game." Managers who expect to become competitive simply by emulating the practices of successful enterprises typically have abandoned the central concept of a strategy.

What is strategy? And what is the role of Operations in framing and executing strategies?

A *strategy* is a description of the manner in which an enterprise intends to gain a competitive advantage. It can be argued that the root cause of the failure of many enterprises in the consumer-centric era is the failure to distinguish between operational effectiveness and *operations strategy*. The operations function enables the enterprise to realize its strategy by providing strategic flexibility: the enterprise's ability to periodically reinvent its existing processes and systems to respond to changing customer preferences. Enterprises that build strategic flexibility are able to compete in a customer-centric world, adapting quickly to changing customer preferences. Strategic flexibility also allows the enterprise to reposition itself when the competitive environment changes.

Consider the general merchandise retailer Target Corporation. In the 1980s and early 1990s, Target was considered a deep-discount retail store. It had relatively poor store layouts and store environments, and poor customer service.

When Walmart aggressively began to establish its position as the leading low-price discount retailer in the United States, Target realized that it could not compete directly with Walmart in this manner. Target completely changed its strategy, targeted a specific market, and set certain expectations for customer experience with regard to store layout, environment, customer service, product selection, and quality. Target deliberately decided to move completely away from its position as a deep-discount retail store.

In the early 2000s, Target's strategy was to provide exceptional value to American consumers through multiple retail formats ranging from upscale discount and moderate-priced to full-scale department stores. Target now aims to remain "committed to providing a one-stop shopping experience for guests by delivering differentiated merchandise and outstanding value with its Expect More. Pay Less. brand promise."* Instead of trying to compete simply by imitating Walmart's best practices, Target demonstrates strategic flexibility by periodically reinventing processes and systems.

The discussion so far can be summed up as follows:

▲ Operational effectiveness and operations strategy are both essential to superior performance, but they work in different ways. Whereas operational effectiveness allows the enterprise to perform *similar* activities better than its rivals, an operations strategy is needed to position the enterprise more effectively in the marketplace.

▲ An operations strategy should help the enterprise gain a relative advantage through actions that its competitors will find hard to follow, allowing the advantage to be extended even further.

▲ The goal of operations strategy is to provide strategic flexibility—well-designed concepts and tools that will move the enterprise ahead of the competition and keep it ahead—through periodic reinvention of processes and systems.

Building Strategic Flexibility

For an enterprise that wishes to continue to grow its business, the biggest threat probably stems from a policy of inaction. For instance, if an enterprise ignores or fails to recognize changing customer preferences, it risks losing market share. If the enterprise is not flexible enough to adapt to changing customer preferences, it faces increased production costs owing to the mismatch between its production capabilities and market preferences, leading to a potential loss of market share.

The decline of the U.S. machine tool industry in the early 1980s provides a stark example of the negative consequences of a mismatch between customer preferences and industry capabilities. The U.S. machine tool manufacturers believed that their customers would continue to prefer highly customized machine tools. Consequently, they continued to organize

*See the Target corporate information Web site at http://pressroom.target.com/pr/news/corporate-information.aspx.

their manufacturing processes to produce low volumes of specialized machine tools. Since every machine tool was virtually a unique product, it required long lead times and was expensive.

During this period, Japanese machine tool manufacturers entered the U.S. market with more standardized and less elaborate machine tools. Anticipating changing customer preferences for simpler machine tools, the Japanese were able to offer quality equipment with short lead times that was inexpensive and far superior in quality to those of U.S. manufacturers. The U.S. manufactures had to spend the next decade scrambling to regain lost ground in the machine tool marketplace.

Intel, on the other hand, is an enterprise that exhibits strategic flexibility as it strives to match or even *anticipate* customer preferences. When we hear the name Intel, one of the first thoughts that come to mind is probably the phrase, "Intel Inside," the familiar slogan displayed by most PCs. With its Pentium, Centrino, and Celeron chips, Intel cemented its superiority over Advanced Micro Devices (AMD). Now probably best known for its Core processors for laptops and desktops and the Xeon processor for servers and workstations, Intel has constantly innovated and stays ahead of the rest of the competition.

Intel has invested heavily in research and development and in capacity, and this investment has paid off. Intel's financial performance continues to dominate the financial performance of AMD, its nearest rival in the central processing unit (CPU) market. For the fiscal year 2010, Intel had a revenue of $43.6 billion and a net income of $11.67 billion, giving it a profit margin of 26.76 percent. The corresponding numbers for AMD for the year 2010 were $6.49 billion, $471 million, and 7.25 percent, respectively. Intel also dominates its nearest rival, NVidia, in the graphic processing unit (GPU) market.

Intel's former CEO, Craig Barrett, has said that Intel is focused on a *demand-pull strategy*, forging closer ties with customers to create products that fit customers' needs, instead of a *technology-push strategy* of designing products no one has asked for. The $7.7 billion acquisition of McAfee, Inc., and the $1.4 billion buyout of the Infineon Technologies AG Wireless Solutions business in early 2011 provide Intel with an opportunity to put security at the center of its foray into mobile computing.

Intel has moved beyond manufacturing chips for PCs, but it is not abandoning its core competency—making standardized low-cost chips for computers. Even as Intel takes a financial risk by investing in new ventures, its factories making chips for PCs, servers, and other established markets are running full speed, producing cutting-edge chips that continue to uphold Moore's Law.*

Increasing customer demands frequently outpace the ability of a business to adapt to these changes, and often there seems to be no consistent way to respond to and support different customer segments with distinct needs. Enterprises that wish to rapidly adapt to changing customer preferences and offer effective solutions thus face challenges. The primary challenge these enterprises face is to align the marketing function with the operations function to evolve a set of marketing and operations strategies that fulfill corporate goals.

Another challenge to overcome is the reluctance of many enterprises to make strategic choices or tradeoffs. Serving one group of customers and excluding others places a real or imagined limit on a corporate model that strives to have flexible response to changing customer preferences. Managers often compromise by taking incremental steps such as extending product lines, adding new features, and imitating rivals' products. Compromises in the pursuit of growth, however, pose a real danger of eroding the competitive advantage of an enterprise. One cannot be all things to all people.

Strategic flexibility is not achieved simply by *offering* new products to adapt to changing customer preferences. Strategic flexibility relates to the ability to *deliver* these new products to the customer.

A Model for Enterprise Growth

What is the right model to follow to promote strategic flexibility? Figure 5.3 presents a model in which enterprises periodically enhance their competitive position by developing new products, processes, and systems. This model, the S-Curve Model, is a series of S-curves, each depicting incremental improvement in process capabilities over time.

Each S-curve represents a new generation of a process or a technology. The initial part of the S-curve represents a period of slow growth in process capability as the enterprise begins to adapt to the process or technology. This is followed by a period of rapid improvement in process capabilities as the enterprise better understands the process or technology. At some point, the rate of process improvements begins to slow no matter how much effort is expended in improving the process or technology, and the S-curve flattens

---

*Moore's Law, attributed to Gordon Moore, the founder and ex-CEO of Intel Corporation, states that computing power should double roughly every 18 months.

Process Capabilities

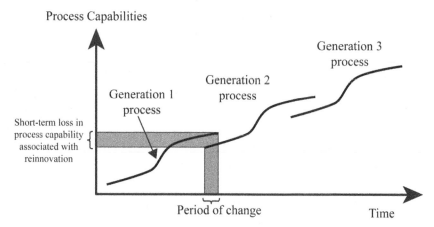

Figure 5.3 A model for enterprise growth.

out. Once the limit is reached, process capability is improved only through a new generation of process or technology.

The step changes in Figure 5.3 may result in a temporary decline in capabilities during periods of transition as the enterprise adjusts to new processes and systems. For instance, Intel's attempt to venture beyond the computer chip business and expand into the Web hosting market failed in 2002, resulting in a $100 million charge. Transition periods present the greatest challenge to enterprises; they promote a policy of inaction, especially for managers in risk-averse enterprises. However, for well-executed operations strategies, such "backward" steps are often followed by a period of robust growth.

The ramification of the S-Curve Model is that for real, continuous improvement, there must be both incremental and innovation improvement. Enterprises must focus on strategic flexibility and be prepared to modify their existing processes and systems as needed. This discussion is summarized by the seventh Lean Supply Chain Principle:

Lean Supply Chain Principle 7

The role of operations strategy is to provide the enterprise with the ability to cope with changing customer preferences. Products and processes should be designed to promote strategic flexibility.

Here are the steps to maintain strategic flexibility, periodically adapting processes and systems to continually deliver customer value:

▲ Maintain a process orientation.
▲ Bring new products to market faster.
▲ Coevolve marketing and operations strategies.
▲ Communicate financial benefits to management.
▲ Enable the operations strategy.

Maintaining a Process Orientation

In the fall of 2002, I visited an organization that fabricated and assembled display racks for major retail stores. A vast majority of the orders the organization received were for standard display racks that required modest customization. When the marketing and sales department received orders that required even a modest degree of customization, it routed those orders through the product design department. Product design approved the design modifications and forwarded the orders to the production planning department. Production planning, in turn, batched these orders and released them to the production department when an "economic production quantity" was reached.

Fabricating and assembling a rack typically required about an hour of labor. However, because of the multiple hand-offs and delays involved, it took about 15 days from the moment marketing and sales received the order until the order was presented to production. The production department took another 15 to 20 days to fabricate and assemble the display rack. This organization had a niche market in the display rack manufacturing industry at the time.

My question was: How could this organization exhibit strategic flexibility if it had to contend with significant competition? The performance of this organization was significantly hampered by its *functional* orientation. The organization needed a *process* orientation that better aligned its internal processes and departments (functions).

Functional Orientation and Functional Silos

Traditional enterprises tend to group similar activities together under functional units such as marketing or operations. A functional orientation is often easier to manage because the "specialists" are grouped together and supervised by people who have similar skills and experience. The functional orientation also provides economies of scale because it tends to centralize similar resources and provides mutual support through physical proximity while clearly defining career paths for employees.

The functional orientation generally works well when the enterprise deals with a steady demand for standard products that do not demand much interfunctional coordination. However, the functional orientation does not easily accommodate changing customer preferences, so it does not facilitate the objectives of the lean supply chain.

The basic tenet of functional orientation is "Just do your tasks as prescribed" or alternately, "My boss is the most important customer." Such an organization results in *functional silos* that promote the familiar *over-the-wall syndrome* shown in Figure 5.4. With the functional silo mentality, communication between functional units is very poor. The series of operations shown in the figure is very reminiscent of the process followed by the display rack manufacturing enterprise I visited in 2002.

Operating with functional silos can lead to bizarre outcomes. Stanford University Professor Hau Lee[4] discusses the case of a well-known automobile manufacturing enterprise in the mid-1990s. The marketing and sales group of this enterprise, faced with an excessive inventory of green cars in the middle of the year, offered special discounts and rebates on green cars

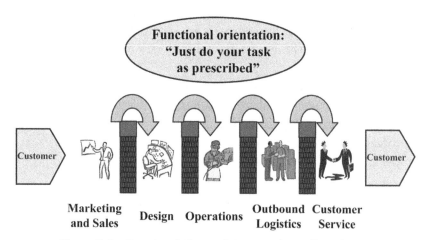

Figure 5.4 Functional silos and the over-the-wall syndrome.

to the distributors. As the sale of green cars increased rapidly in response to the promotion, the supply chain planning group incorrectly assumed that there was a big demand for green cars and decided to initiate production of even more green cars. The lack of communication between marketing and sales and supply chain planning resulted in the enterprise ending the year with a large inventory of green cars.

Developing a Process Orientation

Many enterprises use a *matrix* form of organization. These enterprises are focusing on the processes that deliver the product to the customer as key to promoting a smooth flow of products through the enterprise. Such a focus is a *process orientation*. Figure 5.5 depicts a process-oriented organization structure that is in sharp contrast with the functional orientation in Figure 5.4. The process-oriented structure aims at being customer-focused, trying to execute orders as quickly as possible.

A critical challenge for an enterprise that embraces the process orientation is to reconcile the needs of the individual, the function, the enterprise, and the supply chain in a way that realizes full benefits for the supply chain as a whole. For instance, one problem with the process orientation is that it may require individuals assigned to a cross-functional team to abandon a customary functional path. Another problem is that such assignments may diminish key functions. When individuals and functions feel threatened by so-called streamlined processes, the processes may not stay streamlined for long.

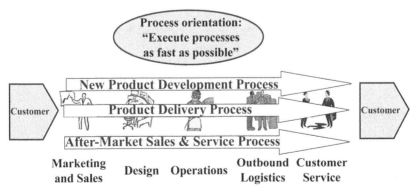

Figure 5.5 A process-oriented enterprise.

Maintaining a process orientation also can be a problem for enterprises whose business is growing. As the business grows, enterprises typically tend to grow in terms of both physical resources and number of employees. During a growth phase, there is a natural tendency for enterprises to become more bureaucratic and erect functional boundaries.

Economist John Kenneth Galbraith once wrote, "So complex, indeed, will be the job of organizing specialists that there will be specialists on organization."[5] Galbraith was trying to show that the American economy, which was growing rapidly in the 1970s, was becoming a planned, bureaucratic economy much like the Soviet economy. He postulated that economists would have to study the corporate sector as a form of planned economy using classic economics.

Galbraith charged that an inevitable consequence of bureaucracy was that "an increasing span of time separates the beginning from the completion of any task." Galbraith was alluding to Ford Motor Company, which delivered its first car in 1903, *less than five months* after the company was formed. The Ford Mustang that was introduced in 1964, however, took three and a half years from the initial planning stage before it was made available to consumers. Galbraith thus deduced that lead times to deliver products tend to increase as enterprises grow in size and age.

Every enterprise follows a predictable, natural pattern of evolution from birth to maturity. The initial stage is characterized by enthusiasm, shared responsibility, and a general desire to respond quickly to customer demands. The emphasis is on learning—to understand the technology, to respond to divergent customer needs, and to develop sources of capital. However, as the enterprise matures, it often falls victim to institutionalization as processes are formalized, rigidity sets in, and democratic processes are replaced by hierarchical rankings. The enterprise that begins life as an informal *learning* organization becomes a formal *hierarchical* organization.

The preceding discussion is summarized as follows:

▲ As enterprises grow and mature, they tend to form hierarchical structures.

▲ Enterprises with formalized, hierarchical structures encourage managers to operate in functional silos, focusing on promoting and protecting their own functional interests with little concern for the greater good of the enterprise.

▲ Enterprises with a rigid hierarchical structure are less responsive to changes in customer demand and slower to adapt to changes in processes and technologies.
▲ Consequently, as enterprises grow and age, they require more time to deliver the product to customers.

A strong case can therefore be made for mature enterprises, especially enterprises that have grown in size over the years, to seek ways to rejuvenate themselves. This is precisely what Jack Welch, former chairman and CEO of General Electric, was alluding to when he sought to get the "soul of a small company" into the "large, muscle-bound, big-company body" that General Electric had become.[6]

Even innovative enterprises are not immune to the functional silo trap when they grow and expand. Michael Dell found that as his business grew, his information systems group, for instance, gradually began to view its role in the enterprise as one of just creating information systems rather than one of facilitating the flow of information to employees, customers, and shareholders. He once stated

> In the thick of our growth, our team had lost sight of our fundamental values: serving the interests of the customer, the shareholder, and the company as a whole.[7]

Dell's employees had fallen into the functional silo trap, and Dell had to consciously work on breaking the silos.

While it is desirable to align as many functional units as possible, some of these alignments are especially critical for the lean supply chain. To determine the critical ones, consider some attributes that Lean enterprises should possess:

▲ A customer focus
▲ Quick response to changing market conditions
▲ Continuous innovation and effective application of new technologies
▲ Close communication and partnership with customers and suppliers

These characteristics highlight the need for a better alignment of the operations function with two key functions: design and marketing. Consider first the alignment of design with marketing and operations.

Bringing New Products to Market Faster

For convenience, the term *design process integration* (DPI) will be used to refer to the set of activities and processes that integrate design with marketing and operations. DPI significantly affects the product cost. It also affects the new-product development (NPD) process and the product delivery process for the lean supply chain.

Consider first product cost. Numerous studies have shown that by the time a product design is complete, less than 10 percent of the total product budget is expended, on average. However, the design phase also commits *80 percent of the cost of the product over its lifetime!* The concept phase of the design process alone typically determines 60 percent of the cost, as shown in Figure 5.6.

Needless to say, once the design is locked in, it is often very difficult to make substantial changes to the design. All too often the result is an endless stream of engineering change notices that attempt to improve on the design or, worse yet, attempt to rectify errors introduced during the design phase. Typically, these changes are incremental and offer "patches" to the existing design, very much like the patches made to software programs.

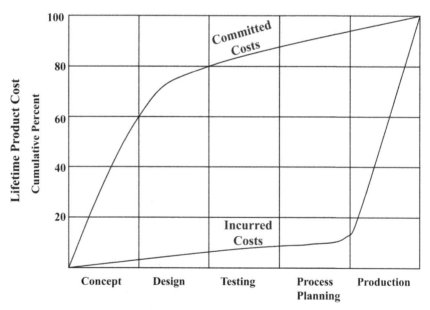

Figure 5.6 Product cost during the life of a product.

Consider next NPD, a major activity for the design function. NPD projects provide the enterprise with an opportunity to develop new skills, new knowledge, and new systems. NPD projects provide such opportunities because they are sufficiently limited in duration and scope to allow enterprises to experiment without incurring major risk. These projects also provide a real-time test of the systems, structures, and values of the enterprise.

Many enterprises believe that the real source of competitive advantage is innovation. The reasoning is that when an enterprise is no longer on the cutting edge of technology, its gross margins shrink, putting pressure on the enterprise to cut costs and commit fewer resources to research and development, thus promoting a vicious cycle.

Whether or not this belief is universally accepted, it is a fact that product life cycles are continuing to shrink. Enterprises are constantly challenged to bring new products to the market faster and cheaper. In order to keep up with or get ahead of the competition, enterprises feel the necessity to develop, produce, and launch products in shorter and shorter periods of time. This is especially true in the computer industry, where Moore's Law is alive and well. Integrating the design function with marketing and operations to bring new products faster to market is vital for survival in such an environment.

One industry that has benefited significantly from DPI is the automobile industry. Product development times for automobiles have dropped significantly over the last two decades. For example, as noted earlier, in 1964 the Ford Mustang took three and a half years from the initial planning stage until it was available to customers. In the early 1980s, it took General Motors more than 60 months to bring a new car into the market—after everyone had signed off on the final design. As a result of DPI, the automakers have succeeded in reducing the time it takes to develop a new vehicle down to as little as 14 to 16 months for specialty vehicles such as the Ford GT. The new goal for automakers is to reduce product development times to 12 months from the time the design is "frozen" until production begins.

Leader Versus Follower Strategies

An issue to be resolved is whether the enterprise wishes to be a leader or a follower in bringing new products to the market. The leader follows a proactive approach that tries to be the first to market with a product that competitors would find difficult to imitate or improve on. The follower adopts a reactive approach that waits until the competition introduces a new product and imitates it if the product proves to be successful.

Each approach has its advantages and drawbacks. The advantage of the proactive approach is that the enterprise gains an edge over the competition both from a market perspective and from a technical perspective. From the market perspective, being first to market better positions the enterprise for establishing brand recognition. Since the enterprise is the first to market, it is aware of the potential flaws with the product design and is therefore in a better position to avoid these flaws in the future. On the other hand, enterprises that adopt the proactive approach must devote resources to research and development and also be prepared for the possibility of making costly mistakes.

The primary advantage of the reactive approach is that the risks and costs associated with development and test marketing of the product have already been shouldered by the competition. However, the reactive approach has the disadvantage that the enterprise is always a follower. Enterprises that adopt a reactive approach have to consider the possibility that they may always be one step behind their competitor, who is very likely following a proactive approach.

Regardless of whether the enterprise follows a proactive approach or a reactive approach, the fact is that in the face of shrinking product life cycles, almost every industry has been forced to rethink its product development and launch strategies. This new perspective on product launch is significantly different from the traditional over-the-wall approach. In particular, the traditional approach, with its functional orientation, results in significantly large product development times. In this regard, DPI assumes even greater importance because, for many enterprises, the design function is itself confounded by fragmented activities, overspecialization, and delays.

Demand Pull Versus Technology Push

As with any other activity, understanding customer expectations is a key initial step in DPI. To maintain a competitive edge by bringing new and innovative products faster to market, enterprises are constantly on the lookout for new processes and technologies. The key is to decide if and when the enterprise should adopt these new technologies and processes. It is important to differentiate between a demand pull and a technology push.

A *demand pull* occurs when an enterprise identifies a marketplace need and then creates a product to meet that need. Demand pull arises in a variety of ways—it can occur when enterprises seek better technologies to reduce their costs of production or to improve the quality of their existing products. Demand pull can also take place simply in response to the business ecosystem. In the latter case, the enterprises that respond to the demand pull often create their own new technologies or processes to address the demand.

Consider how demand pull influenced the automobile ecosystem. The oil embargo in 1973 caused fuel prices to rise, generating a need, partly mandated by governmental regulations, for more fuel-efficient vehicles. The big three automakers responded by investing in developmental efforts that eventually led to microcomputers being installed in automobiles. These microcomputers were intended initially for controlling fuel consumption and improving fuel efficiency, but eventually, the automakers found a variety of other uses for the microcomputers to improve the performance of automobiles.

A more recent example of demand pull is provided by Walmart's requirement that its top 100 suppliers have radio frequency identification (RFID) tags on all their pallets of products by January 25, 2005. The RFID tag is also an example of a product that is driving new technologies and processes to make sure that metal objects located near the RFID reader do not attenuate or distort RFID signals. RFID signals also tend to get absorbed by certain liquids, affecting performance as well. The suppliers of RFID tags are working to overcome these challenges.

Demand pull is more likely to occur in market-driven enterprises searching for products that meet the needs of that marketplace. Market-driven enterprises grow market share by using available technologies; they aggressively seek new technologies only when forced to do so, as in the example of the automobile industry pushed by high fuel prices. Even though many manufacturing enterprises concentrate on demand pull activities, they cannot afford to neglect new technologies. Otherwise, these enterprises run the risk of their competition pulling ahead with a new product line powered by a new technology.

Technology push occurs when enterprises identify an interesting technology, use that technology to create a product or a new application, and then try to find a market for the product or application. A technology push orientation allows enterprises to look beyond the limitations of current technologies. The driving assumption behind technology push is that today's technologies are inadequate for tomorrow's customer needs. The belief is that once the new technologies are developed, market opportunities will appear.

Technology push is more likely to occur in technology-driven enterprises. These enterprises tend to be innovative and entrepreneurial, which promises both risks and rewards. There are many instances where technology-driven enterprises developed products for which there were no known uses at the time. Yet these products became outstanding successes. One example is 3M's Scotchgard.

The discovery of Scotchgard in 1953 by a young chemical researcher, Patsy Sherman, was almost serendipitous.* In the 1950s, 3M had committed major laboratory resources to conduct research on fluorochemical compounds. While 3M had no particular application in mind, its researchers believed that this class of chemicals eventually would have commercial value.

One day a technician spilled a dilute solution of the chemical on Patsy Sherman's new tennis shoes. When she tried to rinse it off, she noticed that the color wasn't changed and that the water beaded up. Patsy Sherman also noticed that over time the shoe that had the chemical spilled on it remained clean, whereas the other shoe got dirty. This was hard evidence that 3M had the potential to make a commercially useful product from its research, a product many experts had written off as "thermodynamically impossible."

Scotchgard eventually proved to be a tremendous success. An unarticulated need of customers for a versatile fabric and material protector was aired—and satisfied.

Needless to say, for every such success story, there are a number of failure stories. Technology-driven enterprises risk not finding an application for a truly innovative product. These enterprises typically need large cash reserves and plenty of patience if they are to succeed with technology push.

The iPod introduction in 2001 presents an interesting combination of demand pull and technology push. The iPod was not the first MP3 player on the market. Apple simply made the MP3 player smaller, better, and cheaper in terms of cost per song. The iPod thus can be viewed as a demand pull

---

*See http://inventors.about.com/library/inventors/blscotchgard.htm.

innovation because it created a new market for existing customers who wanted a portable music player with much more capacity. The iPod's compact hard-drive-based technology represents a technology push innovation.

Coevolving Marketing and Operations Strategies

While there will be conflicting objectives between functional units, it has been claimed that there is more disagreement between marketing and operations than between any other pair of functions. This is not surprising given that the goals of these two functions are often in conflict. A major cause for conflict between these functions is that marketing is charged with generating demand, and operations is charged with satisfying demand.

Consider how these two functions react to a customer order. Marketing is more interested in the order value—how much revenue the order generates. Operations, on the other hand, is more interested in order makeup—how to produce the order.

Consider next the issue of product diversity. To satisfy a wide array of consumer preferences, marketing would like to offer customers a wide variety of choices. Furthermore, marketing's inherent desire to satisfy customers often leads it to promise product modifications for individual customers. Operations, on the other hand, would prefer to work with standard products because every unique product may involve some initial setup or changeover time.

Marketing would like to accept all customer orders that it deems profitable, and this may result in huge swings in the demand on resources under the control of operations. Operations, on the other hand, would prefer to accept orders that balance the load on these resources. With respect to quality control, the conflict is whether to produce a perfect product (arguably, the marketing perspective) or to compromise on what would be acceptable to the customer (arguably, the operations perspective).

The conflict between marketing and operations is especially severe in enterprises with a functional orientation, where such conflicts typically are handled by working *around* them rather than *through* them. That is, the existence of the conflict is assumed as given, and strategies are formulated to work around the causes of conflict.

In the worst cases, the existence of the conflict is ignored, and the marketing-operations conflict typically is "resolved" as follows: Corporate objectives typically are communicated in a hierarchical manner to marketing, which evolves strategies to meet those objectives. The strategies may take the form of increasing the variety of products offered to customers or offering volume discounts. When operations works on these strategies, it evolves its own operating strategies in such areas as inventory policies, make or buy decisions, and capacity allocation. The corporate goals thus result in functional strategies (a marketing strategy, an operations strategy, and a logistics strategy) that are not linked to one another.

In the absence of a proper dialog, marketing-led initiatives usually assume that operations has the capability to respond positively and flexibly to whatever demands are placed on it, and that should be the role of operations. This often has operations functioning in a classic firefighting, reactive role, forced to respond to orders as quickly as it can instead of functioning in a proactive role, determining what levels of demand it can execute satisfactorily.

This situation, of course, is counterproductive for the enterprise as a whole because it would be preferable to have operations functioning proactively and having a say in what levels of demand it can execute satisfactorily. The situation is especially severe because a major portion of an enterprise's cash is invested in resources that are directly under the control of the operations function. *How can an enterprise compete effectively if the functional unit that controls the major portion of the resources operates reactively?*

Any operations strategy should reflect the intended market position of the enterprise. Some enterprises may choose to compete primarily on cost, others on high levels of customer service, and so on. Operations must respond to these objectives by performing appropriately for the intended market position. It is not just a matter of selecting the current market position and then asking operations to adjust the various resources and processes to fall in line. Rather, it is necessary to recognize the competencies or capabilities that these resources and processes provide and exploit them accordingly.

So the question is: Should market position dictate how operations' resources are deployed, or should it be the other way around? One way to resolve this impasse is to provide a framework that will allow operations and marketing to evolve their strategies in consultation with each other. Figure 5.7, an adaptation of a framework set out in the book, *Manufacturing*

Corporate Objectives	Marketing Strategy	Order Qualifiers & Order Winners	Operations Strategy	
			Structural Elements	Infrastructure
Growth Profit ROA Survival	Advertising Branding and Positioning Single Account Penetration Direct Marketing Marketing Channels Leader vs. Follower	Price Quality Delivery Speed Delivery Reliability Product Range Design Brand Image Technical and after Sales Support	Process Choice Inventory vs. Capacity Make or Buy Facility Size and Location	Organizational Structure Workforce Skills Planning and Scheduling Quality Assurance

Figure 5.7   A framework for coevolving marketing and operations strategies.

Strategies,[8] presents an approach for integrating marketing strategies with operations strategies.

This framework essentially identifies corporate objectives, such as growth or return on investment, and translates them into marketing initiatives. Marketing initiatives may involve decisions such as whether to use direct marketing or conventional distribution channels, whether to be a leader or a follower, or whether to be an innovator.

Order qualifiers and order winners provide the opportunity for engaging marketing and operations in a dialog to jointly evolve their strategies. As discussed in Chapter 4, *order qualifiers* are the criteria that must be associated with the product for the customer to even consider purchasing it. The criteria referred to include cost, quality, availability, brand image, and delivery reliability. *Order winners* are criteria that will secure the customer's order.

Order qualifiers and order winners provide a key link between marketing and operations strategies because they articulate the goals for marketing and operations much more effectively. These criteria define, clearly and precisely, what customers expect from a product in a manner that is more easily understood by operations. While marketing will have an important perspective on what these criteria should be, an essential perspective must come from operations.

Order qualifiers and order winners therefore must be determined jointly, perhaps iteratively, by marketing and operations. Marketing now can evolve its strategies for increasing customer awareness on products with a better assurance that operations can deliver the products that satisfy these criteria. Order winners and order qualifiers must be determined for each market segment, and the enterprise may choose to evolve different marketing and operations strategies for fulfilling demand within each segment.

The fast-moving consumer goods organization Hindustan Unilever (HUL), discussed in Chapter 4, provides a good example of how organizations can coevolve marketing and operations strategies and deliver the order winners successfully. HUL markets and sells its products using rural women and local citizens who travel from door to door on bicycle. The marketing strategy is to penetrate rural markets and "create consumers out of nonusers." The order winner is the ease of access to HUL's products, and the operations strategy for delivering this order winner is achieved by enlisting the assistance of women and local citizens.

The delivery structure evolved by HUL to penetrate rural markets supports the TOC philosophy of inherent simplicity because it is a simple and elegant solution to what might have been viewed as a complex problem. The solution also represents a win-win situation. The women get an additional source of revenue, and HUL is able to reach villages where it had no presence earlier.

In general, after the order winners and qualifiers are determined for each market segment, the next step is to translate these order qualifiers and winners into specific product requirements—that is, into equivalent tasks for operations. At issue here is the question of how the enterprise should *respond* to customer orders along these different market segments. This is a critical step in operations strategy development because the decisions involved are structural in nature and require investment in the appropriate processes and possibly infrastructure.

To get organizational buy-in for implementing the operations strategies, it is important to communicate the results expected from these strategies to top management. In turn, it is the responsibility of top management to ensure that such decisions are not approved or rejected using pure economic hurdles.

Communicating Financial Benefits to Management

While it is important to clearly communicate the results expected from operations strategies to top management, it is equally important to communicate the expected results to the chief financial officer (CFO). In particular, when communicating the potential to the CFO, it is important to speak the CFO's language—essentially let her know how these strategies translate into performance that can be measured with standard financial metrics. The *Strategic Profit Model* (also known as the *DuPont Model*) provides a very useful framework for making such a translation.

The DuPont Model

The DuPont model was developed by F. Donaldson Brown, an electrical engineer who joined DuPont Company in 1909 and went on to become financial executive and corporate director for both DuPont Company and General Motors Corporation (GM). When DuPont Company bought 23 percent of the stock of GM in 1918, Brown was charged with the task of cleaning up the automobile maker's tangled finances. The DuPont model that Brown developed allowed GM to manage its decentralized empire very effectively. Alfred Sloan, the chairman of GM from 1937 to 1956, credits a large part of GM's success to Brown's financial model.

The DuPont model uses the enterprise's income statement and balance sheet to determine two key measures of profitability: Return on assets (ROA) and return on equity (ROE). ROA was discussed briefly in Chapter 3; it is the ratio of the net income to the total assets owned by the enterprise. The net income is obtained from the income statement as the sales revenue minus expenses (in the form of the cost of goods sold and other expenses). The total assets is obtained from the balance sheet, and it is the sum of current assets (raw materials, work-in-progress, finished goods, and cash) and fixed assets (buildings, plant, and machinery).

The ROE is the product of the ROA and the financial leverage, where *financial leverage* is defined as the ratio of the total assets to the stockholder equity. The stockholder equity is available from the enterprise's balance sheet.

Any financial performance analysis method has its strengths and weaknesses, but the DuPont model is intuitive, and the underlying formulas for ROA and ROE can be reproduced using a common sense approach. Even managers with a limited math background can quickly determine what metrics need to be emphasized to improve financial performance. The model starts by calculating the ROA:

$$ROA = \frac{net\ income}{total\ assets} = profit\ margin \times asset\ turnover$$

where

$$Profit\ margin = \frac{net\ income}{sales}\ and\ asset\ turnover = \frac{sales}{total\ assets}$$

Once the ROA is determined, the ROE is calculated simply as the product of the ROA and the financial leverage. That is:

$$ROE = \frac{net\ income}{total\ assets} \times \frac{total\ assets}{shareholder\ equity} = \frac{net\ income}{shareholder\ equity}$$

Figure 5.8 depicts the DuPont model in its basic form.

The DuPont Model provides a ready way to link operational performance to financial performance because it captures the essence of operations effectiveness in terms that most laypeople can understand. How efficiently are the assets being used? This information is provided by the asset turnover

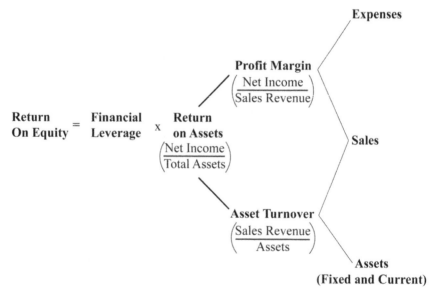

Figure 5.8   The DuPont Model for financial performance.

(the ratio of sales to assets). How effectively is the organization leveraging profits from its income? This information is provided by the profit margin (the ratio of net income to sales).

The DuPont Model can be adapted to present the value of effective supply chain and operations strategies by showing how these strategies translate to a competitive advantage, thus leading to an improved ROA. Figure 5.9 shows how the basic DuPont Model can be adapted to link ROA with supply chain and operations strategies, strategies supported by superior process execution.

In this figure, all the elements presented in the right-most column can be addressed by effective supply chain and operations strategies. These strategies will translate into:

▲ Reduced expenses from improved procurement practices, better use of labor, and improved yields
▲ Increased sales resulting from improvement in quality, delivery, and so on
▲ Improved asset utilization resulting from reduced inventory, a smaller operator footprint, and less equipment used

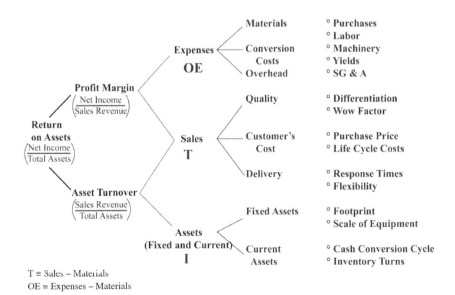

Figure 5.9 Translating process execution to financial performance.

A Ritzy Experience

For an example of how superior process execution translates into improved quality and increased sales revenue, I will relate a personal experience during my first stay at the Ritz-Carlton Hotel in Singapore in 2007. I arrived at the Ritz-Carlton at the end of a 20-hour journey from the United States, and while I was paying the taxi driver who drove me to the hotel from Changi Airport, a bellhop was placing my bags on a trolley. When I got out of the taxi, the bellhop greeted me by my name. Noting my surprise, he explained that he had read my baggage tag to find out my name.

As I walked over to the reception desk, the two women at the counter simultaneously greeted me by my name as well. I was surprised once again by this greeting, but it did not take me long to deduce that the bellhop had radioed the ladies my name and its correct pronunciation.

I found out, subsequently, that the practice of having the bellhop read the baggage tags of hotel guests and having that information relayed to the reception desk is a standard operating procedure* at the Ritz-Carlton. This procedure was instituted by Horst Schulze, a former president and chief operating officer of Ritz-Carlton, who left Ritz-Carlton to launch the West Paces Hotel Group in 2005. In my mind, this is a wonderful example of a Lean tool applied in the service industry.

This produced a true "wow" experience, and it has made the Ritz-Carlton the hotel of my choice for my next visit to Singapore. The *wow factor* identified in Figure 5.9 is an order winner for Ritz-Carlton. It is no surprise to me that the Ritz-Carlton has received the Malcolm Baldridge National Quality Award. Incidentally, Ritz-Carlton is the only service enterprise in America that has won the Malcolm Baldridge Award twice. *Training Magazine* has called Ritz-Carlton the best organization in the United States for employee training.[9]

Linking the DuPont Model to TOC Performance Measures

Figure 5.9 also provides a link between the DuPont Model and TOC performance measures Throughput (T), Investment (I), and Operating Expense (OE). To understand this linkage, consider the items categorized

---

*Standard operating procedure, or standard work, as it is otherwise called, is a Lean tool discussed in Chapter 7.

under expenses in Figure 5.9—materials, conversion costs, and overhead. Of these, materials is a variable expense, whereas conversion costs and overhead typically are fixed expenses.* Thus the metrics T, I, and OE can be used to determine ROA as follows:

T = sales – materials

Net profit = sales – materials – fixed costs = $T - OE$

$$\text{ROA} = \frac{\text{net profits}}{\text{total assets}} = \frac{T - OE}{I}$$

After obtaining support from top management and the CFO, the next task is to plan the execution of the operations strategy. To enable execution of the operations strategy, the enterprise must mobilize the resources and the workforce so that they are aligned with the strategy. The following section discusses the steps the enterprise should undertake to put in place the structural elements and the infrastructure that will enable the operations strategy.

Enabling the Operations Strategy

Enabling the operations strategy involves a series of decisions on structural elements and infrastructure. As indicated in Figure 5.7, decisions on structural elements relate to choice of process, the inventory strategies to cope with variation in demand, make or buy decisions, and facility size and location. Decisions on infrastructure involve the organizational structure, workforce skills, planning and scheduling systems, and quality assurance.

The structural elements discussed in this section relate to decisions on process choices and inventory strategies. Make or buy decisions were discussed in Chapter 2 in the context of systems thinking and the Total Cost of Ownership. From among the infrastructure decisions, this section discusses organizational structure and workforce skills. Planning and scheduling systems are covered in Chapter 8.

---

*Conversion costs include electricity, direct labor, depreciation, and other manufacturing expenses. These are generally fixed costs that do not vary with the output of the enterprise.

Structural Elements: Process Choice

The choice of process is influenced by expected product volumes and the order winners and order qualifiers for the product. If product variety is an order winner, it might suggest the need for a flexible, less capital-intensive process, especially if production volumes are not as high as would be expected for a standard product.

The choice of process dictates and is dictated by other considerations such as scale of operations and cost. The *product-process matrix* presented in Figure 5.10 is a simple tool used to determine whether or not proposed strategic choices lie within the enterprise's area of experience. This matrix also can point out what the enterprise needs to change if it decides proactively to pursue a strategy that is not within its current area of operations expertise.

The lower right-hand corner of the matrix represents an enterprise operating under the classic of *economy of scale* setting, with a high-volume, low-variety mode of operation. This mode encourages large production batches, often using a continuous-flow type of operation. An enterprise that decides to compete in such a market typically will choose to work with a

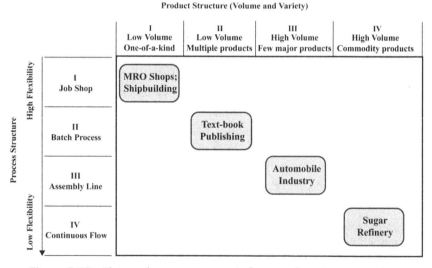

Figure 5.10   The product-process matrix for manufacturing enterprises. *(From R. H. Hayes and S. C. Wheelwright,* Restoring Our Competitive Edge: Competing Through Manufacturing. *New York: Wiley, 1984.)*

highly automated system, sacrificing flexibility for output. On the other hand, an enterprise that works with *economies of scope* would favor a more flexible, perhaps more labor-intensive process (see the upper left-hand corner of the matrix). Thus enterprises typically position themselves along the diagonal of the matrix.

An enterprise may deliberately position itself away from the diagonal to differentiate itself. For instance, a high degree of flexibility is characterized by a position anywhere above the diagonal in the matrix, as shown in the figure. Such a positioning might result in relatively higher costs because the enterprise is using flexible process capabilities to compete with enterprises using automated, dedicated facilities to make similar products.

Similarly, moving to a position below the diagonal typically would imply lower flexibility. Moving to a position below the diagonal also suggests that higher costs may be involved because the enterprise is using capital-intensive assets, typically used in flow-shop operations, to produce at low volumes. Marketing pressures tend to move enterprises toward the lower left-hand corner of the product-process matrix. In other words, there is a pressure on operations to provide increased product variety but at the same time to provide the efficiencies of scale economies afforded by a continuous-flow mode of production.

A similar kind of tradeoff exists in the case of service industries. With service industries, the tradeoff typically is the degree of customization (variety) against the amount of flexibility provided by the service. Figure 5.11 presents a product-process matrix for service enterprises.

The choice of process also should reconcile possibly conflicting objectives on product variety and cost. Once these conflicting objectives are reconciled, the emphasis shifts to determining how the enterprise should *respond* to customer orders. More specifically, the enterprise should evolve plans for delivering products to customers based on their lead-time expectations using the customer-time-based demand profile discussed in Chapter 4.

Aside from the customer-time-based demand profile, Chapter 4 also presented a number of approaches for mitigating customer demand variation. Suppose that demand variation is still present after implementing one or a combination of these approaches. What can the enterprise do to cope with this variation?

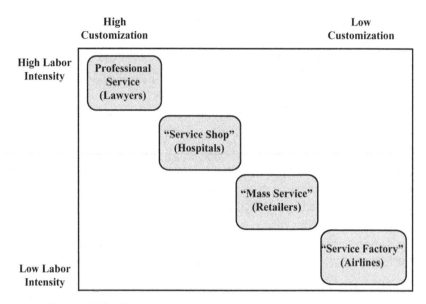

Figure 5.11 The product-process matrix for service enterprises.

Structural Elements: Inventory Versus Capacity

The classic (and traditional) approach to managing demand variation is to resort to finished goods inventory to buffer this variation, but this approach has its own drawbacks. No doubt having the right amount of finished goods inventory in the right place at the right time will significantly improve an enterprise's response to demands made by the enterprise's immediate downstream customer, but this is easier said than done. With uncertain demand, it is very difficult to determine exactly what products to store.

If the enterprise stores finished goods inventory for its customer, this inventory is analogous to WIP inventory from a supply chain perspective. Little's Law, presented in Chapter 1, shows that WIP inventory results in slower responsiveness and longer lead times for the supply chain. Lead times and inventory go hand in hand, creating a problematic and cyclic relationship. In addition, the beer game showed the effect of lead times on supply chain performance. Finally, as noted earlier, if enterprises are forced to commit resources to produce finished goods inventory, they often end up misallocating the resources to produce the wrong kinds of products.

Clearly, there are powerful incentives to reduce inventories in the supply chain. So the question is: how can enterprises cope with demand variation without storing inventory?

Instead of using inventory to buffer variation, a better approach is to buffer demand variation with a small amount of reserve capacity. This approach is likely to be met with some resistance from managers, who do not view the supply chain from a systems perspective but are driven by cost world metrics. The cost world metrics would penalize managers if they do not use up their flex capacity even though the situation may not warrant it. However, a lean supply chain must, by definition, maintain flexibility at every stage in the supply chain. Flexibility is best achieved with capacity, not inventory, and this leads to the eighth Lean Supply Chain Principle.

Lean Supply Chain Principle 8

Buffer the variation in demand with capacity, not inventory.

The Theory of Constraints recommends operating all the nonbottleneck resources at less than 90 percent capacity. This recommendation is not simply a TOC recommendation. Queuing Theory shows that operating a resource at high utilization will result in queues and delays that increase at an exponential rate as the utilization approaches 100 percent.

Infrastructure: Organizational Structure

After the structure is erected, the next step is to fill in the "furniture" within the structure—that is, to build the infrastructure. Most elements of infrastructure do not, individually, require the same level of investment as process choice does, but taken collectively, they can exceed the level of investment in processes and technologies.

Organizational structure was discussed earlier in this chapter within the context of functional silos. It was observed that the functional orientation typically resulted in increased lead time to deliver products within the enterprise, underscoring the need for enterprises to adopt a process orientation. An additional problem that exists with many enterprises is the presence of multiple layers of bureaucracy. Typically, the larger the number of layers in the organizational structure, the longer it takes for decisions to be made. A typical enterprise in the 1900s had 3 levels of management. In the 1960s, this number had expanded to 12 levels. The trend since then has been to reduce the number of levels of management, and hopefully, this trend will continue.

When enterprises continue to flatten their organizational structure, they increasingly empower the workforce. The workforce presents one of the most important elements of infrastructure. Many of the world's most profitable enterprises have employees who are enthusiastic entrepreneurs constantly involved in improving productivity. The success of the workforce in improving productivity is not an accident. Productivity is determined by the social structures of the organization. These social structures include measurement systems, incentive systems, job security, freedom to experiment, and advancement opportunities and everything that affects the work environment.

Infrastructure: Workforce Skills

Whereas operations strategies for process choice and product delivery strategies can provide enterprises with the competitive edge, ultimately it is the energy and creativity of the workforce that result in improved productivity. A motivated workforce significantly assists the enterprise in its efforts to build skill sets and capabilities that provide the ultimate competitive edge.

A combination of organizational resources and processes can bring about a sustainable competitive advantage. Whereas a rival can purchase the same technologies and emulate the processes used by the best-in-class enterprises, it is harder to emulate a combination of activities and processes. Similarly, it is harder to copy expertise that is developed organically—in-house—based on the experience of the employees or expertise that is interconnected with other capabilities developed within the enterprise. As a result, the competitive advantages such organically created skills produce are more likely to be retained over time.

The key is to develop generic skill sets that enable the enterprise to develop flexible responses to changing customer demands. These skill sets can give the enterprise a set of core capabilities and competencies that it can use to establish, excel, and protect itself in the marketplace. Maintaining and improving these core capabilities is one of the key tasks of operations. The two philosophies, the Theory of Constraints and Lean, present significant opportunities for enterprises to help build these generic skill sets.

Conclusions

Then said they unto him, Say now Shibboleth: and he said Shibboleth: for he could not frame to pronounce it right. Then they took him, and slew him at the passages of Jordan: and there fell at that time of the Ephraimites forty and two thousand.[10]

Failure to distinguish between operational effectiveness and operations strategy is unlikely to have as serious a consequence as befell the Ephraimites at the hands of the men of Gilead. Yet the consequences can be quite severe. The difference between operational effectiveness and operations strategy is as follows:

▲ Operational effectiveness seeks to continually improve every situation where there are no tradeoffs, trying to shift the productivity frontier outward in a relentless effort to achieve best practice. While this may produce absolute improvement by raising the bar, it may not lead to relative improvement for the enterprise because rivals can mimic best-in-class practices. Thus operational effectiveness is a necessary but not sufficient condition for competitiveness.

▲ In contrast, operations strategy is all about building *strategic flexibility* and maintaining a competitive advantage by integrating functions and processes effectively. Enterprises therefore must be engaged in an ongoing effort to extend their unique position in the marketplace. Operations strategy should aim at building the competitive edge by developing products and processes that respond flexibly to changing customer preferences.

Building strategic flexibility requires:

▲ A move from a functional orientation to a process orientation. There also must be a concerted effort by enterprises to maintain a process orientation, especially during periods of growth.

▲ A close dialog among design, marketing, and operations to resolve internal inconsistencies and to coevolve strategies. Inconsistencies can arise if, for instance, the enterprise lacks a focus and attempts to market too many products, or if operations performs new tasks but continues with outdated policies and structure, or if the process technology is not suited to the product that is produced.

▲ Order qualifiers and order winners provide a common ground for engaging marketing and operations in an ongoing dialog. Used in conjunction with the customer-time-based demand profile, they can greatly help match customer expectations with operations' capabilities.

▲ Many of the decisions that emanate from an operations strategy are structural in nature and may involve high levels of resource commitments. An enterprise does not have a second chance to correct investment decisions. So care must be exercised to ensure that such decisions are not approved or rejected using pure economic hurdles. Decisions instead should consider how they will help operations to become a competitive weapon.

▲ The DuPont Model allows operations managers to convey the financial impact of their efforts to the CFO and the analysts in a clear and concise manner.

▲ As Lean Supply Chain Principle 8 states, it is better to buffer the variation in demand with capacity, not inventory. As far as possible, the demand variation should be met with additional capacity. While finished goods may allow the enterprise to service customers faster, very often the enterprise ends up carrying the wrong kinds of products.

▲ It is critical to provide the right infrastructure, develop workforce skills, and build generic skill sets so that the enterprise can develop a flexible response capability to changing customer demands. Maintaining and improving these core capabilities is one of the key goals of an operations strategy.

References

1. Andersen Consulting (1994), "Worldwide Manufacturing Competitiveness Study: The Second Lean Enterprise Benchmarking Project Report," Arthur Andersen & Co, SC, London.
2. W. Skinner (1969), "Manufacturing—Missing Link in Corporate Strategy," *Harvard Business Review*, May–June 1969.
3. M. E. Porter (1996), "What Is Strategy?" *Harvard Business Review*, November–December 1996, pp. 61–78.
4. H. L. Lee (2001), "Ultimate Enterprise Value Creation Using Demand-Based Management," Stanford Global Supply Chain Management Forum.
5. J. K. Galbraith (1971), *The New Industrial State*, Houghton Mifflin, Boston.
6. J. Welch (1999), "Letter to Shareholders," in GE Annual Report 1999.

7. M. Dell (1999), *Direct from Dell: Strategies that Revolutionized the Industry*, HarperCollins, New York.
8. T. Hill (2000), *Manufacturing Strategy: Text and Cases*, 3rd ed., Irwin McGraw-Hill, Boston.
9. R. Reiss (2009), "How Ritz-Carlton Stays at the Top: An interview with Simon F. Cooper, president of the Ritz-Carlton Hotel Company"; available at www .forbes.com/2009/10/30/simon-cooper-ritz-leadership-ceonetwork-hotels .html.
10. The Book of Judges 12:5–6.

CHAPTER 6

Partnering in the Lean Supply Chain

"A great marriage is not when the 'perfect couple' comes together. It is when an imperfect couple learns to enjoy their differences." This statement by Dave Meurer, author of the book, *Daze of our Wives*,[1] succinctly presents a pragmatic approach to partnering in the supply chain.

Enterprises seldom work alone when they create and deliver value to the customer; they must also be able to build effective alliances with their supply chain partners. More often than not, such partnerships may involve enterprises that have differing perspectives on how products and services are delivered to the customer. These enterprises must understand and appreciate their differing perspectives and work toward a common goal. The terminology used to describe such partnerships varies, but the phrases *strategic alliances* and *strategic partnerships* are often used.

Developing strategic partnerships can be a complex endeavor. Many enterprises claim that they have formed strategic partnerships, but these relationships often end up as a one-sided "we win, you figure out how you can win" business model. A one-sided business model clearly will not lead to a stable, sustained partnership. Even if the business model subsequently evolves into a compromise solution, some enterprises will be striving constantly to alter the business model to achieve a more favorable outcome if they believe that their position has been compromised.

One-sided business models typically emanate from the notion that an enterprise in the supply chain can improve its profits only at the expense of one or more of its supply chain partners. This notion has some basis, especially in manufacturing enterprises, where direct material costs account for anywhere between 35 and 70 percent of revenue. For a manufacturing enterprise with a fixed cost of 20 percent and a direct material cost equal to

70 percent of revenue, a reduction of 5 percent in direct material costs can increase its bottom-line profitability by 35 percent.

Enterprises have recognized the huge potential savings that can result from reducing direct material costs, but they have been slow to develop effective strategic partnerships with suppliers and logistics providers in their efforts to reduce cost across the supply chain. Instead, their purchasing departments typically adopt an adversarial relationship with suppliers and logistics providers.

Determined to pay as low a price as possible for materials, the purchase departments in some of these enterprises either attempt to engage suppliers in a bidding war or keep the pressure on suppliers to cut costs. Some enterprises in the automobile industry still expect a 5 percent price reduction from their suppliers year after year.

The practice of imposing unconditional price reductions on a supplier may force the supplier to cut corners to stay in business, make the supplier continue to lose money and eventually go out of business, or cause the supplier to exit from the relationship altogether. None of these outcomes benefits the enterprise.

Building supply chain partnerships and alliances requires a more progressive approach, one based on systems thinking. Enterprises should realize that their suppliers' costs are, in effect, their costs. The enterprise is justified in expecting stellar performance from its suppliers at a reasonable cost, but it also should realize that all parties involved should share the goal of reducing costs across the supply chain. The underlying philosophy that should drive partnerships and alliances in the supply chain is summarized by the ninth Lean Supply Chain Principle:

Lean Supply Chain Principle 9

Develop partnerships and alliances with members of the supply chain strategically, with the goal of delivering goods and services as quickly and efficiently as possible.

This Lean Supply Chain Principle facilitates the enterprise's growth strategy. Even while the enterprise strives to build strategic partnerships with the goal of reducing the total cost of providing goods and services, the enterprise also should be seeking collaborative strategies for growing the business with a systems perspective. A prevailing notion surrounding most supply chain relationships is that the pie is fixed, and if one supply chain member takes a larger slice of the pie, the other members will receive a smaller share. In many practical situations, the pie is *not* fixed; rather, there are a number of opportunities for growing the pie so that more than one member in the supply chain will benefit.

This chapter presents guiding principles for establishing partnerships and alliances to build and manage the lean supply chain. For clarity, supply chain partners are separated into suppliers and logistics providers, and the tools and technologies for coordinating suppliers and logistics providers are discussed in the next two sections. A subsequent section discusses a Thinking Process tool, called the evaporating cloud, which creates win-win partnerships. The concluding section presents a case study that demonstrates how the evaporating cloud can be used to develop a collaborative strategy leading to a win-win situation for multiple members in a supply chain.

Partnering with Suppliers

The success of an enterprise's supply chain depends heavily on the capabilities of the suppliers that choose to collaborate with the enterprise in anticipation of higher profits. In general, enterprises collaborate with their suppliers in one of two ways:

▲ *Arm's-length relationships.* The enterprise procures parts or raw materials using a number of suppliers and shops for the best prices each time it requires an input.
▲ *Strategic partnerships or virtual integration.* The members in the supply chain work together to leverage a competitive advantage.

Arm's-Length Relationships

Arm's-length relationships typically are formed when the enterprise outsources its noncore activities to specialist suppliers. In principle, outsourcing noncore activities lowers costs and makes better use of an enterprise's scarce resources, allowing the enterprise to concentrate those resources on its core activities. The enterprise is more flexible and can respond more rapidly to changing market conditions because it does not own the specialized assets needed for the noncore activities. However, arm's-length relationships usually do not lead to long-term partnerships or alliances. Instead, the buyer typically shops for the best prices each time he needs to procure items, awarding contracts to the supplier with the lowest bid, with relatively less attention paid to quality, logistics, or life-cycle costs.

A real challenge with arm's-length relationships is that an enterprise's desire to maximize its own profits often goes counter to the profit objectives of the enterprise adjacent to it in the supply chain, at least for the short term. Thus enterprises are reluctant to trust each other completely or to share information or to engage in any other activities that would result in productivity improvements for the entire supply chain. Since low trust and an absence of good information characterize arm's length relationships, these relationships are often held together by contractual agreements, often specified on paper but seldom followed.

Arm's-length relationships were prevalent during the heyday of mass production, when suppliers typically were treated as adversaries rather than partners. It was not uncommon for the purchasing departments to pit one potential supplier against another and award supply contracts to the lowest bidder without fully understanding the process capabilities of that supplier. Needless to say, such relationships do not instill confidence among suppliers or motivate them to invest in resources for building and delivering a better-quality product.

The parties involved in an adversarial relationship implicitly recognize the negative dynamics that can accompany such an arrangement and will react accordingly. For instance, the suppliers will be tempted to bid low to acquire the contract and to subsequently negotiate prices upward based on contingencies. Such actions will, of course, result in a continual cycle of bidding and contract awards.

There is another pitfall to be avoided. More than a few enterprises resort to outsourcing to rid themselves of problems that they could not solve on their own. The real reason for outsourcing should be to better leverage core competencies by outsourcing noncore activities to suppliers that provide the same product to a number of other customers and therefore are in a better position to exploit economies of scale.

Strategic Partnerships

The JIT movement that gained popularity in the 1980s was based on the Japanese philosophy that cooperation rather than confrontation maximizes the benefits for both parties. As a result, instead of working with arm's-length relationships, enterprises began to form strategic, collaborative partnerships.

In addition to promoting stable and cooperative relationships, strategic partnerships have numerous other benefits, a significant one being that the boundaries between the buyer and the supplier begin to fade, leading to increased *virtual integration*. It is not unusual to find Lean enterprises such as Toyota or Honda temporarily assigning employees to work with their suppliers as resident engineers. These employees are better positioned to help the suppliers with quality problems because they can better communicate the problems back to their own design and manufacturing departments. It is also not unusual to find Lean suppliers sending their design or manufacturing engineers to a buyer's facility to rectify problems at the source and/or to develop solutions that will prevent further problems at the buyer's facility.

As Figure 6.1 suggests, strategic partnerships involve more relational arrangements than arm's-length relationships, where transactional arrange-

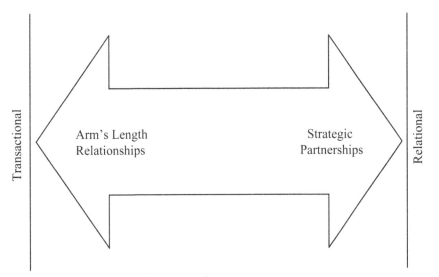

Figure 6.1 Types of partnering arrangements.

ments are commonplace. The nature of these strategic partnerships will differ depending on whether the enterprise is dealing with a supplier or a logistics provider.

Consider the relationship between a buyer and a supplier. By entering into strategic alliances, the buyer and supplier gain significant benefits that are both strategic and operational. The strategic benefits include easy entrance into new markets and the potential to attract new customers. Operational benefits emerge as a result of information transparency, which leads to lower costs, higher reliability, and better quality. The characteristics of effective partnerships between suppliers and buyers are as follows:

▲ Virtual integration is possible with suppliers.
▲ The buyer's production schedules are more visible to the supplier.
▲ The buyer uses blanket purchase orders* and has single-source suppliers.
▲ The supplier and the buyer jointly decide where to hold strategic inventory.

Virtual Integration

Virtual integration, a characteristic of strategic partnerships, offers the advantage of the tight coordination expected from vertically integrated enterprises. At the same time, virtual integration facilitates the focus and customization that are derived from outsourcing to a specialist. Whereas an arm's-length relationship works well if the supplier is providing a commodity, virtual integration works well with suppliers that provide products of high value or products that require a high degree of interdependence between supplier and buyer.

One organization that exploited virtual integration very successfully is Dell. When it started operations, Dell could not afford to create every piece of the supply chain. It decided to buck the industry trend favored by Compaq, IBM, and Hewlett-Packard, organizations that designed and manufactured most of their products. Instead, Dell dedicated itself to the task of assembling and delivering computer systems to its customers. Such a focus led Dell to outsource a number of its activities, which gave Dell a number of advantages. Unlike the other major PC makers, Dell did not

---

*A blanket purchase order represents an agreement between the enterprise and a supplier to transact multiple purchases under a single purchase order number.

require a lot of fixed assets to assemble its products. Therefore, Dell did not have to worry about recovering sunk costs in fixed assets.

Dell soon found that building strategic partnerships with key suppliers such as Sony allowed it to react to customer demands much more quickly than vertically integrated enterprises could. If there was a problem with a new product launch, for instance, engineers from Sony would immediately arrive at Dell's assembly plants.

As Dell began to forge strategic partnerships with its suppliers, it was able to adapt much more rapidly to technological advances. For instance, when Intel introduced a new chip, Dell could rely on its strategic partners to redesign their products to match the new chip design. Since Dell did not have many fixed assets, it could move much faster than its competitors could. Enterprises adopting Dell's successful business model have moved further away from arm's-length relationships.

Increased Visibility to Suppliers

How did Japanese automakers leverage JIT across the supply chain so much more effectively than their American counterparts in the twentieth century? Not only did they believe in long-term partnerships and alliances with their suppliers, but they also were willing to grow that joint effort by sharing their production plans with suppliers. For example, Toyota gives its supplier, JTEKT Automotive Tennessee-Vonore, Inc., its production schedule for the coming two weeks. JTEKT Automotive thus can see two weeks into the future what it has to supply Toyota, which, in turn, allows JTEKT Automotive to communicate its own production plans to its raw materials suppliers. Because of this visibility of production schedules throughout the supply chain, JTEKT Automotive is able to operate with less than two days of raw materials inventory for meeting Toyota's demand while supporting a strong relationship with its own raw materials suppliers.

Greater visibility and information sharing thus facilitate an integrated supply chain. The increased visibility on end-user demand also allows the managers of supply chains to better understand the customers' expectations.

Single Sourcing and Blanket Purchase Orders

Single sourcing implicitly can enhance long-term partnerships and collaboration. In addition to the motivation and commitment to mutual success it generates, single sourcing has other benefits, among them improved quality, innovation sharing, reduced costs, and better coordination of production and delivery schedules.

Establishing single-source suppliers implies that these suppliers are certified as quality suppliers. The trust placed on the supplier's ability to provide high-quality materials relieves the customer of having to inspect each incoming shipment for quality. It also implies that the suppliers are reliable and will deliver the right quantity at the right time. Unfortunately, many suppliers have hurt their cause through the "overpromise, underdeliver syndrome," or they bid low to secure contracts and then resort to creeping price escalation. Therefore, a large number of enterprises that do believe in the benefits of single sourcing maintain an alternate source of supply in case the primary supplier cannot deliver at the rate and quality levels specified. Having an alternate supplier also discourages the primary supplier from seeking unsubstantiated price increases.

Another approach to engaging suppliers in long-term contracts is to use blanket purchase orders. A *blanket purchase order* is a contract to buy a certain number of items over a specified time interval. Once the initial contract is executed by the purchase department, requests for deliveries typically are generated directly by the production department.

The use of blanket purchase orders is not new. In fact, it has been in existence in many countries at least since the early 1960s. However, in the past, when relationships between suppliers and customers were traditionally adversarial, the motivation for using blanket purchase orders often was either to eliminate paperwork or to ensure commitments from the suppliers that they would deliver. These days, there is a subtle but perceptible shift in the way blanket purchase orders are viewed. The intent now is to stress long-term relationships with key suppliers.

For a while it appeared that many manufacturers were moving toward single-sourcing. However, that trend seems to be reversing. In particular, as supply chains have become increasingly vulnerable to global events, from natural disasters to the global credit freeze in 2008, manufacturers are revisiting alternate sourcing strategies. Cisco, for example, now strives to have two sources qualified for each component as far as possible.[2] While the trend reversal is disturbing, some comfort can be drawn from the fact that the reversal stems from a desire to manage risk rather than to pit one supplier against another.

Inventory Ownership and Consignment Inventories

Many enterprises have consignment inventory arrangements with their suppliers. Under this arrangement, the suppliers place inventory on consignment at the customer's site, either directly at the point of use or at a warehouse, but the goods are not deemed delivered to the customer until they are actually consumed. This arrangement effectively benefits the customer, who does not have to worry about payment until the product is actually used in production.

At first glance, such an arrangement may suggest that the customer is taking unfair advantage of the supplier. This may be true to some extent, but the supplier benefits as well. When the customer picks up a consignment for production, it is a pull signal to the supplier that provides better visibility on demand to the supplier, who now can better plan production. When the partnership operates in this mode, it is more of a win-win situation. In fact, it is the basis for *vendor-managed inventory* (VMI).

Vendor-Managed Inventory

VMI is not a new concept, but there has been renewed interest in it as enterprises analyze their core competencies and work on outsourcing noncore activities. With VMI, the supplier is responsible for stocking the customer's shelves. The quantity replenished typically is based on data obtained through EDI, although the supplier makes regular visits to the customer sites to determine replenishment quantities.

VMI is referred to by different names depending on the industry. The apparel industry calls it *efficient consumer response*, the grocery industry uses *efficient consumer response* and *JIT distribution*, and the automobile industry uses *VMI* and *JIT distribution*.

VMI reduces the number of transactions for the purchasing, inspection, and storage functions. It also gives the supplier clear visibility on the rate at which its products are being consumed. With VMI, suppliers do not have to rely on a customer's purchasing department to give them delivery schedules. Instead, suppliers now control how they replenish their stock at a customer's facility based on shared demand information.

VMI lets suppliers prioritize their delivery schedules based on which customer is expected to stock out. With VMI, there is no temptation for the supplier to induce bulk buying by the customer to take advantage of quantity discounts. As observed from the beer game, discounts produce unpredictable demand surges in the supply chain.

Another compelling reason for enterprises to consider VMI is that it enhances collaboration in the supply chain. Figure 6.2 indicates how implementing VMI has an immediate impact on a customer's production. Absent a VMI program, the production department typically transmits a request to the purchase department. The purchase department, in turn, generates either a purchase order or a delivery request for the supplier (sometimes inflated by the purchasing department depending on how it perceives the supplier's ability to deliver the requested material). This sequence of hand-offs, each with potential for error, is short-circuited by a VMI program.

In summary, the advantages of VMI include:

▲ *A virtual shortening of the supply chain.* The production function in the downstream enterprise now has direct contact with the supplier.
▲ *Frequent communication of inventory levels, stock-outs, and planned promotions.* The supplier now has better visibility. EDI linkages facilitate this communication.
▲ *Reductions in inventories and stock-outs.*

Despite the numerous benefits it has to offer, implementing VMI can pose challenges. The problem is not merely one of logistics. When a supplier

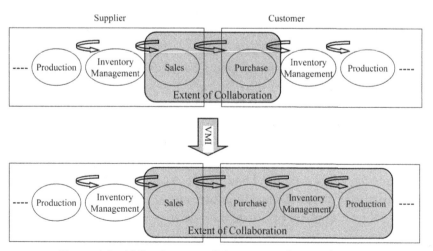

Figure 6.2   VMI enhances collaboration in the supply chain.

tries to implement VMI, it can encounter resistance from its sales force. At issue are the roles played by each participant, the skills required, the degree of trust, and the acceptance of power shifts. Sales may view VMI as a threat to incentive bonuses, especially if the bonus depends on how much salespeople are able to sell to their customers. There may be skepticism about whether the process will function smoothly. There also may be a concern that the reduced inventory that usually follows from a VMI program will result in less shelf space, generating a perception of a loss in market share.

If there is an intermediate distribution channel, distributors may have concerns about VMI, especially if they lose control over what they receive. The distributors may perceive the VMI program as trying to push inventory onto them. Since they do not have any control over what they stock, they also may worry that the supplier eventually could take over the distributor's function, supplying products directly to the customer. When Barilla SpA[3] introduced VMI in the pasta manufacturing industry, the biggest challenges came from distributors who feared that their right to order what they wanted was being denied.

Partnering with Logistics Providers

Logistics is a system of related activities to manage an orderly flow of material within and between firms. The term, as understood here, covers inventory management, materials handling, warehousing and storage, and transportation from one enterprise to another. Services provided by the logistics function range from activities undertaken in-house by the users of the services, such as storage or inventory control at a manufacturing plant, to the operations of external service providers. Logistics services comprise physical activities such as transportation and storage as well as nonphysical activities such as choosing contractors and negotiating freight rates.

The importance of logistics integration in the lean supply chain cannot be overstated. It allows logistics providers to make timely deliveries of quality goods to their customers. Logistics integration significantly facilitates supply chain decisions about where to position strategic inventory to provide better customer service. It also allows suppliers and customers to work effectively with minimal inventories without having to buffer uncertainties in the logistics process with extra inventory or capacity.

It is not possible to treat the logistics function in a single section or even a chapter. The intent here is to underscore the importance of logistics integration and of partnering with logistics providers. A large number of enterprises are building such partnerships. For example, Home Depot partnered with the logistics provider, J. B. Hunt, to ensure the delivery of quality products from warehouses to retail stores. The trucking company installed drop bars in its trucks to secure the different pallet shapes and sizes that it carried for Home Depot.

Logistics providers now ensure timely deliveries of small lot sizes at regular intervals. The concepts of *milk runs* and *less-than-truckload (LTL) quantities* have made it possible for enterprises to streamline their operations. Milk runs are delivery routes set up by logistics providers to deliver goods to enterprises at fixed times during the day so that enterprises can rely on timely arrival of goods to their stores. In combination with LTL shipments, milk runs facilitate delivery of small lots at frequent intervals, considerably enhancing the supplier's ability to respond quickly and flexibly to changing customer demands. Since the deliveries typically are in small lot sizes from nearby locations, the next delivery can be modified more easily than otherwise would be the case if full-truckload quantities were delivered less often.

Many of the factors that promote effective partnership with suppliers also apply to partnering with logistics providers. Long-term contracts, single sourcing of logistics providers, and better visibility on shipping and delivery schedules lead to more sustainable relationships between the enterprise and the logistics provider, although logistics has some unique characteristics not found in buyer-supplier relationships, such as the presence of *third-party logistics providers* (3PLs).

3PLs and 4PLs

When the industrial environment became more competitive in the 1980s and 1990s, there was tremendous pressure on suppliers to deliver products faster, cheaper, and in small lots. Many enterprises were reluctant to cope with these pressures either because they did not have the resources to invest in a logistics infrastructure or simply because it did not add to their core competencies. After all, their main focus was to manufacture a product. The burden of coordinating the logistics activities thus fell on the willing shoulders of the 3PLs.

A 3PL is an enterprise that provides logistics services such as warehousing, order management, distribution, and transport services to its customer using its own assets and resources. 3PLs were embraced by enterprises eager to contract out logistics activities; there has been a tremendous growth in demand for their services.

The 3PL provides integrated transport- or warehousing-related solutions to the shippers. The primary services contracted from 3PL providers are inbound and outbound transportation, cross-docking (described in a following section), warehousing, freight bill auditing and payment, and freight consolidation and distribution. A key differentiating factor between a 3PL and a typical transportation or other logistics service provider is that the 3PL also manages some of the information needs of the enterprises for which it provides logistics support.

There are a number of advantages to partnering with 3PLs. The better 3PL providers are able to constantly update their IT and equipment. Thus the shippers do not have to be concerned with constantly updating their technology in this area but instead can focus on their core competencies. In fact, the retailers they ship to may have different and probably changing delivery and technology requirements that 3PLs are better positioned to meet in a more cost-effective manner.

The 3PLs also give shippers greater flexibility. For instance, suppliers who have to provide rapid replenishments may require regional warehouses, but by using 3PLs to handle the warehousing, the supplier does not have to invest time and money building and maintaining warehouses. 3PLs are also in a better position to consolidate low-volume LTL shipments from different suppliers for delivery to customers.

The services provided by 3PLs inherently depend on long-term relationships oriented toward solving problems for the enterprise, sharing risks and benefits, and recognizing mutual interdependencies. The preferred mode of operation is for the enterprise to negotiate with a single 3PL that agrees to provide a broader set of order-fulfillment activities from storage to order picking to transportation to financial management. The 3PL may be given responsibility to design the logistics network and to monitor and control logistics processes.

Such a long-term arrangement demands a long-term commitment of assets on the part of the 3PL. In return, the enterprise, whether shipper or receiver, must be willing to commit to a long-term relationship to make the work of the 3PL economically feasible.

The 3PLs were the result of the enterprise's desire to outsource its logistics activities. As 3PLs became more sophisticated at moving goods from one place to another, there was a perception that they were still not offering some activities that could well be outsourced to them. For instance, speedy transfer of and access to information was still missing. Enter the *fourth-party logistics providers* (4PLs).

4PLs represent further outsourcing. They were the product of consulting enterprises, in particular, Andersen Consulting (Accenture), which trademarked the term in 1996. The 4PL is, in theory, a logistics integrator that manages the 3PLs in addition to a set of other supply chain-related activities such as IT management. It is an additional service layer between the 3PL and its customer that, in effect, tries to manage these activities without necessarily carrying any assets.

Postponement in Logistics

Postponement, the philosophy adopted in lean supply chains, is in direct contrast to *speculation*, where channel members assume risk rather than shifting it. Speculation exploits the economies of large-scale production; its goal is to minimize stock-out and order-processing costs. In a manufacturing context, postponement refers to the situation where a manufacturer begins production or assembly of components or sub-assembled parts only after receiving a firm order.

Postponement in logistics shifts the risk of owning goods from one channel member to another. Just as a manufacturer may refuse to produce goods until it receives a firm order, similarly, an intermediary may postpone owning inventories by purchasing from sellers who offer faster delivery, or on consignment, or only when a sale has been made. Consumers postpone ownership by buying from retail outlets where products are in stock.

3PL's participate in postponement strategies in a number of ways. They may mix pallets for individual customers as orders are received, repackage products to fit specific customer or country requirements, or perform final assembly or customization on site.

Cross-Docking

Cross-docking is a process by which products are moved from one enterprise to another enterprise through an intermediate warehouse, where they are not stored for more than a few hours. The goal of cross-docking is to be able to transfer these products directly from incoming to outgoing trailers or vehicles without having to store them. Cross-docking is used to change the type of conveyance, to sort materials intended for different destinations, or to combine materials from different origins into transport vehicles or containers bound for the same destination. Basically, cross-docks are an effective alternative to picking orders and delivering in small quantities to each retail outlet using LTL shipments. They enable economies of scope.

Cross-docks are essentially marshaling yards in the old railroad sense. Trucks arrive with products that must be sorted, perhaps consolidated with other products, and then loaded onto outbound trucks. The incoming trucks typically arrive from an upstream enterprise, and the outbound trucks typically are destined for a manufacturing enterprise or a retail outlet. Figure 6.3 shows a cross-dock. Workers place pallets in lanes corresponding to the receiving doors, a second team of workers sorts pallets into shipping lanes, and a third team loads them onto outbound trailers.

What are some obvious difference between cross-docking and the traditional warehousing operation? In traditional warehousing, the ware-

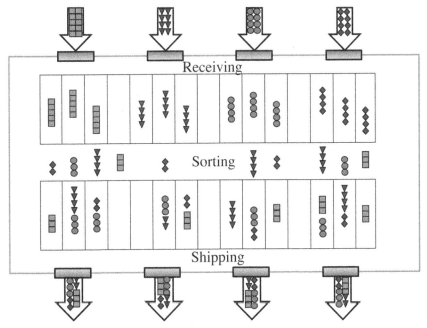

Figure 6.3 A representation of a cross-dock.

house receives products, updates its inventory records, and moves the product into a specific location in the warehouse. The product sits there in inventory until it is required by a customer, at which time it is picked, packed, and shipped, and then the inventory records are adjusted.

On the other hand, cross-docks typically do not have any inventory records to update because that is unnecessary. Instead, the products are shipped as soon as possible with possibly a little waiting time for other trucks to arrive with products bound for the same destination. The product does not go into long-term storage.

Cross-docking promises certain benefits over a traditional warehouse. Benefits include:

▲ Improved product flow, with quicker deliveries to the customer
▲ Reduced labor costs (Products no longer need to be picked and stored in warehouses.)
▲ Reduced warehouse space because there is no requirement to store the products
▲ Reduced inventories with less opportunity for pilferage

To be effective, cross-docking demands advance knowledge of the inbound product and its destination and a system for routing the product to the proper outbound vehicle. A specific system must be in place to ensure efficient exchange of both product and information and to match and schedule inbound and outbound shipments so that the product flows through the warehouse as quickly as possible.

Cross-docking does not come without headaches. It requires extensive coordination among suppliers, the distributor, and customers. A cross-docking operation imposes restrictions on suppliers and customers: suppliers may be asked to deliver small shipments more frequently or to attach bar codes to packages. Customers may be scheduled to receive supplies on certain days. These restrictions can lead to extra costs and coordination for channel partners. Good information systems are required if the cross-dock facility has to know what is on each inbound truck before it arrives.

Improved technology in the form of warehouse management systems, electronic data interchange, and radio frequency identification (RFID) technology have helped the use of cross-dock programs considerably. Advance ship notices also help to determine potential cross-dock opportunities and allow for better scheduling of events.

Supply Chain Metrics

When the directors of an enterprise ask the CEO, "How are we doing?" what is the typical response? The CEO probably would talk about the performance of the enterprise in terms of measures such as return on investment, profitability, inventory turns, and material costs. These are important metrics to gauge the financial health of the enterprise, but they are all internal measures that may not address the performance of the enterprise adequately in the future.

As discussed previously, the battleground has shifted from rivalry between enterprises to rivalry between supply chains. The financial health of an enterprise in the supply chain is directly affected by the overall performance of the chain. Outstanding performance at one location in the supply chain is no longer adequate if the performance of other key supply chain members is not on par. Locally focused measures of cost and other performance measures are incomplete and lead to suboptimal decisions. Enterprises must focus not only on performance within their four walls but also on performance across the supply chain.

The objective of supply chain metrics is to provide a basis for evaluating the performance of the whole supply chain as one system. That performance is the result of policies and procedures that drive various critical segments of the supply chain. Properly designed supply chain metrics help to clarify the interrelationship between enterprise performance and supply chain performance and help enterprises to better align their activities.

In all probability, the current strategy and its resulting structure are a consequence of the individual segments in the supply chain making isolated decisions that make sense to them from their local perspective. These individual decisions result in an unsynchronized supply chain characterized by long lead times and many pockets of inventory.

Consider a supply chain with two enterprises, A and B, where A supplies products to B. Suppose that A is measured on finished goods inventory levels and responds accordingly by reducing this inventory. From a local perspective, A has done well, but if the inventory reduction at A is carried out in isolation without any change in the pattern of B's demands on its supplier, A may be putting itself in jeopardy because it is now unable to react promptly to unforeseen changes in demand from B. From B's perspective, A will be perceived as less flexible, so B may decide either to carry some inventory of its own or to find another supplier. The lack of supply chain metrics has led the manager of *A* to make local improvements that did not improve the performance of the supply chain as a whole.

To provide another simple example of the effect of locally focused decisions, consider an enterprise that produces and ships products in large batches. This enterprise has minimized its production and transportation costs, but it has increased the inventory for the buyer. In fact, viewed from the perspective of the supply chain, the long lead times created by big batches and shipping quantities are very costly. Shipping products in large batches forces large amounts of WIP in the supply chain, reduces flexibility and responsiveness, and promotes the bullwhip effect.

Many enterprises claim to have true supply chain metrics. However, quite often measures currently identified as supply chain metrics are in fact simply measures of internal logistics operations. Typical metrics used to measure delivery performance, such as fill rate and on-time performance, will be applied in a different context if a systems perspective is adopted. For example, note that as inventory moves across a supply chain and gets closer to the point of consumption, it increases in value from a customer perspective. Hence an improvement in inventory turns at a retailer is likely to have a more significant impact on overall supply chain performance than a corresponding improvement in inventory turns at a supplier.

So what is the approach to follow when designing supply chain metrics? When developing these metrics, it is important to keep in mind the fact that a product manufactured and delivered by the supply chain should be considered as sold only when the end customer has paid for it. To sharpen the focus on the metrics that really matter, it is worth asking the following questions for each metric considered. These questions should be asked in the order presented below.

▲ Will the metric help to sell more products profitably to the end user (increase *T*)?
▲ Will the metric help to reduce investment in resources in the supply chain (reduce *I*)?
▲ Will the metric help to reduce supply chain expenses long term (reduce *OE*)?

If the answer is "No" to all these questions, then that metric may not serve any useful purpose. The last section in this chapter is a case study that demonstrates how it is possible to devise win-win solutions to address all these questions satisfactorily. These questions, however, serve to surface the key driving metric on which the supply chain should focus: throughput. The tenth Lean Supply Chain Principle captures this focus:

Lean Supply Chain Principle 10

Formulate supply chain performance metrics that focus on improving throughput.

While the focus should be on throughput, the question on investment in resources is also very important. A question that might be asked is: is there a way to optimize inventory costs across the entire supply chain?

In the past, the question would have been dismissed as a theoretical exercise, but today this question is rapidly changing from a theoretical to a practical one as managers of supply chains face increasing pressures on customer service and asset performance. Sony, for instance, is acutely aware of the fact that any inventory of its products at Best Buy and Walmart ultimately affects its profitability if it remains on the shelf for more than a few days, and so it has changed its delivery metric from *sell-in* to *sell-through*. The former metric allowed the Sony sales department to chalk up a sale when the product was shipped to Best Buy or Walmart; the latter metric chalks up a sale only when the product is paid for by the customer. Similarly, Procter & Gamble uses its VMI process to routinely measure both its own inventory and the downstream inventories of its products.

A well-designed measurement system thus can help the focus on throughput significantly by aligning processes across the supply chain and targeting the most profitable market segments. Goldratt says, "Tell me how you will measure me, and I will tell you how I'll behave"[4] to emphasize how metrics drive behavior. According to Goldratt, if there is a conflict between the local metrics (metrics for the enterprise) and global metrics (supply chain metrics), it is a clear indication that the rules governing the business relationships between the enterprises are wrong. To resolve such conflicts and to help enterprises arrive at the right metrics, the TOC Thinking

Process provides a set of cause-effect logic tools that result in simple solutions to seemingly complex problem situations.

One of the Thinking Process tools is the *evaporating cloud*, a technique that uses necessity-based logic to describe and resolve conflicts that, at first glance, do not appear to have a satisfactory solution. The evaporating cloud helps to identify the right measures and policies that will resolve conflicts in a win-win manner. While it is was developed originally as one of five Thinking Process tools, the evaporating cloud is also a very effective stand-alone tool that finds application in a wide variety of situations.

Creating Win-Win Partnerships: The Evaporating Cloud

The evaporating cloud was discussed briefly in Chapter 3, where it was noted that it provides an un-common sense solution to conflict resolution: "in order to resolve conflicts, ignore the conflict." The evaporating cloud is based on the belief that there are no conflicts in nature, only erroneous assumptions. According to Goldratt, a conflict exists because of an incorrect assumption someone has made about reality. Therefore, instead of focusing on the conflict, the idea is to focus on the assumptions that lead to the conflict. The technique helps to resolve conflicts quickly and arrive at a solution that is not a compromise but a real breakthrough.

The evaporating cloud helps to find win-win solutions because it emphasizes that both parties involved in the conflict are trying to reach the same ultimate goal, even though they may have entirely different perspectives. The evaporating cloud technique uses a diagram called the *cloud*. This diagram is sometimes referred to in the literature as a *conflict-resolution diagram*. The cloud has five entities labeled *A*, *B*, *C*, *D*, and *D'* (Figure 6.4).

The first entity, represented by the box *A* in the figure, is the objective— an objective shared by both parties in the conflict. The objective is translated into the requirements specified by the two parties in the conflict. The requirements for the conflicting parties are presented in boxes *B* and *C* in the cloud. These requirements also can be viewed as the assertions made by the two parties that ultimately lead to the conflict.

The conflict is manifested in the boxes labeled *D* and *D'* in the figure. These two boxes identify what the two parties want, which results in the

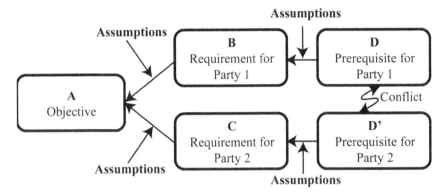

Figure 6.4 The generic cloud.

conflict. Box D' represents a want that is diametrically opposed to the want expressed in box D. The evaporating cloud technique sometimes refers to these wants as *prerequisites*.

The evaporating cloud uses necessity-based logic. The arrows connecting the boxes provide the causality. After the cloud is drawn, it is a good idea to read the boxes aloud in the following sequence to make sure that the logical connections are captured correctly.

▲ In order to have objective A, we must have requirement B.
▲ In order to have requirement B, we must have prerequisite D.
▲ In order to have objective A, we must have requirement C.
▲ In order to have requirement C, we must have prerequisite D'.

Finally, the conflict arising from boxes D and D' should be presented in a manner such that it should be clear to the reader that "There is no way we can have D and D' at the same time." The cloud also must be carefully verified to ensure that the conflict is manifested only in the boxes D and D'.

The arrows connecting the boxes are now examined carefully. The assumptions underlying the arrows are reviewed, and each one of them is challenged.

The evaporating cloud is illustrated with a couple of examples. The first example deals with a conflict between two points of view, more specifically, a conflict faced by a conscientious office worker. The resolution of this conflict results in a unique cross-docking system of operation. In a subsequent section, the evaporating cloud illustrates how multiple parties in a partnership can work together to arrive at a win-win solution.

The Office Worker's Dilemma

The following description of the office worker's dilemma is based on an actual case study that dates back to the 1890s. In the late 1800s, the city of Mumbai was growing rapidly. Migrants from different communities and states came to Mumbai looking for a job in the city. These migrants had different tastes and food preferences, but there were no restaurants or cafeterias in Mumbai that catered to the multiple tastes at that time.

In a popular account of this time in history, many migrants were employed by the British, who were ruling the majority of the Indian subcontinent at that time. While these migrants were eager to please their employers, they did not care for the Western cuisine served in the cafeterias operated by the British and sought alternatives for their lunch needs. Regardless of whether this version of history is authentic or not, the fact remains that these migrants traveled to the city from distant locations, and the lunch break did not did not give them enough time to go home for lunch.

In a more modern setting, the migrant's dilemma still manifests in an office setting. Consider the operation of a call center. The office worker—the operator handling the calls—has to be available to respond to customer queries throughout the day, leaving him with little time for breaks. The call-center operator's objective is to perform stellar work, which requires him to remain mentally alert and productive through the day. However, the absence of a proper meal during the day results in needless fatigue. Because the operator is unable to go home for lunch, and because there are no restaurants or cafeterias that cater to his needs, the dilemma is how to provide him with a nourishing lunch every day. Figure 6.5 illustrates the office worker's dilemma as a cloud.

The conflict presented in boxes D and D' in this figure is to either "eat a nutritious, freshly prepared lunch that will keep me mentally alert and productive the entire day" or "eat an unwholesome lunch at the cafeteria so that I can cope with my workload." The requirements that lead to this conflict are presented in boxes B and C.

Consider boxes A and C. The necessity logic connecting these boxes is verbalized as follows: "in order for me to do stellar work, I have to spend all my time working at my desk." The assumption that drives the operator to be tied to his desk is that he should be on call to undertake critical decisions. Similarly, consider boxes C and D'. The logic connecting these boxes is verbalized as follows: "in order for me to be at my desk, I have to visit the

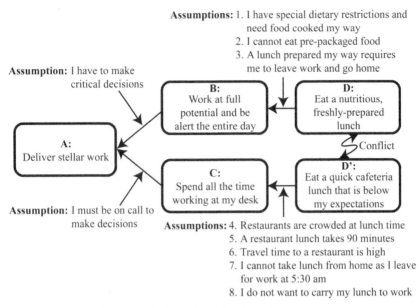

Figure 6.5   The cloud for the office worker.

cafeteria to eat a lunch that is well below my expectations." The assumptions driving this logic are shown in the figure. Reading the cloud with the assumptions included proceeds in a similar manner. For example, "In order to be at my desk, I must eat a quick cafeteria lunch because lunch at a restaurant will take 90 minutes."

After ensuring that the objective, the requirements, the prerequisites leading to the conflict, and the assumptions are correct by verbalizing them, the evaporating cloud technique tries to break the conflict by challenging the assumptions. Each assumption is examined carefully to see if it provides a direction to the solution. Some assumptions may be clearly invalid—these assumptions point the way to new ideas or potential solutions to break the conflict. Assumptions that are not clearly invalid are scrutinized to identify conditions that can invalidate them. Is there a new idea or reality—an *injection*—that will eliminate the conflict? In the ideal case if it is possible to find an injection for each assumption there will be more opportunities to arrive at a breakthrough solution to the conflict.

In summary, the cloud helps to find a way to satisfy the common objective and both requirements with a win-win *injection*—an action that will invalidate an assumption. For the office worker's dilemma, the assumption "A lunch prepared my way requires me to leave work and go home" is overcome by an injection. This injection is delivered by the *dabbawala*, a person whose job is to carry freshly prepared home-cooked food to the office worker in a lunch box.

The Injection for the Office Worker's Dilemma: The Dabbawalas

A *dabbawala*, literally meaning a "person with a box," is a person who provides a lunch service to office workers in the city of Mumbai. The origin of the *dabbawala* lunch service dates back to 1890, when Mahadeo Havaji Bacche, a migrant to Mumbai from the city of Pune in Maharashtra, started this service to cater to the needs of Mumbai's migrant workers. He set up a service to deliver home-cooked meals to these workers using the *dabbawalas*.

The *dabbawalas* currently serve about 200,000 customers, office managers, workers, and students, charging a fee of just $6 per customer per month. There are 5,000 *dabbawalas*; many of them can hardly read or write, and the average literacy rate is at about the eighth grade level.

The *dabbawalas* employ an intricate delivery system using Mumbai's metropolitan railway and bus transportation networks. Each lunch box carries a code that identifies the home address from where the box originated, the train station where the box ultimately should be unloaded, and the building address where the box has to be delivered.

A *collecting dabbawala*, usually traveling on a bicycle, collects the lunch box from the worker's home at around 9:00 a.m. and takes it to a designated sorting place, typically the nearest train station, where he works with other *local dabbawalas* to sort and bundle the lunch boxes onto pallets based on the code. The pallets are placed in a designated railcar.

The coding system is used by the local *dabbawalas* to move the boxes through the metropolitan railway and bus transport networks, often using hand-off points typically located at selected train stations. At the train station, the lunch box could be taken out, placed on a different pallet, and possibly transported by a different *dabbawala* to another train station. The lunch box thus conceivably could change hands three or four times before reaching its final destination. At the train station closest to the destination, the boxes are handed over to a local *dabbawala*, who delivers them to the customers by around 12:30 p.m. The empty boxes are collected and sent back to the respective homes.

This intricate set of activities involving multiple splits and merges is strongly reminiscent of the cross-docking operation practiced by logistics providers today to transport goods across large distances. Unlike modern cross-docking systems that use sophisticated systems to track the progress of shipments in the supply chain, the *dabbawalas* use a simple coding system with colors and numbers to denote origin and destination points.

What is noteworthy about the *dabbawala* operation is that it has performed so well over the past 100 years with uninterrupted service even on days of extreme weather such as during Mumbai's monsoons. The delivery accuracy is also remarkable. In 1998, *Forbes Global* magazine conducted a quality assurance study on the *dabbawalas'* operation and gave it a Six Sigma efficiency rating of 99.999999 percent accuracy, an error rate of less than 1 in 16 million deliveries. Remarkably, too, over the years, the *dabbawalas* have been able to transport the lunch boxes from origin to destination without the use of any electronic communications device or advanced technology.

More recently, the *dabbawalas* have begun to use technology, booking delivery orders through text messaging (SMS) or their Web site (www .mydabbawala.com). The Web site has allowed the *dabbawalas* association to solicit donations and sell merchandise, with the proceeds going into a social security fund that pays for their life and medical insurance. The *dabbawalas* have also started to advertise and market products for large organizations that find it very cost-effective to advertise in this manner. In one such arrangement, the *dabbawalas* place pamphlets advertising Microsoft products with the lunch boxes. If the customer buys the product advertised, the *dabbawala* receives a 100 rupee (approximately $2) bonus from Microsoft Corporation.

The *dabbawalas* have created a win-win scenario. The customer gets a home-cooked meal for a nominal cost, and the *dabbawala* gets a comfortable salary with fringe benefits such as life and medical insurance.

The following case study presents an application of partnering in an automobile manufacturer's supply chain. The case also demonstrates how the evaporating cloud technique can help to identify a win-win situation that benefits multiple members in the supply chain.

CASE STUDY

The Reo Motors Supply Chain*

Reo Motors is an automobile manufacturer that sells vehicles through a dealer network. The dealers receive monthly allotments of automobiles from Reo Motors to sell to customers. Reo Motors has partnered with a railroad company, Grand Trunk Railroad (GTR), and has enlisted a trucking company for its outbound transportation needs. As part of the partnership arrangement, GTR reserves railcar capacity to meet any demand surge Reo Motors might experience. These railcars are not placed constructively and thus are not subject to demurrage. Vehicles in transit are owned by Reo Motors. Figure 6.6 presents the Reo Motors supply chain.

Reo Motors   Grand Trunk Railroad   Haddy Lane

Figure 6.6 The Reo Motors supply chain.

The Current State for the Reo Motors Supply Chain

Reo Motors sells 2 million vehicles a year through the dealer network, charging the dealers $25,000 per vehicle. Reo Motors also provides a discount of $1,200 directly to customers. The cost of goods sold (COGS) is 84 percent of Reo Motors' revenue, or $21,000 per vehicle. Selling, general, and administrative expenses (SG&A) account for 8 percent of Reo Motors' revenue, or $2,000 per vehicle.

Financials for Reo Motors—Current State

The cost to transport the vehicles to the dealers averages $400 per vehicle, of which $160 is paid to GTR and $240 is paid to the trucking company.

---

*This case is adapted from the Integrity Motors case developed by Dr. James M. Reeve.

CASE STUDY

The trucking company transports vehicles from the assembly plants to the railroad and also from the destination railway terminal to the dealers. The net profit for Reo Motors is currently $400 per vehicle (see Table 6.1).

Table 6.1 Income and Investment for Reo Motors—Current State

		Explanation (calculation)
Dealer price	$25,000	Given
Customer rebate	$1,200	Given
COGS	$21,000	= 84 percent of $25,000
SG&A	$2,000	= 8 percent × $25,000
Freight	$400	Given
Income from continuing operations	**$400**	
Inventory	$3,500	= (60/360) × $21,000
Accounts payable	($1,750)	= (30/360) × $21,000
Accounts receivable	$3,125	= (45/360) × $25,000
Property, plant, and equipment	$6,000	= $12 billion/2 million
Total investment per vehicle	**$10,875**	

Reo Motors operates its plants 360 days a year. The total lead time, from start of production until the vehicle is delivered to the dealer, is 60 days. The 60-day lead time includes 15 days of transportation time. Reo Motors values the 60 days of inventory at COGS. Accounts payable to suppliers is 30 days of inventory, again valued at COGS. The accounts receivable, the money outstanding with the dealers, is 45 five days of sales, and it is valued at dealer cost.

The 60 days of inventory represents an investment of (60/360) × $21,000 = $3,500 per vehicle. Accounts payable is calculated similarly as (30/360) × $21,000 = $1,750 per vehicle, and accounts receivable is (45/365) × $25,000 = $3,125 per vehicle. Note that accounts payable appears as a debit item on the balance sheet because it represents short-term debt payments to suppliers and banks.

Reo Motors has invested $12 billion in property, plant, and equipment. This investment supports sales of 2 million vehicles per year, which

CASE STUDY

translates to an investment of $12 billion ÷ 2 million vehicles = $6,000 per vehicle. The total investment per vehicle thus is $10,875, as shown in Table 6.1.

Financials for Grand Trunk Railroad—Current State

The shipping and transportation industries typically use a metric called *revenue ton miles* (RTMs) to determine profits and expenses. In particular, the RTM metric is used widely in the railroad industry. GTR charges customers 8 cents per RTM.

The weight of a vehicle is 1.25 tons, and Reo Motors vehicles are transported an average of 1,600 miles by rail. Transporting each vehicle thus amounts to 1.25 × 1,600 = 2,000 RTMs, providing GTR with a revenue of $0.08 × 2,000 = $160 per vehicle.

Expenses for GTR are calculated based on RTMs: wages are $0.015 per RTM, fuel is $0.012 per RTM, equipment costs are $0.010 per RTM, railroad maintenance and depreciation expenses are $0.005 per RTM, and SG&A is $0.024 per RTM. The total RTM-based costs amount to 2,000 × ($0.015 + $0.012 + $0.010 + $0.005 + $0.024) = $132 per vehicle.

GTR incurs costs at the terminals: Spotting and loading costs of $120 per railcar, and switching and classifying costs of $180 per railcar. Since each railcar can carry 15 vehicles, the total terminal cost charged per vehicle is ($180 + $120) ÷ 15 = $20 per vehicle. The total cost per vehicle is the sum of RTM expenses and terminal costs, $132 + $20 = $152 per vehicle, giving GTR a profit of $8 per vehicle (see Table 6.2).

Table 6.2 Income and Investment for Grand Trunk Railroad—Current State

		Explanation (calculation)
Freight revenue	$160	= 2,000 RTM × $0.08
Wages, fuel, equipment, maintenance, and SG&A	$132	= $0.015, $0.012, $0.010, $0.005, $0.024 per RTM
Spotting and loading, switching, and classifying costs	$20	= ($180 + $120)/15 vehicles per car
Income from continuing operations	**$8**	

CASE STUDY

Table 6.2   Income and Investment for Grand Trunk Railroad—Current State
(continued)

		Explanation (calculation)
Materials and supplies (revenue allocation)	$2.40	= ($160/$6 billion) × $90 million
Accounts payable (revenue allocation)	($22.40)	= ($160/$6 billion) × $840 million
Accounts receivable (revenue allocation)	$12	= ($160/$6 billion) × $450 million
Property and equipment (RTM allocation)	$200	= ($16 billion/160 billion RTM) × 2,000
Total investment per vehicle	**$192**	

To calculate investment per vehicle, GTR uses selected balance sheet data on investment in materials, accounts payable, and accounts receivable. These costs are allocated to the Reo Motors operation with a revenue-allocation method.

GTR receives revenue of $160 per vehicle. The total revenue for GTR across all of its operations is $6 billion. Expenses for materials and supplies last year were $90 million. So the materials and supplies charged per vehicle using the revenue-allocation method amount to ($160/$6 billion) × $90 million = $2.40 per vehicle. Similarly, with the revenue-allocation method, accounts payable and accounts receivable were $840 million and $450 million last year, resulting in per-vehicle costs of $22.40 and $12, respectively.

The total property and equipment is $16 billion. The allocation to vehicle operations is based on RTMs. GTR generates 160 billion RTMs a year.* Since each vehicle accounts for 2,000 RTMs, the RTM allocation per vehicle is ($16 billion/160 billion RTMs) × 2,000 RTMs per vehicle = $200 per vehicle.

---

*Automobiles account for 10 percent of the Grand Trunk Railroad traffic. Reo Motors' share of the automobile traffic is 25 percent, so Reo Motors effectively accounts for 2.5 percent of all traffic.

CASE STUDY

Haddy Lane, Inc., is a dealer in Knoxville, Tennessee, that sells vehicles manufactured by Reo Motors. Haddy Lane sells 480 Reo Motors vehicles a year on average. These vehicles are delivered by GTR to the Knoxville Northern Terminal, from where they are delivered to Haddy Lane, Inc., by truck.

Financials for Haddy Lane, Inc.—Current State

The manufacturer's suggested retail price (MSRP) for the vehicle is $30,000, and Haddy Lane provides an average customer discount of $2,000 off the MSRP. The net customer price after factoring in the $1,200 manufacturer's rebate is $30,000 – $2,000 – $1,200 = $26,800.

Haddy Lane's COGS is the $25,000 per vehicle it pays to Reo Motors, and its operating costs are 10 percent of COGS. Haddy Lane keeps 60 days of inventory of these vehicles on its parking lots. Customers either pay cash or finance their vehicle purchase, so Haddy Lane has no accounts receivable, but it has 45 days of accounts payable to Reo Motors. Haddy Lane has invested $4 million in property and equipment for its sales and service operations, 60 percent of which is allocated to sales of Reo Motors' vehicles.

The income from operations per vehicle for Haddy Lane is the MSRP of $30,000 less its expenses. The expenses are the dealer discount of $2,000, the COGS of $25,000, and the operating costs of $2,500, which add up to $29,500. Haddy Lane therefore earns a profit of $500 per vehicle sold.

The inventory investment per vehicle is (60/360) × $25,000 = $4,167. The accounts payable is (45/360) x $25,000 = $3,125. The property and equipment allocation per vehicle is (60 percent × $4 million) ÷ 480 vehicles = $5,000 per vehicle. Table 6.3 summarizes the profit and investment calculations for Haddy Lane.

Table 6.4 summarizes the information for the Reo Motors supply chain. The return on assets (ROA) in the table is the ratio of the net income from operations to the total investment per vehicle.

CASE STUDY

Table 6.3 Income and Investment for Haddy Lane, Inc.—Current State

		Explanation (calculation)
MSRP	$30,000	Given
Dealer discount	$2,000	Given
Dealer COGS	$25,000	Given
Operating costs	$2,500	= 10 percent × COGS
Income from operations	**$500**	
Inventory	$4,167	= (60/360) × $25,000
Accounts payable	($3,125)	= (45/360) × $25,000
Accounts receivable	$0	
Dealer property and equipment	$5,000	= (60 percent × $4 million) ÷ 480 vehicles
Total investment per vehicle	**$6,042**	

Table 6.4 Summary Information for the Reo Motors Supply Chain—Current State

Current state	Reo Motors	Grand Trunk Railroad	Haddy Lane, Inc.
Income per vehicle	$400	$8	$500
Investment per vehicle	$10,875	$192	$6,042
Pretax ROA	3.68 percent	4.17 percent	8.28 percent

The information in this table shows low ROAs for Reo Motors and GTR. The railroad industry, with its sizable investment in assets, typically experiences low ROAs. Both Reo Motors and GTR are actively seeking opportunities to make more profits.

As noted earlier, the objective of this case is to demonstrate how partnering will result in a win-win scenario for multiple members in the supply chain. Creating such a win-win scenario also will lead to a more sustainable mode of operation.

CASE STUDY

Creating a Win-Win Scenario: The Cloud

Reo Motors, the key player in the supply chain, develops the cloud for its operations. Figure 6.7 presents the cloud. This cloud presents a few key assumptions.

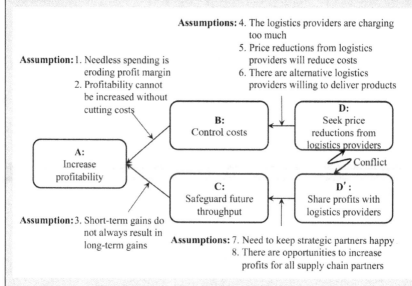

Assumptions: 4. The logistics providers are charging too much
5. Price reductions from logistics providers will reduce costs
6. There are alternative logistics providers willing to deliver products

Assumption: 1. Needless spending is eroding profit margin
2. Profitability cannot be increased without cutting costs

Assumption: 3. Short-term gains do not always result in long-term gains

Assumptions: 7. Need to keep strategic partners happy
8. There are opportunities to increase profits for all supply chain partners

B: Control costs

A: Increase profitability

C: Safeguard future throughput

D: Seek price reductions from logistics providers

D′: Share profits with logistics providers

Conflict

Figure 6.7 The cloud for Reo Motors.

An examination of the cloud provides the injection. The injection overcomes the assumption underlying the arrow connecting box *A* and box *B*: "Profitability cannot be increased without cutting costs." The injection provides two possible opportunities for Reo Motors to consider: Either increase profits by generating more sales, or increase profits by redesigning the current mode of operation. In this case, Reo Motors decides to embark on a "have it your way" strategy by which customers will have automobiles built to their specifications.

CASE STUDY

Reo Motors Embarks on a BTO Strategy

The new supply chain strategy is to move Reo Motors from its current build-to-stock (BTS) mode of operation to a build-to-order (BTO) mode of operation. In this mode of operation:

▲ Customers will order cars from a kiosk or Internet web site.
▲ The order will be transmitted electronically to Reo Motors, and a vehicle will be built and delivered to customer specifications.
▲ Vehicles will be designed under a modular concept, and the assembly plant will need to have plug-and-play capabilities.
▲ The vehicle will be designed to shrink the supply base from about 3,000 parts to around 30 modules and options.

Under this strategy, the dealers will serve as intermediaries, helping Reo Motors sell vehicles to the customers for $26,000, a better price than the $26,800 that customers currently pay for a vehicle after the manufacturer's discount. Customers will visit the dealer showrooms to test drive a model Reo Motors vehicle and to place orders.

In return for the sales support provided, dealers earn a commission of 3 percent on the sales price. Dealers no longer pay Reo Motors for vehicles but act only as commission agents that do not take ownership of the vehicles. To simplify the analysis, assume that sales are unaffected by the change in mode of operation and that the 2 million vehicles are all built under the BTO mode of operation.

Dealer operating costs such as interest, space, and property taxes are expected to drop significantly from the reduction in overhead costs. The reduction in overhead operating costs, however, will be slightly offset by higher selling expenses.

Haddy Lane estimates that operating costs now will equal 70 percent of its commission revenue. With just a few models on its parking lots, the property investment needed to sell Reo Motors' vehicles will be reduced by 75 percent. Thus the investment in property and equipment drops from the original $5,000 per vehicle to $1,250 per vehicle. Table 6.5 presents expected BTO scenario profits and investment for Haddy Lane.

CASE STUDY

Table 6.5 Income and Investment for Haddy Lane, Inc.—BTO Scenario

		Explanation (calculation)
Dealer's commission	$780	= 3 percent × $26,000
Operating costs	$546	= 70 percent × $780
Income from operations	**$234**	
Dealer property and equipment	$1,250	= $4 million × (60 percent × 25 percent) ÷ 480 vehicles
Total investment per vehicle	**$1,250**	

The modular approach to assembling automobiles is expected to reduce inventory at Reo Motors from 60 days down to 6 days. Reo Motors still will have a 30-day accounts payable to its suppliers, but accounts receivable will change dramatically. Now Reo Motors will collect cash from customers 5 days *before* the vehicle is delivered to the customer, in a manner similar to the approach pioneered by Dell, which collects cash from its customers as soon as they place orders, before the computer is assembled.

To support the BTO operations, Reo Motors incurs an additional SG&A expense of $500 million and additional manufacturing expenses of $1.2 billion per year, which increases its COGS. Reo Motors also incurs some one-time investment costs. It has built kiosks at each dealer location, at a cost of $108,000 per location. Additional investment in IT support and engineering and manufacturing support amounts to $1 billion.

The BTO system guarantees delivery of the vehicle to the customer in 5 days. In addition to reducing its manufacturing lead time, Reo Motors is working with GTR to reduce the transportation lead time from its current value of 15 days. Reo Motors will now pay $500 to transport a vehicle, paying $225 per vehicle to GTR and $275 per vehicle to the truck fleet operator. In return, the truck fleet operator and the railroad have agreed to reduce transport time from 15 days (3 days with truck fleet and 12 days with the railroad) down to 3 days (1 day with the truck fleet and 2 days with the railroad). Table 6.6 presents financials for Reo Motors under the BTO scenario.

CASE STUDY

Table 6.6 Income and Investment for Reo Motors—BTO Scenario

		Explanation (calculation)
Dealer price	$26,000	Given
COGS	$21,600	= $21,000 + $1.2 billion/2 million
SG&A	$2,250	= $2,000 + ($500 million/2 million)
Commission to dealer	$780	Given
Freight	$500	Given
Income from continuing operations	**$870**	
Inventory	$360	= 6/360 × $21,600
Accounts payable	($1,800)	= 30/360 × $21,600
Accounts receivable	($361)	= -5/360 × $26,000
Kiosk investment	$225	= $108,000 ÷ 480 vehicles per dealer
Additional IT, engineering,	$500	= $1 billion/2 million vehicles and manufacturing
Property, plant, and equipment	$6,000	= $12 billion/2 million vehicles
Total investment per vehicle	**$4,924**	

GTR is expected to incur additional operating costs of 2 cents per RTM under the BTO scenario. It has invested $50 million to support the BTO operations. Since it moves 2 million cars each year for Reo Motors, the additional BTO investment per vehicle = $50 million ÷ 2 million vehicles = $25 per vehicle.

Under the current mode of operation, a vehicle is in transport for 15 days, the railroad accounting for 12 of these days. Under the BTO mode of operation, a vehicle is expected to be in transport for 3 days, with the railroad accounting for 2 of these days. The railroad has reduced its effective time to transport BTO vehicles from 12 days down to 2 days, an 83 percent reduction. Correspondingly, the railcars reserved for BTO operations will be used more efficiently. That is, GTR could make the same revenue shipments with fewer railcars or ship more volume with the existing assets.

CASE STUDY

The investment per vehicle therefore is adjusted for BTO shipments as follows: Of the total $16 billion investment in assets by GTR, $3 billion is invested in railcars. Since the RTM allocation for property and equipment is $200, the benefits from decreased railcar travel time is $(10/12) \times$ ($3 billion/$16 billion) $\times$ $200 = $31.25. Table 6.7 presents the profit and investment per vehicle for GTR under the BTO scenario.

Table 6.7   Income and Investment for Grand Trunk Railroad—BTO Scenario

		Explanation (calculation)
Freight revenue	$225	
Wages, fuel, equipment, maintenance, and SG&A	$132	$0.015, $0.012, $0.010, $0.005, $0.024
Spotting and loading, switching, and classifying	$20	= ($180 + $120)/15 vehicles per car
Additional BTO operating costs	$40	= 2,000 RTM × $0.02
Income from operations	**$33**	
Materials and supplies	$2.40	From current mode of operation
Accounts payable	($22.40)	From current mode of operation
Accounts receivable	$12	From current mode of operation
Property and equipment (RTM allocation)	$200	= ($16 billion/160 billion RTM) × 2,000
Additional BTO investment	$25	= $50 million/2 million vehicles
Benefit from decreased railcar travel time	($31.25)	= (10/12) × ($3 billion/$16 billion) × $200
Total investment per vehicle	**$185.75**	

Table 6.8 presents the consolidated results for the three supply chain partners under the BTO scenario. The table shows that the partnering arrangement will result in a true win-win for all three partners. Furthermore, the customer is also paying less for the vehicle. The reduced price to the customer eventually should result in increased sales as well.

Compared with the current state values presented in Table 6.4, every one of the three members requires much less investment per

CASE STUDY

vehicle and will increase ROA by a significant amount. The profit per vehicle has increased for Reo Motors and for GTR, but it has gone down for Haddy Lane, Inc.

Table 6.8 Summary Information for Reo Motors' Supply Chain—BTO Scenario

Current state	Reo Motors	Grand Trunk Railroad	Haddy Lane, Inc.
Income per vehicle	$870	$33	$234
Investment per vehicle	$4,924	$186	$1,250
Pretax ROA	17.67 percent	17.77 percent	18.72 percent

If Haddy Lane, Inc., now will make less profit per vehicle, how can Reo Motors persuade the dealer to accept the BTO mode of operation? There are at least two ways by which Reo Motors can persuade the dealer.

The first option is to point out that Haddy Lane now will increase its ROA and also free up 75 percent of its capital investment. In fact, the dealer now carries practically no inventory of Reo Motors' vehicles. If the dealer can apply the capital to generate a return on investment of more than 8.28 percent—the ROA under the current state—then the dealer will come out ahead. What really matters is not the absolute measure of profit per vehicle but the profit generated per unit of investment.

If Haddy Lane is still reluctant to buy into the strategy, Reo Motors can consider sharing some of its increased profits with Haddy Lane. Reo Motors is expected to more than double its profit per vehicle and now stands to make an additional $470 per vehicle. Even if it shares half this amount with Haddy Lane, Reo Motors still will make additional profit from the BTO mode of operation.

Takeaways from the Reo Motors Case

The Reo Motors case provides a number of learning points. The case shows how the supply chain can improve sales revenue and Throughput (*T*) by:

▲ Better understanding customer needs
▲ Being quicker to adapt, market, and innovate, making the customer the focal point in the supply chain

The supply chain can increase asset efficiency—improve Investment (*I*)—by:

▲ Using information and better decision making to achieve increased *T* across capital assets
▲ Using Lean techniques to reduce delivery cycles, apply the RAP (postponement) principle, and reduce variation

The supply chain can reduce costs—reduce Operating Expense (*OE*)—and improve profit margins by:

▲ Streamlining process, product, and information flows
▲ Collaborating to remove non-value-added costs from the supply chain

The Reo Motors case also demonstrates that supply chain collaboration results in a win-win solution for all parties. In addition, the customer is paying less for the vehicle, and that should eventually result in increased sales revenue for all three partners.

In sum, the case shows that:

▲ Growing the pie is much easier if the members understand and work with the joint metrics that matter to them. An important metric for Reo Motors will be fill rate. For Grand Trunk Railroad, on-time delivery will be an important metric. The ROA should be an acceptable metric for all three members.
▲ ROA can be improved in several ways. Doing so will increase shareholder value.
▲ Most important, integration that increases the ROA of the entire supply chain is sustainable.

Conclusions

In the twenty-first century, the spotlight has shifted from competition between enterprises to competition between supply chains. Managers of these enterprises have to contend with the fact that some of the biggest challenges they now face relate to actions that must be coordinated jointly with their upstream and/or downstream partners. To promote effective supply chain partnering, enterprises should consider the following:

- Establish a long-term partnership with the supply base. Enterprises should move away from their traditional adversarial, arms-length relationship with suppliers toward more collaborative partnerships and strategic alliances.
- Enterprises should provide increased visibility to their suppliers on their production plans.
- Trust must be developed so that those sharing information do not have to be concerned about the data being used against them. The trust is nourished by working with few suppliers on long-term contracts.
- The burden of inventory should be shared in strategic locations to minimize the total cost of holding inventory. The 3PLs can use their information and resources to have the right product in the right quantity at the right place when wanted.
- The vision of supply chain performance metrics is no longer a distant dream owing to the advances in IT and the Internet. However, developing supply chain metrics requires the members in the supply chain to set aside concerns about sharing what is deemed to be confidential information.

To sharpen the focus on the metrics that really matter, it is worth asking the following questions for each metric considered in the order presented below:

- Will the metric help to sell more products profitably (increase T)?
- Will the metric help to reduce investments in resources (reduce I)?
- Will the metric help to reduce payments/expenses long term (reduce OE)?

Setting supply chain metrics with a systems perspective requires supply chain members to focus on win-win scenarios when developing partnerships. Compromise solutions do not work because, by definition, a compromise solution will leave some party feeling cheated.

The evaporating cloud:

▲ Is a technique aimed at conflict resolution that helps members in the supply chain arrive at win-win solutions

▲ Helps to find win-win solutions because it emphasizes that both parties involved in the conflict are trying to reach the same ultimate goal, even though they may have entirely different perspectives

▲ Can quickly focus ideas on problem areas requiring attention

▲ Helps to resolve conflicts quickly and get to a solution that is not a compromise but a real breakthrough

▲ Provides an un-common sense solution to conflict resolution. Instead of addressing the conflict, it focuses on the assumptions that lead to the conflict.

As demonstrated by the Reo Motors case, with the help of the evaporating cloud, it is possible to create win-win scenarios that benefit multiple members in the supply chain.

References

1. D. Meurer (2000), *Daze of Our Wives: A Semi-Helpful Guide to Marital Bliss*, Bethany House Publishers, Bloomington, MN.
2. Harrington and J. O'Connor (2009), "How Cisco Succeeds," *Supply Chain Management Review*, July–August 2009, pp. 10–17.
3. J. H. Hammond (1994), "Barilla SpA (A)," Harvard Business School Case 9-694-046, 1994.
4. E. M. Goldratt (1989), *The Haystack Syndrome: Sifting Information Out of the Data Ocean*, North River Press, Great Barrington, MA.

CHAPTER 7

Streamlining the Value Stream

Unlike Theory of Contraints, which owes its origin to one individual, Eli Goldratt, Lean evolved through the collective effort of a number of individuals over the years. A widely held notion is that the principles and concepts of Lean originated from Japan. What is probably not as widely known is that a number of these principles and concepts were developed originally in the United States. It is therefore instructive to begin this chapter with a brief voyage back in time to discover the origins of Lean. In addition to underscoring the fact that a number of the principles of Lean originated from the U.S. automobile industry, the voyage will identify potential stumbling blocks that an enterprise might encounter as it embarks on its own Lean journey.

From Craft Production to Mass Production to Lean Production

A little known fact is that the first company formed exclusively to build automobiles was a French enterprise, Panhard et Levassor, which also introduced the first four-cylinder gasoline engine. In 1889, Rene Panhard and Emil Levassor, partners in a woodworking machinery business, obtained a license from Daimler to build engines for automobiles.* Panhard and Levassor built the first car in 1890. Not seeing a future in this business, they granted Armand Peugeot the right to use Daimler engines in self-propelled vehicles.

---

*Benz in 1885 and Daimler in 1887 produced the first gasoline automobiles. However, they were inventors who experimented with automobile designs to test their engines. They licensed patents and sold engines to automobile manufacturers before becoming full-fledged manufacturers in their own right.

Peugeot made 5 cars in 1891 and 29 cars in 1892. These cars were built using the *craft production technique*, and no two cars were alike. By 1905, fewer than 15 years after Panhard and Levassor built their first car, hundreds of enterprises in Europe and the United States were producing cars in small volumes using craft production techniques. Craft production techniques for automobiles, however, were heading for extinction owing to the pioneering efforts of the "father of mass production" Henry Ford.

Henry Ford and the Origin of Mass Production

Henry Ford was not the first mass producer in the United States. This title probably belonged to Ransom E. Olds, after whom both the Oldsmobile and REO brands were named. However, Ford changed the way the world perceived manufacturing by introducing the concepts of flow and throughput velocity. To create flow, Ford instituted the moving assembly line in the Highland Park plant that built the Model T automobile.[1] The moving assembly line reduced assembly time of automobiles from 12 worker-hours down to about 1½ worker-hours in 1914. For the first time in history, one plant was building 1,000 cars a day.

Henry Ford's goal was to reduce waste in any form—not just within the factory walls. He reduced waste and leveraged flow across the entire supply chain. In his book, *Today and Tomorrow*, he claimed, "Our production cycle is about 81 hours from the mine to the finished machine in the freight car, or 3 days and 9 hours instead of the 14 days we used to think was record-breaking."

Ford's relentless attention to removing waste from every step in the process slashed production costs. As those costs fell, he passed on some savings to customers. His innovations led to a sharp drop in the price of the automobile from $1,000 down to $260. The sharp increases in productivity that accompanied these innovations kept inflationary pressures down and led to periods of "benign deflation."[2]

Not all of Henry Ford's contributions to management were beneficial. He equated throughput velocity with product uniformity by insisting on a standard model with a single color.* Henry Ford's managerial style, combined

---

*Henry Ford's famous quote, "The customer can have any color so long as it is black," is believed to have a twofold reason: the fact that it reduced setups and also the notion that black paint dried faster and thereby allowed Ford to increase throughput velocity.

with his strategy to produce only a single model, resulted in the Ford Motor Company losing market share to General Motors between the 1920s and World War II.

Under the leadership of Alfred P. Sloan, General Motors took advantage of a perceptible shift in the buying patterns of the American consumer. While Ford continued to produce the same model every year, GM's Chevrolet division introduced an annual model change. In 1921, Ford had 55 percent of the U.S. market, but by 1927 its market share was under 15 percent.

Despite his shortcomings, Henry Ford's contribution to manufacturing cannot be denied. In addition to making a number of contributions to mass production, he also inspired many of the concepts and tools used in the Toyota Production System.

The Toyota Production System

The Toyota Production System (TPS) owes its origins to two individuals, Kiichiro Toyoda and Taiichi Ohno, although the latter is more widely acknowledged as the creator of TPS. Inspired by Henry Ford's book, *Today and Tomorrow*, Kiichiro Toyoda had formulated, as early as 1936, a clear mental picture of the production system he wanted. The basic idea was to put in place a pull system—to initiate a production run only when it was needed rather than to produce in anticipation of a demand. Toyoda applied this idea in the automobile department he had started within his father's enterprise, the Toyoda Automatic Loom Works. Slips of paper were passed around to specify the number of parts to be processed that day. This was the origin of the *kanban* method of production, and it provided the basis for the JIT production management system.

In 1950, Kiichiro Toyoda's cousin, Eiji Toyoda, toured Ford Motor Company. An important process he learned during the trip was the Ford Motor Company suggestion system. Eiji Toyoda instituted the concept, and it is considered to be one of the major building blocks of continuous improvement (*kaizen*). On his return to Japan, he sought the help of Taiichi Ohno to produce cars in small batches more efficiently than the big U.S. enterprises were able to.

Ohno was an ardent admirer of Ford and credits his contributions to TPS to two main concepts.[3] The first concept, taken from Henry Ford's book *Today and Tomorrow*, was the moving assembly line that provided the basis for the production and assembly system used in TPS. The second concept was inspired by a supermarket operation that Ohno and his team observed during a visit to the United States in 1956. The team observed how the supermarket operation replaced products on the shelves as and when customers purchased them. Ohno set up a pull system in which each production process became a supermarket for the succeeding process. Each process would produce to replenish only the items that the downstream process had used.

Like Ford, Ohno emphasized waste reduction. Ohno's contention was that waste is prevalent in many instances, and it is not eliminated because people learn to live with it or they work around it. Ohno, however, modified Ford's ideas to reflect modern market demands. Ford had offered automobiles to his customers in only one color to reduce changeover times between paint colors. Subsequent efforts to introduce product variety into the U.S. automobile industry were hampered by those large changeover times. This apparent inflexibility had become a corporate millstone for U.S. automakers.

The Japanese refused to accept changeover times as a constraint. Instead, they focused relentlessly on reducing changeover times. By significantly reducing changeover times, they were able to provide product variety without having to produce in large lots. As noted by Shingo, "The Toyota production system is the antithesis of large-lot production, *not* mass production."[4]

The U.S. Response

The Japanese automakers were now more competitive against the U.S. and other foreign automakers both in quality and in cost. When the Arab-Israeli war in 1973 and the accompanying oil price increases caused U.S. consumers to purchase smaller, more-fuel-efficient cars, the U.S. automakers were taken by surprise and started to study the Japanese production methods in more detail.

The U.S. automakers studied the Toyota Production System and identified a number of TPS tools that they believed could be transplanted into their factories. In their enthusiasm to catch up with the Japanese competition, they attempted to implement JIT tools within a very short time frame and in a piecemeal fashion.

The U.S. automakers first tried to drastically reduce their inventory of automobile components. At the same time, the automakers asked suppliers to deliver components just when they were needed. However, they did not first ensure that their own internal processes were reliable. Because their internal processes were unreliable, the automakers were unable to give suppliers clear visibility on their production schedules.

Left in the dark about when the next delivery request would come, suppliers built up finished goods inventory so as to better respond to requests for JIT supplies. Invariably, the suppliers ended up building the wrong products. Furthermore, relationships with the suppliers at that time were (and in too many cases, still are) adversarial. There were no long-term contracts, and components generally were sourced from multiple vendors, with vendor selection based mainly on price. These factors made the position of suppliers even more tenuous.

Lessons Learned

This brief journey back in time shows that a number of TPS elements, such as *kaizen*, flow, and the focus on eliminating waste, were inspired by Henry Ford. At the same time, the journey also reveals the need for enterprises to avoid adopting tools and techniques in a piecemeal manner but instead to adopt a systems approach. Without a complete understanding of the core concepts and principles of Lean, there is considerable potential for creating more harm than good with piecemeal implementations.

For example, JIT emphasizes working with *kanbans* and minimal inventories, but just trying to reduce inventories without considering other factors can have serious consequences because the system is now much more vulnerable to disruptions.

The U.S. manufacturers probably had misunderstood the intended meaning of JIT. The JIT philosophy articulated by Kiichiro Toyoda merely stated that components for an automobile should not be produced before they were needed but instead should be made just in time using pull signals. The implication was that every step in the supply chain had to work in harmony to produce products when they were needed, not a single moment before. This philosophy never intended, for example, to have the supplier maintain a stock of finished goods inventory to supply material just in time.

TPS was built on partnering arrangements that provided mutual benefits for both Toyota and its suppliers. Not only were the suppliers given ample visibility on Toyota's assembly schedules, but these schedules were adhered to fairly stringently. This made it easier for the suppliers to plan their own production schedules accordingly and deliver supplies in a timely manner without having to hold a large inventory of finished goods.

Even as attempts are made to reduce inventory levels, other major elements that should be in place are reliable processes, preventive maintenance systems, cross-trained workers, setup reduction, and reliable suppliers. If these elements are not already present in a factory, then putting them in place takes time—it cannot happen overnight. Toyota spent more than 20 years perfecting the system before the U.S. automakers observed TPS in action.

Figure 7.1 uses a "river and rocks" analogy that relates the water level to the inventory level in a facility. A higher water level hides potential blemishes in the process, such as unreliable suppliers, scrap loss, and machine breakdowns. These problems surface as the water (inventory) level is lowered, forcing management to correct the defects. The key is to resist the temptation to reduce the inventory level too quickly. Rather, the idea is to lower the inventory level a little, break apart the newly exposed rocks (obstacles), and then lower the inventory level once again.

In 1996, the book, *Lean Thinking*, by Womack and Jones[5] reiterated the core concepts of TPS and presented five steps for Lean: (1) understanding

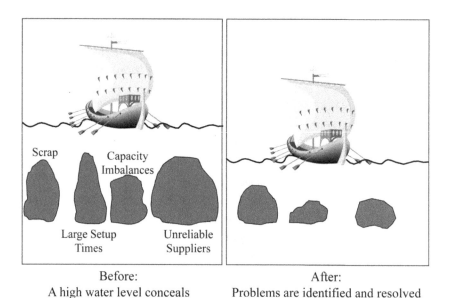

Before:
A high water level conceals
many underlying problems

After:
Problems are identified and resolved
when the water level is lowered

Figure 7.1 Inventory hides defects.

customer value, (2) value-stream mapping, (3) creating flow, (4) pull, and (5) the pursuit of perfection. Womack and Jones emphasized that the goal of Lean is to eliminate *muda*, or waste—any activity that absorbs resources but creates no value. Implicit in this message was the understanding that the freed resources could be applied productively elsewhere.

Lean: A Growth Strategy

Simply put, Lean is a *growth strategy*, a strategy aimed at uncovering additional capacity that could be deployed for further growth. Another benefit of Lean stems from the money that enterprises do not have to spend now—by not having to build new plants, or not having to invest in a new warehouse. The ultimate goal of Lean is to deliver products that the customer values as quickly as possible.

Enterprises often focus on inventory reduction because it reduces inventory carrying costs. However, there are three other reasons for inventory reduction that are more important—reasons that are more customer-focused:

▲ Large finished goods inventories of certain products suggest that the enterprise has built the wrong kind of products, perhaps because it built products in large batches to exploit scale economies.
▲ Reduction in inventory levels reduce lead times,* enabling the enterprise to ship the product to the customer faster. If the enterprise has two weeks of WIP inventory on the shop floor, then a new order processed using the first-come-first-served principle will take at least two weeks to complete. With reduced inventory levels, the enterprise is also more responsive to changing customer preferences.
▲ Finally, reducing inventory exposes problems such as poor quality, unreliable suppliers, scrap, and large changeover times (see Figure 7.1).

Figure 7.1 also conveys two other important messages:

▲ For the boat to move faster, all oarsmen should row at the same time and at the same pace—this is the concept of *Flow Balance*. Balancing the flow implies that all processes should work at the same rate. There is

---
*Little's Law, presented in Chapter 1, states that average work-in-progress (WIP) = average lead time × throughput.

no point in having some of the resources work faster than the others because that invariably will pile up inventory in front of the slower processes.

▲ The boat will move faster if there is no turbulence. In a production context, this situation is analogous to the movement of products in a system with low variation in the process.

These two messages are particularly important for enterprises that produce products in anticipation of future demand. When enterprises use forecasts to drive their production schedules, they follow a push mode of operation. Forecasting methods impede flow because these methods are never 100 percent accurate. For example, if a poor forecast results in raw materials not being available when the customer demands a product, there is a mismatch between the rates of demand and delivery. To address such possible mismatches in flow, enterprises working with push systems rely on an inventory of finished goods to buffer against variation in customer demand.

Push systems thus schedule production and let inventory absorb variation. As a result, enterprises that work with push systems commit their resources to often-unneeded products and are often unable to react quickly to a firm customer order.

In contrast, a *pull* system waits for a demand signal before committing resources to make products. A pull system will have less variation in the system and lower inventories than a comparable push system owing to the simple fact that pull systems place a limit on inventories and use capacity to absorb demand variation. The *kanban* system, which is presented in more detail later in this chapter, is a pull system. Other methods for effecting pull are presented in Chapter 8.

Although it is desirable to use pull systems wherever possible, enterprises still have to anticipate customer demands—they must rely on forecasts. The key is to resist the temptation to *execute* the production schedule based on a forecast. Rather, the idea is to use demand forecasts to *plan* production and use pull signals based on true customer demand to *schedule* production. In addition, a system that responds to pull signals inherently has less variation than a system that pushes products through the supply chain. The eleventh Lean Supply Chain Principle captures this discussion:

Lean Supply Chain Principle 11

Use forecasts to plan and pull to execute. A system that reacts to pull signals will have less variation than a comparable system that adopts a push mode of operation.

Taiichi Ohno is reputed to have said that inventory is the root of all evil. He probably should have stated that "variation is the root of all evil" because variation is the root cause for such inventory buildup. Variation exists in two forms—*system variation* and *process variation*. System variation is determined by how the supply chain is structured. In particular, a supply chain that reacts to pull signals will experience less system variation than a comparable push system, as will be explained in more detail in Chapter 8.

Process variation results from a wide variety of causes: variation in quality, variation in processing capability, equipment breakdown, or missed supplies. Process variation typically is addressed by the *Six Sigma* methodology. Many enterprises have included the Six Sigma methodology in their Lean efforts to develop Lean Six Sigma programs. The synergies between TOC, Lean, and Six Sigma present a powerful combination. Figure 7.2 shows how these three methodologies can work together.

This figure presents TOC and Lean as prescriptive methodologies; they set the direction for the enterprise, defining the path from the as-is (current) state to the to-be (future) state. Six Sigma concepts and tools help to reduce the variation at specific process steps. Six Sigma concepts are not discussed

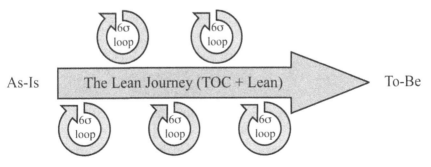

Figure 7.2 Synergies between TOC, Lean, and Six Sigma.

in this book, but Chapter 8 discusses how to exploit synergies between TOC and Lean to enhance flow in the supply chain. The twelfth Lean Supply Chain Principle summarizes this discussion:

Lean Supply Chain Principle 12

Reduce variation in the system. Reduced variation allows the supply chain to operate with higher throughput, lower investment, and lower operating expense.

Lean Supply Chain Principle 12 builds on the previous Lean Supply Chain Principle to convey how Lean and Six Sigma can help to improve on the three TOC measures T, I, and OE. In particular, the second Lean step prescribed by Womack and Jones, value-stream mapping, presents an opportunity for exploiting the synergy among TOC, Lean, and Six Sigma.

Value-Stream Mapping

The *value-stream map* typically is the starting point for an enterprise embarking on the Lean journey. A value-stream map illustrates the flow of physical goods and information in the enterprise and highlights areas in the enterprise that need more attention. *Value stream* is a rather generic term that can represent the processes that add value within an enterprise, or it can represent key process steps across the supply chain.

There is a considerable amount of literature available on value-stream mapping. A typical practice is to first select a product family for which the value stream should be mapped. The choice of product family is often based simply on the products bought by the enterprise's largest or most important customer. The next step is to draw a value-stream map of the current state— the *as-is map*.

Figure 7.3 shows the as-is map for an enterprise that produces brake pads for the automobile industry. The value stream identifies the flow of physical goods from left to right, as shown in the figure, starting with the key supplier of raw materials for brake pads identified on the top-left corner of

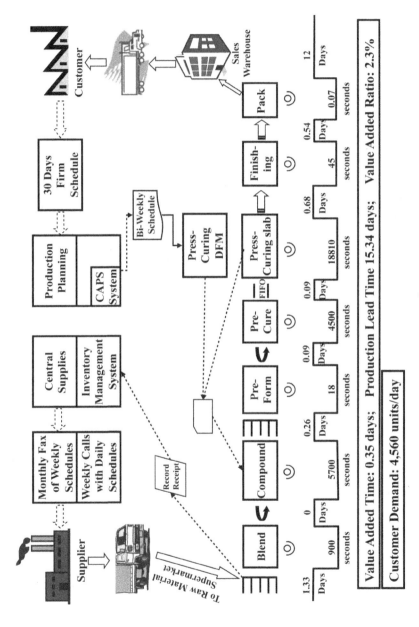

Figure 7.3 As-is value-stream map.

Blend	Compound	Pre-Form	Pre-Cure	Press-Curing slab	Finishing	Pack			

Value Added Time: 0.35 days; Production Lead Time 15.34 days; Value Added Ratio: 2.3%

Customer Demand: 4,560 units/day

Customer

30 Days Firm Schedule

Production Planning

CAPS System

Bi-Weekly Schedule

Press-Curing DFM

Central Supplies

Inventory Management System

Monthly Fax of Weekly Schedules

Weekly Calls with Daily Schedules

Supplier

Record Receipt

To Raw Material Supermarket

Sales Warehouse

FIFO

1.33 Days — 900 seconds
0 Days — 5700 seconds
0.26 Days — 18 seconds
0.09 Days — 4500 seconds
0.09 Days — 18810 seconds
0.68 Days — 45 seconds
0.54 Days — 0.07 seconds
12 Days

234 I Chapter 7 Streamlining the Value Stream

the map. The physical flow ends with the delivery of finished brake pads to the finished goods warehouse.

The as-is map also shows the information flows from the customer to the enterprise and from the enterprise to the supplier. The information flows from right to left in the map.

The value-stream map captures other information, such as the time line for the product flow, the value-added and non-value-added activities, and the *value-added ratio*. The value-added ratio is obtained by adding up the time required to complete all the value-added activities and dividing the result by the lead time, which is the total time taken to complete all these activities, including the time spent on non-value-added activities. The brake pad enterprise in Figure 7.3 operates 24 hours, or 86,400 seconds, every day. The value-added ratio is typically expressed as a percentage.

The value-stream mapping exercise aims at uncovering three possible forms of waste. These three forms of waste are specified by three Japanese words, *muda*, *mura*, and *muri*, which translate to "wastefulness," "unevenness," and "overburdening," respectively. The term *muda* is fairly self-explanatory; it represents any form of activity that does not add value to the product or service. Many Lean practitioners in the Western world only refer to *muda* when they discuss waste elimination. However, the other two forms of waste, *mura* and *muri*, usually are more insidious and should be tackled first.

Mura, or unevenness, in any form represents a waste, whether it is unevenness in demand, unevenness in production schedules, or unevenness in quality. With unevenness in demand, the supply chain is more prone to the bullwhip effect. Unevenness in quality may create similar ripple effects through the supply chain. Unevenness in production schedules may well be the result of a batch production policy that attempts to exploit scale economies, or it could be the supply chain's efforts to cope with uneven demand. Regardless of how the uneven production schedule is generated, the result is an uneven loading on resources, which causes some of these resources to work at full speed for a while, only to experience subsequent periods of idle time. Clearly, the Six Sigma methodology can be applied to address *mura*.

Muri, or overburdening of resources, represents another significant source of waste in Lean because these overburdened resources typically work at full speed while the other resources stand idle. Furthermore, operating these resources at full speed often results in missed deliveries or needless errors.

After the as-is map is complete, key structural elements are examined in detail to identify how they should be managed. From an operational point of view, there are several key areas of concern in any product flow. These include:

▲ *Segments of the value stream that have large flow times.* Lead-time reduction provides a vital competitive edge, so the segments that are unable to respond quickly to changes must be scrutinized and managed carefully.

▲ *Any segment or path that contains physical constraints in the form of either material constraints or capacity constraints.* Effective management of the value stream is impossible without knowing where the constraints are and how they influence the performance of the value stream as a whole.

▲ *Points where there is a high degree of resource sharing.* Resource contention arises when the same resource is required to process a variety of products and any mismanagement of these resources can result in missed deliveries.

▲ *Points where common materials are used by or diverge into different product streams.* An example is the steel-making process in an integrated steel mill, where pig iron is converted into different alloy steels. Misallocations at these points of divergence cannot be reversed. Allocating materials to the wrong product stream could result in unnecessary inventory and could also result in an urgent shortage of the product that should have been produced instead.

▲ *Points where multiple materials must come together.* These are assembly points. Since the assembly process requires all required materials to be available, the logistical challenge of ensuring timely arrival of all the different materials required is significant.

▲ *Points of excessive variation.*

It is usually hard to determine the degree of detail that is useful for a value-stream map. The manager of an enterprise is interested mainly in the immediate linkages the enterprise has with its upstream and downstream partners, so broadening the map to include enterprises beyond these enterprises can result in loss of detail. Yet, if the flow can be mapped to second-tier suppliers and the customer's customer, it may be easier to visualize the kinds of systems that must be in place to improve customer service.

A comprehensive value-stream map highlights the weakest links and the points in the value stream that have high lead times. The map can help identify where resources are insufficient to manage supplier relationships, whether there is a proliferation of suppliers, or whether the size of the supply chain facilitates good supplier development strategies.

The next step is to determine the sources of waste that must be addressed first. Based on this determination, a map of the desired end state, otherwise referred to as the *to-be map*, is drawn next. Figure 7.4 shows the to-be map for the brake pad producer.

The value-stream map should be revisited periodically. Lean is a journey that never ends, and the pursuit of perfection will continue to reveal *muda, mura,* and *muri.* The next section presents the tools and techniques used by Lean to help the enterprise reach the desired end state prescribed by the to-be map.

The Tools and Techniques of Lean

The Lean tools presented here are applied to the process steps identified by the value-stream maps. The important tools and techniques used by Lean to promote flow are:

- ▲ 5-*S*
- ▲ Flowcharts
- ▲ *Takt* time
- ▲ Average labor content and minimum manning
- ▲ Mixed-model scheduling and small-batch production
- ▲ One-piece flow
- ▲ Cellular layout
- ▲ Standard work
- ▲ Pull replenishment
- ▲ Point-of-use material storage
- ▲ Mistake-proofing and method sheets
- ▲ Total Productive Maintenance

Although these Lean tools were originally developed for manufacturing enterprises, many service enterprises find these tools very useful. Therefore, as these tools are discussed, think about how they apply in a service setting. For example, the final product might be a piece of paper that can reach its

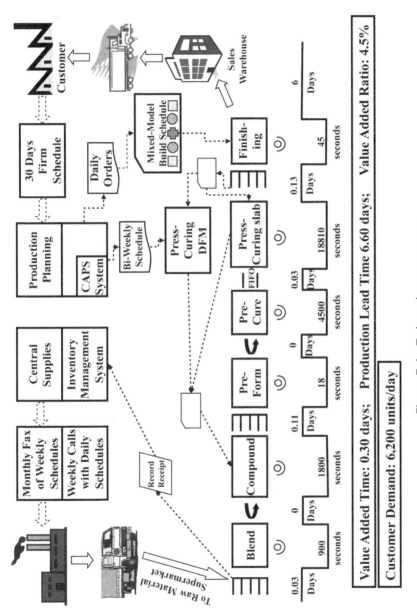

Value Added Time: 0.30 days;   Production Lead Time 6.60 days;   Value Added Ratio: 4.5%

Customer Demand: 6,200 units/day

Figure 7.4   To-be value-stream map.

destination more quickly. How often has an operator sat idle waiting for the next order to present itself? How often has a service delivery been delayed, waiting for the paperwork to be completed?

5-S

The term 5-S is used to denote a systematic process for organizing the workplace based on five simple, yet powerful activities, each of them represented by a Japanese word that begins with an S: *Seiri* ("tidiness"), *Seiton* ("organization"), *Seiso* ("cleanliness"), *Seiketsu* ("neatness"), and *Shitsuke* ("discipline") (Figure 7.5). There are five corresponding English words beginning with the letter S that convey nearly the same intended meaning. Some enterprises add a sixth S for *Safety*.

The first step, *Seiri*, refers to discarding unnecessary items. Every item in the work area is classified as either necessary, unnecessary, or red tag. A red tag indicates that it is unclear whether or not the item is needed, and such items are put up for auction; they are discarded if no one bids on them as necessary items.

The second step, *Seiton*, organizes items so that they can be picked up easily for use. The words *Seiri* and *Seiton* are often used in combination as *Seiri-Seiton* because there is not much difference in their meanings. In any case, the second step is intended to create storage systems and provide visual information about what is stored and how much should be stored in a given spot. Convenient locations are created for tools and devices used in the work

Japanese	Definition	English	Example
Seiri	Tidiness	Sorting	Throw Away Rubbish
Seiton	Organization	Storing	30-Sec. Doc. Retrieval
Seiso	Cleanliness	Sanitizing	Individual Responsibility
Seiketsu	Neatness	Standardizing	Clear Written Instructions
Shitsuke	Discipline	Sustaining	Do 5-S Activities Daily

Figure 7.5 The five S's and their definitions.

area. Tools are typically hung on boards with a silhouette (*shadow box*) of the tool painted on the board where the tool is to be hung. Drawers sometimes are filled with Styrofoam with cutouts of the items stored in the drawers.

The third step, *Seiso*, implies taking pride in a workplace that is well organized. This step goes beyond simply making the area more pleasant by sweeping the floor and cleaning up leaks and spills. Aside from making the area more conducive to work in, the *Seiso* step provides other practical benefits: a clean machine enables the discovery of oil leaks before a catastrophic equipment failure, and an aisle kept clean and free of any oil spills minimizes the chances of an accident.

The fourth step, *Seiketsu*, is the basis for standardization. Literally, *Seiketsu* refers to a condition where there are no smears, stains, or blemishes. This step covers both personal and environmental cleanliness, prescribing what the normal condition should be, as well as how an abnormal condition should be corrected. Visual management is an important ingredient of *Seiketsu*. Color-coding and standardization of colors are used for easier visual identification of problems. Personnel are trained to detect such problems using one or more of their five senses and to correct them immediately.

The final step, *Shitsuke*, relates to building discipline that will sustain the first four steps. Literally, *Shitsuke* refers to making a person maintain a rule or order through training. The rationale is that it is often easier to clean up an area than it is to keep it clean, so an integral part of a 5-S program should be a system for maintaining the first four S's. The Shitsuke step commits to maintaining orderliness and practicing the first four S's continually, and it requires full support from top management. Initially, top management might have to provide incentives to have this step performed on a regular basis. Once the inertia is overcome, the process becomes self-sustaining.

The 5-S program improves safety, work efficiency, and productivity and gives employees a sense of ownership. These activities ensure a clean and orderly working environment. Employees become aware of their working environment and the condition of the tools and machinery they use.

In many enterprises, the benefits of a 5-S program are so dramatic that there is a real danger that the enterprise may step away from a full-blown Lean implementation at this stage, thinking that its mission is complete. It therefore must be emphasized that the 5-S program is just the starting point in the Lean journey. It also must be emphasized that the 5-S program may actually hinder the Lean journey unless the vital fifth step (*Shitsuke*) is strictly followed.

Flowcharts

In a work environment, it is often easy to miss the simple flow of a process from one step to the next. The flowchart is a powerful visual tool to describe practically any process, be it a manufacturing process or a service process. Flowcharts enable quick identification of process steps that should be eliminated. Identifying and eliminating or at least reducing a non-value-added activity is key to streamlining a process.

There are numerous flowcharting methods available to capture value-added and non-value-added activities. One of them is a *process flowchart* that captures the logical sequence of activities involved in delivering the product. The process flowchart is usually used in conjunction with a *spaghetti diagram* that describes the physical movement of products through the plant or office.

A process flowchart typically uses standard symbols, as shown in Figure 7.6, to categorize the activities. The value-added activities are color-coded green, and the non-value-added activities are typically color-coded yellow.

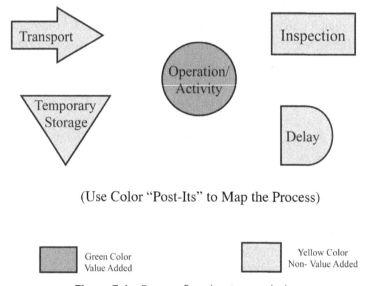

(Use Color "Post-Its" to Map the Process)

Green Color
Value Added

Yellow Color
Non- Value Added

Figure 7.6   Process flowcharting symbols.

The process flowchart also captures the time required to complete the activities.

Deciding what is a value-added activity and what is a non-value-added activity can sometimes be contentious. Does the marketing function add value? Does the logistics function add value? If so, which logistics activities are value-added? One way out of the contention is to define a value-adding activity as an activity that either actually transforms the product or as an activity that the customer would be willing to pay for it to happen.

Figure 7.7 presents a process flowchart for a mortgage loan application. In this figure, the value-added ratio is the ratio of the actual value-added work expressed in time units divided by the elapsed time for the process to complete. The summary data in the figure presents the value-added ratio as 1.8 percent, a remarkably low number, which is, unfortunately, all too typical of the value-added ratio for a majority of processes in the real world. The low value-added ratio highlights the huge opportunities for Lean efforts to remove waste. It is difficult to specify what the value-added ratio should be because it depends on the industry although a ratio of 10 percent sometimes has been specified as a goal for some mass-production industries.

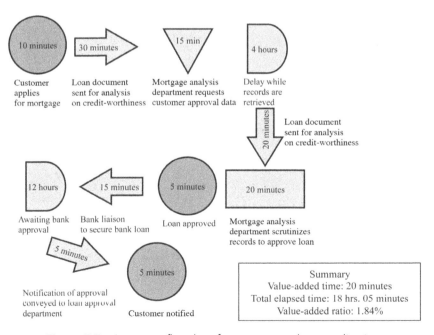

Figure 7.7 A process flowchart for a mortgage loan application.

The value-added ratio formula, however, does not consider the actual effort expended in delivering the product. It is not uncommon for some steps, value-added or otherwise, to involve multiple employees. In such situations, a more meaningful value-added ratio would have the total person-hours of value-added effort required to produce one unit in the numerator and the sum total of all the person-hours employed by the enterprise to produce one unit in the denominator.

The spaghetti diagram is used to represent the distance traveled by the product. Figure 7.8 shows a spaghetti diagram for the same mortgage loan application process. The spaghetti diagram, in conjunction with the process flowchart, can give the analyst valuable information for streamlining the process. While the process flowchart reveals the non-value-added activities, the spaghetti diagram highlights the extent of travel, including any backtracking the product may undergo, suggesting how the process could be streamlined through a better process layout.

The process flowchart preferably should be drawn after the 5-S program is in place; otherwise, the lack of attention to simple housekeeping activities may obfuscate some of the non-value-added activities on which the enterprise needs to focus. For example, operators may be taking more time to change tooling simply because they cannot locate the tools, and the extra time may be reflected in time standards set for tool changeovers.

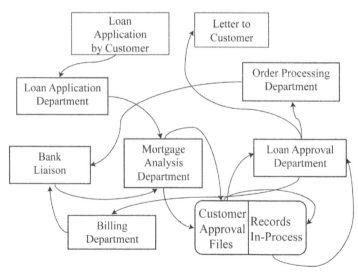

Figure 7.8 The spaghetti diagram for a mortgage loan application.

Takt *Time*

If someone compiled a dictionary of terms used in Lean, they would notice the slew of Japanese words in the compilation. *Takt*, however, is a German word for a musical meter, and this word has found a place in the Lean lexicon, even in Japan.

When German aerospace engineers helped Japan build aircrafts during the 1930s, they used the word *takt* to present an analogy of a conductor waving his baton to set the rhythm for the entire orchestra. After World War II, Toyota adopted this word and the accompanying concept as the basis for linking its production capacity to customer demand in the Toyota Production System. Customer demand became the cadence that dictated the pace of operations on the shop floor.

How do enterprises apply *takt* time? First, *takt* time represents the customer demand and it is calculated as follows:

Takt time = available time per period ÷ demand per period

The duration of the period may be minutes, hours, days, or weeks so long as the same unit of time is used in both the numerator and the denominator. To illustrate the concept, consider a simple example of an enterprise working on a single product.

Dadford & Sons, Inc.

An insurance agency, Dadford & Sons, Inc., processes applications for property insurance. Processing an application involves four steps:

1. Data gathering and data entry (*distribution*)
2. Risk analysis (*underwriting*)
3. Computing the premium (*rating*)
4. Policy writing

Customer demand for this product is 20 policies per day. Dadford & Sons operates a single shift that is eight hours long.

The first step in calculating *takt* time is to determine the available time per shift. Essential breaks for lunch and bio breaks typically are deducted from the shift duration to arrive at an available time of, say, 400 minutes each day. *Takt* time then is 400 ÷ 20 = 20 minutes per application, indicating that the enterprise must process one policy every 20 minutes. (If the enterprise operates two shifts each day, the available time per day is 800 minutes, and the *takt* time is 800 ÷ 20 = 40 minutes per unit.)

Since the customer demand is one unit every 20 minutes, the enterprise should match its internal resources to meet this demand. Suppose that the average times to process the four steps (the *cycle times*) are 14, 22, 6, and 12 minutes, respectively, and that an operator is dedicated to each of the four steps. Figure 7.9 presents a *load chart*, a chart that depicts how these operators are loaded.

One of the main uses of the *takt* time calculation is to match the resource capacities with external demand. The load chart helps to determine whether the work is assigned equitably and whether anyone is overloaded. In Figure 7.9a, it is clear that the operator in charge of underwriting is overloaded beyond the *takt* time. This operator is presumably either working overtime or working faster than called for, creating opportunities for errors. At the same time, the load chart helps to determine whether there is slack in the system. In Figure 7.9a, it is apparent that operators 1, 3, and 4 are underutilized.

What options do Dadford & Sons have at this stage? If some of the underwriting work is reallocated to the operator of the distribution activity, then the operator of the underwriting activity now could get his work done within *takt* time. Additionally, the workload for operators 3 and 4 could be combined and assigned to one operator. Figure 7.9b shows the scenario after

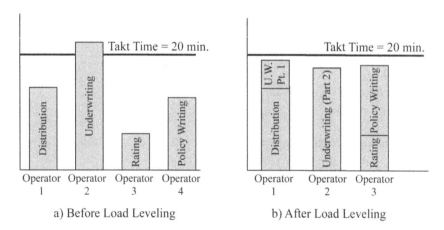

a) Before Load Leveling   b) After Load Leveling

Figure 7.9 Load chart for Dadford & Sons, Inc.

the workload is balanced by shifting five minutes of work from operator 2 to operator 1. The loads on the three operators now are 19, 17, and 18 minutes, respectively.

This discussion assumes that the time to perform each activity is accurate, an assumption that must be validated quite early in this decision process, perhaps through some time studies. Once this issue is resolved, the next step is to determine how the individual operators should be loaded.

If operators are underutilized, there is a likelihood that the work expands to fill the time available, resulting in inefficiencies. On the other hand, loading each operator close to 100 percent may lead to errors, particularly if the workload is highly variable with prolonged periods where the operator is loaded beyond capacity. As Lean Supply Chain Principle 8 indicates, variation ideally is buffered with capacity, not inventory. Loading operators close to 100 percent leaves no room for accommodating increased customer demand without reallocating resources.

Note that the *takt* time goes *down* when demand increases. If the demand at Dadford & Sons increases by 10 percent, to 22 policies per day, then the *takt* time goes down to 18 minutes per job, and operator 1 becomes overloaded. Nevertheless, in some situations, it is advisable to keep operators loaded close to 100 percent because that may motivate them to find creative ways of managing the workload so that the resulting cycle time is well within the allotted *takt* time.

The Dadford & Sons example used task times that were very discrete. If it were possible to subdivide tasks even more finely, it would be possible to load each operator as close to *takt* time as desired. If such a fine division of tasks were possible, what would be the best way to load each operator? In the Dadford & Sons example, the total workload is (19 + 17 + 18) = 54 minutes, so tasks could be allocated to give each operator a cycle time of 18 minutes. However, that would uniformly underutilize each operator.

A better alternative may be to have the first operator loaded with tasks that add up to the *takt* time of 20 minutes, leaving the other two operators loaded only up to 17 minutes each. Since the load on the second and third operators is less than the *takt* time, conceivably they could help operator 1 if she falls behind schedule. Chapter 8 will discuss why it is often preferable to have only one resource in the system loaded close to capacity.

Pacing each operator to *takt* time automatically limits overproduction, a primary cause of inventory buildups. Limiting overproduction also stabilizes the system, preventing the frequent stops and starts that inhibit a smooth flow. When a team of operators paces work according to *takt* time, there is a heightened awareness of the output rates and potential problems that detract from achieving the desired output rate. Operators obtain immediate feedback if they miss *takt* time on a given cycle and make corrections accordingly. If feedback is provided only after many cycles, the window of opportunity to correct errors may have passed.

At the same time, *takt* time should be applied judiciously. This concept is more applicable in a *flow shop* that processes a set of products with relatively predictable demand that does not fluctuate much. *Takt* time may not be very relevant in a job-shop environment, but calculating *takt* time is still useful because it helps to determine the number of operators that must be assigned to a process.

Recalibrating *Takt* Time

How often should the *takt* time change? This depends on the industry. If *takt* time decreases for a manufacturing cell, it is not simply a matter of reallocating work to different operators. There might be equipment-related issues. Adjusting *takt* time daily could cause chaos. At the same time, if the enterprise is not flexible enough to react quickly, this may result in missed opportunities to fill demand or, conversely, lead to inventory buildups.

The key is to distinguish between noise and actual trends. A *run test* could be applied to determine when the *takt* time should be changed. Consider the sequence of demands presented in Figure 7.10. The planned production rate (or *takt* time) could be reevaluated if the demand rate exceeds the set production rate for, say, five consecutive days, as shown in the figure.

Toyota evaluates the customer demand at 10-day intervals and resets its production rate and the corresponding *takt* time as necessary. If the demand outpaces the set production rate, Toyota may resort to overtime because changing the production rate on an automobile assembly line can be a major undertaking. On the other hand, a small manufacturing cell may be able to change its production rate or *takt* time weekly or even daily and adjust the number of operators accordingly.

Takt time is one of the most misunderstood concepts of Lean. I have been to several enterprises where management prominently announces the *takt* time to be, say, "100 pieces per hour." *Takt* time is time per piece, not

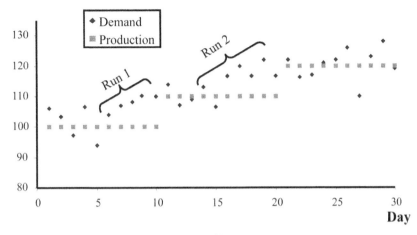

Figure 7.10   Recalibrating *takt* time.

pieces per time. It is also not uncommon for managers to state that their machines have a *takt* time of five minutes. But *takt* time is a measure of external demand; it has nothing to do with machine capacity.

Sometimes *takt* time also has been confused with lead time or flow time. Quite often this is so because enterprises simply go through the motions and implement Lean piecemeal without fully understanding what they are doing. The primary purpose of *takt* time is to match external demand with internal capacity. To sum up the discussion on *takt* time:

▲ *Takt* time is used to represent the customer demand. It is expressed in terms of the time available to make one unit to keep pace with customer demand.

▲ The primary purpose of calculating *takt* time is to match external demand with internal capacity.

▲ *Takt* time should be adjusted only when it is clearly evident that customer demand has changed. Adjusting *takt* time too often to respond to small fluctuations could result in chaos. The key is to distinguish between noise and a trend.

So far the discussion on *takt* time has been based on a single product. The *takt* time calculation does not change when there are multiple products, but the calculations on operator loading are a little more involved. The calculations are demonstrated by expanding on the Dadford & Sons example.

Dadford & Sons, Inc., Revisited

Dadford & Sons, Inc., processes four different kinds of property insurance applications: requests for underwriting (RUNs), requests for price quotes (RAPs), requests for additional insurance on an existing policy (RAINs), and annual renewals of existing policies (RERUNs). The daily demand for each type of application is provided in Table 7.1.

Table 7.1 Demand Data for Dadford & Sons, Inc.

	RUNs	RAPs	RAINs	RERUNs
Jobs/day	4	12	6	18
Percent of total	10 percent	30 percent	15 percent	45 percent

Each product type requires some or all of the four steps defined earlier: distribution, underwriting, rating, and policy writing. The workload varies by product type. Table 7.2 presents the average labor content for each product type.

Table 7.2 Operation Times for Dadford & Sons, Inc.

	RUNs	RAPs	RAINs	RERUNs
Distribution	58 minutes	50 minutes	44 minutes	28 minutes
Underwriting	43 minutes	40 minutes	23 minutes	19 minutes
Rating	72 minutes	65 minutes	68 minutes	75 minutes
Policy writing	67 minutes	0 minutes	55 minutes	50 minutes
Total labor	240 minutes	155 minutes	190 minutes	172 minutes

The *takt* time for this example is determined simply by adding all the demands to obtain a total daily demand of 40 units. Although each product has different time requirements, it is not a matter of concern at this stage because *takt* time considers only external customer demand, not internal resource requirements. Assuming that the enterprise works 400 minutes per day as before, the *takt* time is obtained as $400 \div 40 = 10$ minutes per unit.

Average Labor Content and Minimum Operator Requirement

The next step is to compute the minimum number of operators required to sustain operations. From the data given in Tables 7.1 and 7.2, the average labor content for a job is the weighted average of the labor content for each product type:

Average labor content = 0.10 × 240 + 0.30 × 155 + 0.15 × 190 + 0.45 × 172 = 176.4 minutes

Since the *takt* time is 10 minutes per unit, a minimum of 18 operators (176.4 ÷ 10 = 17.64) are needed to manage customer demand. Clearly, there will be some sharing of tasks because there will be at least 18 operators available to perform the four activities.

Workload balancing issues must be resolved. As a starting point, the number of operators required for distribution is determined. The average labor content for this activity is 0.10 × 58 + 0.30 × 50 + 0.15 × 44 + 0.45 × 28 = 40.0 minutes. Since the *takt* time is 10 minutes, the minimum number of operators needed for this task is 40.0 ÷ 10 = 4 operators.

The average labor content for the other activities is computed similarly and works out to be 28.3 minutes for underwriting, 70.65 minutes for rating, and 37.45 minutes for policy writing. A minimum of three operators is required for underwriting (28.3 ÷ 10 = 2.83), seven for rating (70.65 ÷ 10 = 7.065), and four for policy writing (37.45 ÷ 10 = 3.745). Workload balancing and related issues thus may require more than 18 operators. A load chart can now be constructed to determine how much each operator is loaded.

This exercise demonstrates the importance of scheduling the jobs judiciously and avoiding batching to achieve scale economies. Consider the operators doing policy writing. The RUNs, RAINs, and RERUNs demand at least 50 minutes of effort per job. However, RAPs do not require any time from policy writing operators. If the jobs are scheduled in batches, there will be long periods during which the policy writing operators may be overloaded if they are processing a RUN, RAIN, or a RERUN. There will be a subsequent period during which policy writing operators will be idle because the other Dadford & Sons operators are processing RAPs. On the other hand, if a *mixed-model scheduling approach* is used, it is possible to level-load the operators and manage them much more effectively.

Mixed-Model Scheduling and Small-Batch Production

A characteristic of an efficient production system is that products flow smoothly through the enterprise with no delays. The production schedule is crucial for having this smooth flow. In a perfect world, when the customer pulls a product from the final assembly station, a signal will be generated on each upstream resource to produce exactly what is pulled by the customer. The reality is that production constraints such as changeovers, material availability, and operator availability restrict how products flow through the enterprise. In particular, changeover times significantly influence the extent of batching. Plants that make a variety of different products usually tend to produce those products in large batches to exploit economies of scale.

Large-lot production, of course, sends a ripple effect throughout the enterprise. In the beer game discussed in Chapter 1, a single change in demand at the retailer caused huge variations in demand four stages upstream at the brewery. Likewise, within the enterprise, a small change in demand at a downstream operation can cause significant variations in demand at upstream resources. Batching only exacerbates this problem.

Typically, such demand variations are absorbed by carrying large amounts of WIP between each stage. In-process buffers are one way to level production and work with large batches, but large WIP inventories increase the lead time.

There is a better way to level the production schedule. It is simply to produce every product as quickly as possible at the same rate at which customer demands are made using mixed-model scheduling. The Japanese term for mixed-model scheduling is *heijunka*, which refers to distributing the production of different product types evenly over the course of an hour, day, week, or month.

Suppose that an enterprise makes three products, *A*, *B*, and *C*, each of which requires 10 minutes of assembly time. Assume that the final assembly shop works 10 hours each day five days a week. Suppose that the customer is demanding these products at a rate of three, two, and one per hour, respectively. Although the customer could be demanding these products every hour, the enterprise may choose to produce them in large batches for the reasons already discussed.

Suppose the final assembly shop produces one week's demand of each product each time. The weekly schedule is 150 A, 100 B, and 50 C. Instead of receiving products every hour, the customer receives them once a week. Either the customer or the final assembly shop will carry an average finished goods inventory of 75 A (half the batch size, on average), 50 B, and 25 C. If the final assembly shop instead had produced according to a mixed-model assembly schedule of 3 A, 2 B, and 1 C, the finished goods inventory would be negligible because production would exactly match hourly demand. The six units produced in an hour could be sequenced even more finely as follows: ABACAB.

The preceding exercise assumed that the assembly time is the same for each product. Mixed-model scheduling does an even better job of smoothing flow when different products have different processing times, as with the Dadford & Sons, Inc., example. No doubt true mixed-model scheduling requires that changeover times are not significant. As changeover times become more significant, it can be argued that the batch sizes should increase correspondingly. While there is some truth to this statement, short-cycle scheduling is still achieved by producing in small batches when changeover times are large so long as the resource producing the batch is not the constraint.

To sum up the discussion in this section, large-batch production:

▲ Creates an uneven workload
▲ Creates uneven demand for upstream processes, making pull impossible
▲ Causes production to be out of synch with customer demand

On the other hand, mixed-model production:

▲ Creates a smooth workload
▲ Creates a smooth demand for upstream processes
▲ Allows production to match customer demand

Mixed-model scheduling helps to level the workload at each work center, but its true benefit is realized when it is used in conjunction with another Lean concept: *one-piece flow.*

One-Piece Flow

In the extreme case of a mixed-model schedule, each successive item processed at a resource is a different product type corresponding to products being processed in lots of size one. *One-piece flow* refers to the concept of moving products one unit at a time between workstations rather than the other extreme of processing and moving an entire batch of parts from one workstation to the next. Mixed-model scheduling in combination with one-piece flow keeps WIP inventories at the lowest possible levels.

The goal of one-piece flow is to reduce the lead time or, equivalently, reduce WIP inventory. Recall Little's Law, presented in Chapter 1, which states that the average lead time is equal to WIP divided by throughput. If there is a week's worth of WIP inventory sitting at an output queue waiting to be transferred to the next station, one week has been added to the average lead time at that stage.

To elaborate on how one-piece flow affects lead time, consider the example shown in Figure 7.11, which consists of a process with four stages of operation. Suppose that the production rate at each stage is 100 per week and that parts are transferred 60 units at a time, as in Figure 7.11*a*. Since the total WIP inventory in the system is 240 units, Little's Law gives the average lead time as WIP ÷ throughput = 240 ÷ 100 = 2.4 weeks.

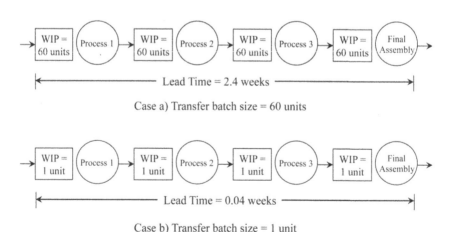

Case a) Transfer batch size = 60 units

Case b) Transfer batch size = 1 unit

Figure 7.11 One-piece flow and its impact on lead times.

On the other hand, if the items are transferred one piece at a time, as shown in Figure 7.11b, the total WIP inventory in the system is four units, so the average lead time is $4 \div 100 = 0.04$ week.

One-piece flow also helps to improve product quality because it shortens the duration of the feedback loop. When parts are transferred one at a time, the downstream workstation is able to determine if the upstream workstation is producing defective items almost immediately. If a week's worth of WIP is transferred at a time, the entire week's output could be defective without anyone noticing the problem. The feedback delay is thus at least one week.

One-piece flow does not necessarily mean that just one piece or one part is transferred between two processes each time. The unit of transfer could well be a pallet of parts, although clearly the smaller the number of units transferred at a time, the lower is the resulting WIP. One-piece flow is an ideal that managers should aim for because it minimizes the hand-off time. Products do not sit in the output queue of the upstream workstation waiting for a batch of products to accumulate before they are transferred to a downstream workstation.

While one-piece flow is typically regarded as an ideal, it might be counterproductive if the cell processes a large variety of products with different processing times and routings. There are a number of other situations where one-piece flow is simply not practical. For example, if the upstream process is a heat-treatment operation that necessarily has to produce a batch at a time, it may not be very meaningful to move these parts one at a time because they would come out of the furnace all at once. Similarly, if the downstream operation requires a setup each time it begins work on a new product, then it may not make sense to move parts to this operation one at a time.

Finally, if material transfers are done by the operators themselves rather than via an automated conveyance system, then it does not make sense for the operator to be moving the parts one piece at a time if the part transfer and processing times are of similar duration. In other words, if materials handling costs are high, then it may be more economical to transfer the parts in small batches rather than one piece at a time.

To implement one-piece flow, it is desirable that there be little variability in process times and process quality at each of the steps in the one-piece flow. If one step is delayed, it stops the flow of the entire process. The processing steps also must be located adjacent to each other in order to facilitate moving only one piece at a time.

Cellular Layout

One-piece flow is significantly enhanced when the various processes are organized in a *cellular layout* (also called a *product layout*). A cell consists of the operators and the workstations required for performing the process steps, with workstations arranged in the processing sequence. The cellular layout is to be contrasted with a *process layout*, where the workstations are grouped by departments or functions.

When workstations are placed close to one another, products moving from one workstation to the next do not have to traverse a long distance, which facilitates one-piece flow. Keeping workstations close to one another allows the operator at the downstream workstation to see what is being produced by the workstation upstream and eliminates any paperwork that may be needed for coordinating these workstations if they were separated by a significant distance.

A common layout used for manufacturing cells is a *U-shaped cell configuration*. The U-shaped layout has a number of advantages, one of which is that it provides more flexibility in allocating tasks among the operators. Consider the assembly cell shown in Figure 7.12, which has eight assembly tasks, each of duration 15 seconds. The *takt* time is currently 15 seconds, and hence each assembly task requires one operator.

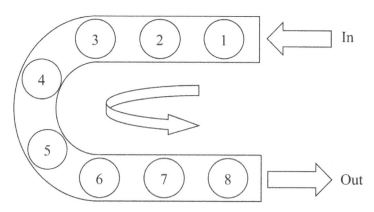

Figure 7.12 A U-shaped cell.

Now suppose that the *takt* time increases to 30 seconds. Since each assembly task still requires only 15 seconds, it is possible to operate the cell with four operators, allocating two assembly tasks to each. The U-shaped cell allows more flexibility in the allocation of tasks. It is now possible to allocate tasks 1 and 8 to an operator who is now responsible for monitoring parts coming in and going out of the cell—a task allocation that would not have been possible with a straight-line layout. The U-shaped layout also allows for easy replenishment of materials from outside the cell and promotes teamwork because the operators are located closer to one another.

Since the U-shaped cell allows for more flexibility in allocating multiple tasks to operators, there is better employee utilization. The cell shape facilitates reallocation of tasks among operators when an operator is added or removed in response to a change in *takt* time. Other common cell configurations include the T-shaped cell, the L-shaped cell, and a serpentine arrangement (a series of adjoining U-shaped cells).

In summary, some of the benefits associated with one-piece flow and cellular manufacturing include:

▲ WIP reduction
▲ Better space utilization
▲ Reductions in lead time
▲ Productivity improvement—more flexibility in allocating tasks to operators and rebalancing production lines to accommodate absenteeism
▲ Quality improvement—immediate feedback on defects
▲ Enhanced teamwork and communication, with more support for coworkers who fall behind
▲ Better visibility of all tasks and operations

The next step is to identify the best method for performing a particular task and then to develop a standard work procedure that should be followed by anyone working on this task. This is the concept behind *standard work.*

Standard Work

Standard work or *standard operating procedure* relates to a clear specification of how tasks should be performed. The tasks are first organized in the most effective sequence using the most effective combination of resources. This task sequence and combination of resources then is fully documented, and every operator is required to adhere to the sequence and use the same resources. The intent is not to take away from operator creativity. Rather, it is to make every operator follow recognized best practices.

There are a number of reasons why standard work is important. First and foremost, standard work promotes consistency and continuous improvement. It is very difficult to improve a process if each operator performs tasks in a different way. A documented standard makes it easier to effect continuous improvement and increases the likelihood that the results will be consistent.

Second, standard work improves safety. Unsafe practices are mitigated when all operators follow the same routine for specific tasks. Moreover, with standards established, it now becomes easier to measure performance equitably. It is possible to establish a fair output rate and judge everyone by the same standards. Standard work is particularly useful when training new employees.

Standard work recognizes that the best practice may be a moving target. Operators performing tasks are encouraged to come up with a better method for a task, in which case the standard work practices will change. If operators are involved in defining standard work, they will be more likely to do their jobs correctly and will help with continuous improvement efforts in the future.

The goal for setting standard work is to give each operator an amount of work less than or equal to the *takt* time while creating a compact footprint for each operator. Since standard work represents a set of tasks allocated to an operator, it will change when the *takt* time or the model mix changes. Many enterprises have created standard work charts for different *takt* times requiring various numbers of operators. These enterprises are able to respond very quickly to *takt* time changes with minimal disruption because the standard work plan is already prepared.

Pull Replenishment and Kanbans

Pull replenishment is a very convenient and effective way to control product flow. The goal of pull replenishment is to contain inventory. Pull replenishment is achieved by using *kanbans* (Japanese for "sign or signal"), although there are other methods for effecting pull (discussed in Chapter 8).

Pull replenishment using *kanbans* is quite simple in concept. The basic idea is to transfer production responsibility to the operators themselves rather than have a production controller decide in advance what each operator should be producing at a given time. Control of operations is decentralized by having each downstream operator signal upstream operators when parts are needed; *kanbans* provide this signaling mechanism. To use *kanbans*, the following conditions typically must be met:

▲ Demand for the item must be relatively repetitive.
▲ Lead times must be relatively short.
▲ Components must be available so that an item can be produced on demand when the visual signal is generated.

The first step in designing a *kanban* system is to determine the amount of inventory that will be used to buffer the downstream operator from the upstream operator. Two types of *kanbans* typically are used: *in-process kanbans* and *material kanbans*.

In-process *kanbans* typically are used when the upstream and downstream operations are close enough so that the upstream operator is triggered simply by a visual signal from downstream. In-process *kanbans* can be implemented simply by allocating a physical location between the two operations and specifying the maximum amount of WIP inventory that the upstream operator can place in this location. If the in-process *kanban* is full, the upstream operator stops production until inventory is drawn from the *kanban* location.

It is common practice to paint a square or a rectangle on the shop floor between the two operations indicating where the part or container of parts should be placed. With multiple part types, each part type might have a different color code. Each location or container will have a WIP inventory limit.

Material *kanbans* are used in a variety of ways. A production facility may use them to signal a need for replenishment of material from:

▲ A supermarket or warehouse (a *withdrawal kanban*)
▲ Another production facility (a *production kanban*)
▲ A supplier (a *supplier kanban*)

A production *kanban* is used in place of an in-process *kanban* if the upstream and downstream processes are far apart and the upstream operator has no visibility on the needs of the downstream operator.

The replenishment signals usually are transmitted either through a card or an electronic signal. Each card requests that a specific number of items be replenished. At any point in time, the number of *kanban* cards (equivalently, containers of parts) in circulation is determined using the following formula:

$$\text{Number of kanban cards} = \frac{\bar{D} \times KCT \times (1 + SF)}{kanban \text{ size}} + 1$$

where $\bar{D}$ is the average demand per time period, KCT denotes the *replenishment lead time* (*kanban* cycle time), and SF is a safety factor to buffer the combined variations in the demand, the replenishment lead time, and supply quality.

The safety factor SF is determined, using the approach presented in Chapter 4, to calculate the additional inventory needed to buffer variation at the points of consumption in a distribution system as follows: the term $\bar{D} \times KCT \times (1 + SF)$ in the *takt* formula represents the average demand during the *takt* cycle time $\bar{D} \times KCT$ plus a buffer, $\bar{D} \times KCT \times SF$, to accommodate variation. If the enterprise can gather data over a certain time period—say, the past three months—on the demand that takes place while a *takt* is replenished and returned to the enterprise (the demand during a *takt* cycle time), then the enterprise can calculate the average and standard deviation of this demand.

By definition, the average demand during a *takt* cycle time will be $\bar{D} \times KCT$. Let $\sigma_{\bar{D} \times KCT}$ denote the standard deviation of the demand during the *kanban* cycle time. Suppose that the enterprise wants to set the safety factor equal to three standard deviations of the demand during the *takt* replenishment time; that is, suppose that the enterprise wants to guarantee material availability 99.87 percent of the time. Then the value of $\bar{D} \times KCT \times SF = 3\sigma_{\bar{D} \times KCT}$.

The *kanban* formula assumes that the signal to replenish a container of parts is triggered when the container becomes empty. This formula has two unknown values: (1) the number of *kanban* cards in circulation and (2) the *kanban* size (the term commonly used to denote the number of items in a container). Typically, *kanban* size is determined in consultation with the supplier, the upstream facility, or the supermarket based on a variety of factors such as ergonomic issues and standard container sizes. The formula thus will determine the number of cards in circulation.

Some enterprises use a *two-bin system* of replenishment: they start with two *kanban* cards and use the formula to determine the *kanban* size. If the value obtained for the *kanban* size is unsatisfactory, then the number of cards is increased by one, and the computation is repeated until a satisfactory *takt* size is determined.

The *kanban* system requires a minimum of two cards because there should always be one container at the workstation from where the operator will pull parts. These *kanban* signals typically are generated from a production facility that maintains materials at point of use.

Point-of-Use Materials Storage

Point-of-use materials storage places the materials in the production process at locations that allow for quick access. The upstream process or external supplier usually delivers the materials directly to the point of use, typically based on *kanban* pull signals.

Typically, materials are stored on flow-through racks just outside the cell. Flow-through racks are storage locations with shelves that can be replenished from the back and consumed from the front, like the beverage coolers in convenience stores. Flow-through racks preserve first-in, first-out material usage and allow materials to be replenished from outside the cell.

For material that cannot be stored at point of use, supermarkets (nearby storage locations) are often used in place of centralized storage. A supplier may deliver a large batch of parts that are used by several cells to a supermarket located near the cells. A cell that produces in small batches may store only the materials for one product at the point of use at any given time, whereas the materials needed for all the other products are stored at the supermarket.

Total Productive Maintenance

Total Productive Maintenance (TPM) is a term used to denote the systematic execution of maintenance by all employees. The goal of a TPM program is to significantly increase productive capacity and decrease process variation. TPM is a management strategy originally developed by Toyota to support their Toyota Production System, and it evolved from the Total Quality

Management (TQM) movement pioneered by Deming and Juran. TPM resembles TQM in a number of ways, and the similarities are not coincidental. When the problems of maintenance were examined as a part of the TQM program, the general TQM concepts did not seem to fit or work well in the maintenance environment. To solve this problem, the original TQM concepts were modified to suit this environment. These modifications elevated maintenance to the status of a separate yet integral part of the overall quality program, and gave it the name TPM.

TPM is a continuous-improvement philosophy that emphasizes the importance of people and the importance of production and maintenance staff working together. The focus is on maintaining the equipment *and* the processes that support manufacturing. Because there is a natural tendency for people to follow the "if it ain't broke, don't fix it" philosophy, TPM requires top management commitment for sustaining the initiative.

Mistake-Proofing and Method Sheets

Mistake-proofing and *method sheets* are tools used to improve quality. Mistake-proofing (*poka yoke* in Japanese) prevents defects from being passed on to the next process. Mistake-proofing requires that quality checks be built into both operations and equipment using appropriate sensors to detect errors and to stop the process if necessary. Combined with other Lean tools, mistake-proofing works to ensure that 100 percent quality is built into the process and the product. An example of mistake-proofing is the three-prong electrical plug: there is only one way you can plug it into a socket.

Method sheets are visual instructions located at a workstation that show how a job must be done, the quality checks necessary, and the tools to be used. The instructions show pictures of each step as it is to be performed. The goal is to make instructions so clear and unambiguous that a new operator can understand them immediately.

Continuous Improvement and the Pursuit of Perfection

Complacency may be the toughest challenge in any Lean transformation process. Lean is not a one-time effort, nor is it a quality program of the month. It is an ongoing journey that requires a sustained effort at continuous improvement. The Lean transformation is not accomplished simply by applying a few techniques; it is a whole new way of looking at the operations of the enterprise.

As with any continuous-improvement initiative, Lean tools and techniques require a sustained effort. Enterprises that do not aim to continue their upward momentum will fall behind the competition. It is essential to continuously reexamine processes and look for ways to take out waste and non-value-added activities if enterprises are to see significant lasting improvement in financial performance.

To sustain Lean implementations, it is therefore necessary that enterprises constantly initiate *kaizen* (continuous-improvement) events. Typically, *kaizen* events must be initiated by employees. At the same time, there is a need for *kaikaku** events involving the radical redesign of processes and methods geared for achieving breakthrough performance and growth. Once a *kaikaku* step is applied, *kaizen* becomes a powerful follow-up drive to perfect the processes and methods. The sequential application of a *kaikaku* step followed by a series of *kaizen* events results in performance improvements that effectively match the S-curve model presented in Chapter 5.

Dreaming about perfection is fun. However, Lean provides ways to make these dreams a reality. Applying Lean and implementing the tools and techniques to create flow result in a fundamental change in the way the enterprise thinks about operations. The employees soon realize that there is no end to the pursuit of perfection—to reduce effort, time, space, cost, and mistakes in the process of producing and delivering a product. When products flow faster through the enterprise, they expose hidden waste in the value stream. The harder the pull, the more obstacles are revealed, and the more easily they can be removed.

While Lean implementations must have commitment and support from top management, shop floor personnel are also critical to the success of Lean. Many enterprises have initiated their Lean efforts from the bottom up. *Kaizen* events play a vital role in getting employees engaged in the Lean journey, and that pays dividends. Managers at all levels became Lean thinkers and change agents.

A truly Lean enterprise makes it much easier for everyone—shop floor employees, supervisors, Lean champions, subcontractors, and first-tier

*This step is often referred to as a *kaizen blitz*.

suppliers—to discover better ways to create value. Because feedback loops are shortened significantly, there is faster feedback to employees, providing a more conducive environment for pursuing perfection.

Conclusions

Thomas J. Watson, Jr., former President of IBM, once said, "Whenever an individual or a business decides that success has been attained, progress stops." Lean is a journey—an ongoing journey that requires sustained effort to generate and maintain the momentum. At the same time, once initial resistance is overcome, it becomes much easier to maintain the tools and techniques of Lean. There is a sharpened awareness among employees of the waste present in the system, and this awareness will be accompanied by a concerted effort to maintain the momentum if the right incentives are provided.

All types of enterprises can benefit from Lean, regardless of whether they are involved in manufacturing, healthcare, distribution, software, or financial services. Important points that enterprises should keep in mind when embarking on a Lean journey are these:

▲ While the goal of Lean often has been identified as the removal of *muda*, removing *muda* is just a means to an end. The real goal of Lean is to reduce lead time. Lean is all about lead-time reduction and creating flow.

▲ Lean works in conjunction with Six Sigma to remove variation in the process. Reduced variation addresses the three principal measures of TOC—it results in increased throughput, lower inventories, and lower operating expense.

▲ Forecasts should be used to plan, and execution should be driven by pull signals. A system that reacts to pull signals will have less variation than a comparable system that adopts a push mode of operation.

▲ Some of the more important steps that enterprises can take to create flow are *takt* time, standard work, pull replenishment, and 5-S. Incidentally, all these are steps that readily apply in a service setting as well.

▲ Steps such as 5-S and *takt* time are often misunderstood or misused. For example, the fifth step in the 5-S program, *sustain*, is vital for sustaining the momentum. Once a 5-S program is put in place, some enterprises neglect to practice this step. Lean is a *journey*—one that really never ends.

▲ Enterprises that embark on the Lean journey should start by identifying a product family on which they can apply Lean principles.

▲ Lean must be applied to all process steps in the enterprise. The idea is not to simply Lean out some process steps and create a few islands of excellence. Some waste may be removed by creating such islands, but the products flowing out of these islands will end up waiting elsewhere. In particular, they will queue up in front of the constraint resources, underscoring the need to apply Lean in conjunction with TOC.

▲ Finally, the lean supply chain is the ultimate goal. It is the responsibility of the Lean enterprise to collaborate with upstream and downstream supply chain members to streamline the supply chain successfully.

References

1. H. Ford (1926), *Today and Tomorrow*, Doubleday, New York; reprinted by Productivity Press, 1989; and H. Ford (1930), *Moving Forward*, Doubleday, New York.
2. E. M. Kerschner, T. M. Doerflinger, and M. Geraghty (1999), "The Information Revolution Wars: Fighting for 'Digitizable GDP,'" Paine Webber, Inc., New York.
3. T. Ohno (1988), *Toyota Production System: Beyond Large-Scale Production*, Productivity Press, Cambridge, MA; translated from the Japanese book, *Toyota seisan hoshiki*, Diamond, Tokyo.
4. S. Shingo (1989), *A Study of the Toyota Production System*, p. 84, Productivity Press, Portland, OR.
5. J. P. Womack and D. T. Jones (1996), *Lean Thinking*, Simon & Schuster, New York.

CHAPTER 8

Creating Flow Through the Supply Chain

Have you ever visited a facility where a manager enthusiastically displayed a Lean cell his team has created, a cell that puts out products at a very impressive rate with minimal delays between operations within the cell? At the same time, you may have observed that the products flowing out of this cell create a pocket of WIP or finished goods inventory that waits a long time before it is picked up by the downstream process.

No doubt by creating a Lean cell the manager has eliminated *muda*. However, her actions have not created a smooth flow of products across the enterprise. Unless the products are picked up by the customer at the same rate at which the cell operates, all that the manager has done is create an island of excellence that, at best, serves as a showcase for visitors.

In a larger context, the situation just described is not very different from a situation where one of the enterprises in the supply chain is extremely efficient, processing products with minimal delays. However, if these products either end up as finished goods that wait for a long time before the customer picks them up or end up at the customer's facility as raw material that the customer does not intend to use right away, then once again, all that the enterprise has done is create inventory in the supply chain.

This book has repeatedly emphasized the importance of reducing lead times in the supply chain. Lead times are directly influenced by the rate at which products flow through the supply chain. Long lead times are symptomatic of poor flow, and conversely, the lack of flow results in long lead times.

Reduced lead times and improved flow thus work in concert, creating a virtuous cycle. Therefore, when managers focus on improving flow in the supply chain, such a focus will result in lower lead times, higher throughput, lower inventories, and the capability to respond flexibly to changing customer preferences.

This chapter develops some principles for improving flow through the supply chain, building on some of the concepts and principles presented in previous chapters. In particular, Chapter 3 presented TOC concepts and principles and described a systematic approach to identify and manage constraints that inhibit flow and prevent the system from generating more profit. Chapter 7 presented tools and techniques for Lean, aimed at creating flow within an enterprise by removing waste at key steps in the process.

The following section shows how TOC and Lean can work together to create flow. A subsequent section presents a simple example and uses insights from the example to present two Lean Supply Chain Principles that relate to creating flow, especially in systems with dependent activities that are subject to variation.

Creating Flow: Synergies Between TOC and Lean

TOC and Lean have the goal of reducing lead time. Both philosophies address the need for enterprises and supply chains to remain competitive through a process of ongoing improvement, albeit in slightly different ways. While TOC advocates the Five-Step Focusing Process presented in Chapter 3 to achieve the throughput objective of the supply chain, Lean emphasizes continuous improvement and the pursuit of perfection to create and maintain flow across the enterprise or supply chain.

Comparing TOC and Lean Philosophies

Both TOC and Lean promote the notion of continuous flow and attack the batch-and-queue method of production. The two philosophies work on surfacing hidden capacity and minimizing inventory, especially WIP and finished goods inventory, emphasizing *pull* production although the exact methods of implementing pull differ. TOC emphasizes a model that reacts to pull signals from the bottleneck, whereas Lean emphasizes *kanban* pull signals.

There are some other differences in the philosophies. A key difference in perspective relates to how *muda* is eliminated. The Lean purist would attempt to remove all forms of waste. The TOC purist would argue that such efforts may dilute or diffuse the efforts of the enterprise. The TOC purist would argue that the supply chain should focus its efforts on removing wasteful activities only at bottlenecks.

The TOC purist's arguments have some validity. From a systems perspective, there is a danger that reducing waste in any form may detract focus from removing waste at the key leverage points in the supply chain. Furthermore, there is a danger that the absence of a systems perspective might result in poor decisions. For example, if attempts to remove waste result in a resource having a relatively low workload, the cost world perspective might result in a rebalancing of workload in which this resource is removed and the remaining resources are loaded close to the *takt* time.

A simple example will be presented shortly to show that a focus on simply balancing the capacities of all resources can, in fact, limit the potential of the system, especially in the presence of variation. The example will serve to illustrate that the focus instead should be on balancing flow, not capacity.

Thus the TOC purist probably may not even attempt to remove excess capacity at nonbottleneck resources because these resources necessarily should have protective capacity; otherwise, they also would become capacity constraints. In other words, a purist would argue that TOC and Lean are in direct conflict here because what Lean considers waste in the form of excess unassigned capacity would be something that TOC would deem important to maintain.

On the other hand, the argument that the focus should be on *only* removing waste at bottleneck resources could well result in missed opportunities. Over time, the amount of waste that builds up at nonbottleneck resources may go unrecognized unless it is monitored periodically. A Lean effort thus may free up resources from nonbottleneck operations that could well be redeployed to assist the bottleneck operations and thereby generate more throughput.

Both philosophies advocate reducing the variation that causes inventories to exist. However, the TOC purist will leave inventory buffers in place until the variability is removed or at least reduced. The diehard Lean proponent would probably first try to reduce inventory so that it exposes the problems that cause such variation and then attack those problems.

There is, however, some convergence taking place between these two philosophies. There is better awareness among many Lean practitioners that the bottleneck resource should be the first candidate to be considered for improvement. These practitioners recognize that attempts to reduce process time variation should first be directed at the bottleneck resource, followed by attempts to reduce process time variation at nonbottleneck resources that have the least protective capacity. In other words, they are subscribing to the principle of balancing flow and not capacity. At the same time, more TOC practitioners are starting to use many of the Lean tools for improvement efforts that, at first glance, have only a local impact.

Exploiting the Synergy Between TOC and Lean to Create Flow

Moore and Scheinkopf[1] suggest that it is possible to exploit the synergy between TOC and Lean to create flow, capturing the best of both worlds, by adopting a framework based on the TOC Five-Step Focusing Process as follows:

▲ *Adopt a throughput world perspective.* It is much easier to promote a growth model within the enterprise compared with a model that has the goal of cost cutting. The latter goal will encounter considerable resistance from employees fearful about losing their jobs.

▲ *Define the system to be improved, its purpose, and the measures to be used.* Start with the system that is within the enterprise's control. Gain internal control before trying to change or control customers and/or suppliers. By gaining control within the enterprise, the credibility needed to influence customers and suppliers is earned.

▲ *Identify the system's constraint.* Map the value stream, as suggested by Lean. The value-stream map will reveal waste that can be eliminated quickly—the intent here is not to reduce cost; rather, it is to quickly reduce the number of dependencies and increase protective capacity. A *kaikaku* approach, as suggested by Lean, can be applied at this stage.

▲ *Decide how to exploit the system's constraint.* This step is an ideal step for applying Lean techniques. The system's constraint is a resource that limits the output of the entire system. Identify the root cause for why the constraint is limiting throughput, and look for ways to implement *kaizen* and/or *kaikaku* events that will free up capacity at the constraint or remove variability at the constraint. Is waste associated with setups? Is waste associated with skilled laborers being diverted to performing tasks that an unskilled worker could perform? It is often useful to establish a throughput-per-constraint-unit value for constraint operations. Is the constraint being used to generate the best throughput possible, or should the constraint be deployed to work on other products? Would employing another employee help to improve throughput, even if this employee is underutilized?

▲ *Subordinate to the system's constraint.* The concept of subordination applies to both TOC and Lean. In TOC, the Drum-Buffer-Rope system limits or subordinates the release of material into the system, just like the *kanban* system in Lean. There are a number of support activities that should be subordinated to the constraint operation as well. For example, if the constraint goes down, then plant maintenance should attend to the constraint immediately, even if it means setting aside unfinished work on a nonconstraint. The quality-control personnel should focus on inspecting any item before it is worked on a defective item. Similarly, engineering design personnel should focus their efforts on improving tooling and fixtures at the constraint.

▲ *Elevate the constraint.* This step, as prescribed by the Five-Step Focusing Process, should be undertaken only after the exploit step. The exploit step is often sufficient to remove internal constraints and avoids having to buy additional equipment or employing additional resources. Quite often the exploit and subordinate steps increase the capacity of the constraint by a significant amount. Like TOC, Lean also emphasizes capital avoidance. Even if additional capital resources are needed, the equipment does not have to be new.

▲ *Avoid inertia. Identify the next constraint if a constraint is broken.* Enterprises always have at least one constraint. As soon as one constraint is broken, another constraint will surface somewhere in the enterprise. Awareness of this fact will help to maintain the process of ongoing improvement.

Creating Flow: The Impact of Variability and Dependency

Two factors that have a significant impact on flow are variability and dependency. Variability seriously degrades flow, but it is a factor often neglected or overlooked in the design of product delivery systems. Many enterprises design their work flow assuming a deterministic scenario. These enterprises design their processes assuming that everything will function according to plan.

Processes do not function in a deterministic manner for a number of reasons: customer orders get canceled, operators are absent, machines break down, tools required to perform a specific operation are not available when needed, the logistics provider is delayed by a traffic backup, or the supplier's deliveries are affected by a strike. If enterprises run their resources at high levels of utilization, the presence of variation will lead to large queues that build up in front of these resources.

Dependent events, too, are pervasive. Sales cannot provide a quote to the customer until engineering has reviewed the desired specifications, the order cannot be placed unless a quote is presented, the product and process must be developed by engineering before they can be handed over to operations, funds must be available before supplies can be ordered, operations cannot begin work on the product unless the suppliers have delivered raw materials, the order cannot be shipped until the logistics provider arrives, and so on.

Although dependencies are pervasive, typically they are assumed away during the system design phase, and the various activities, events, and processes involved in the delivery of the product are often designed and developed in isolation. Complex tasks are broken down into a large number of simpler tasks, and managers focus on optimizing these simpler tasks, adopting the classic local optimization stance. With no variability or interdependencies in the system, such an approach potentially could achieve the global optimum. However, in the presence of variation, efforts to optimize dependent activities in isolation will fail to produce desired results.

The Frontier City Clinic

To clarify the preceding discussion, consider a health-care clinic that has leased a facility in Mt. Juliet, Tennessee, to test patients for cardiac care. The clinic specializes in a test that determines the flow of blood through the heart muscles. The test involves three steps: preparing the patient by administering a small dose of a nuclear medicine (prep), a stress test involving a treadmill exercise (test), and a monitoring of the patient after the stress test, which involves taking a series of pictures of the heart (monitor).

The test activity takes an average of 60 minutes per patient, and this activity must be administered by a physician. The test activity should begin no later than one hour after the prep activity is completed, otherwise the effects of the nuclear medicine will wear off and render the test useless. Similarly, the monitor activity should begin no later than one hour after the test activity is completed.

The enterprise has hired a physician to work eight hours a day from 8:00 a.m. to 4:00 p.m. at a rate of $750 per hour. The physician works overtime if necessary, at $1,500 per hour.

The prep and monitor activities each average 28 minutes per patient. The enterprise has hired two laboratory technicians for these activities, paying each of them $100 per hour. The overtime rate for a laboratory technician is $200 per hour if the technician works more than eight hours on a given day. Figure 8.1 represents this process graphically. The facility lease cost is $1,000 per day, including the cost of equipment, and utilities. The cost of supplies is $800 per day. The enterprise charges $2,500 per patient treated.

There is a big demand for the services provided by this clinic, and the more patients that the clinic can serve, the more revenue it will generate. Assume, too, that patients in Frontier City arrive exactly at the scheduled time and that the prep activity can be started on a patient immediately on arrival.

How many patients can the clinic service every day, and what is the resulting profit?

To answer these questions, let's first assume that activity times are constant. It is clear that the physician is the bottleneck. The physician takes 60 minutes to test a patient, whereas each laboratory technician works with a patient for only 28 minutes. Since the physician works eight hours a day, it is logical to conclude that Frontier City Clinic treats eight patients every day. However, there are some scheduling issues to consider.

The three activities, prep, test, and monitor, are *dependent* activities in the sense that there is a specific sequence of steps required to complete the

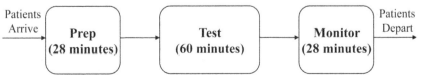

Figure 8.1 A clinical process with three activities.

process. So the approach would be to schedule patient arrivals and the work for the laboratory technicians in such a way that the physician—the bottleneck—never has to wait to test the next patient. Lean Supply Chain Principle 13 articulates this approach:

Lean Supply Chain Principle 13

Focus on bottleneck resources because they control the flow. Synchronize flow by first scheduling the bottleneck resources on the most productive products; then schedule nonbottleneck resources to support the bottleneck resources.

Note that this principle is in line with steps 2 and 3 of the Five-Step Focusing Process, exploiting the constraint and subordinating everything else to this decision. Using Lean Supply Chain Principle 13, it is possible to schedule eight patients per day.

The laboratory technician who performs the prep activity now is scheduled to start work at 7:30 a.m., which will allow the physician to see the first patient at 8:00 a.m. Thereafter, the physician can test patients exactly every hour, with the last test starting at 3:00 p.m. Purely for ease of presentation, assume that the physician and the two laboratory technicians take short bio breaks as well as a lunch break while the patients are being treated. Table 8.1 presents the schedule for the deterministic scenario.

Table 8.1 Schedule of Visits to the Clinic: Constant Activity Times

Patient	Arrival time	Prep		Test		Monitor	
		Start	Finish	Start	Finish	Start	Finish
1	7:30	7:30	7:58	8:00	9:00	9:00	9:28
2	8:30	8:30	8:58	9:00	10:00	10:00	10:28
3	9:30	9:30	9:58	10:00	11:00	11:00	11:28
4	10:30	10:30	10:58	11:00	12:00	12:00	12:28
5	11:30	11:30	11:58	12:00	1:00	1:00	1:28
6	12:30	12:30	12:58	1:00	2:00	2:00	2:28
7	1:30	1:30	1:58	2:00	3:00	3:00	3:28
8	2:30	2:30	2:58	3:00	4:00	4:00	4:28

With this schedule, the laboratory technician who performs the prep activity works from 7:30 a.m. to 3:30 p.m. every day, giving him a little more than a half hour to clean up after he completes the prep on the last patient at 2:58 p.m. The technician performing the monitor activity works from 9:00 a.m. to 5:00 p.m. every day, giving him a little more than a half hour to clean up after he completes the monitor activity on the last patient at 4:28 p.m.

The total daily expense of operating the clinic includes the physician's charge of $6,000 ($750 per hour for 8 hours), the $1,600 in wages paid to the two laboratory technicians (two technicians at $100 per hour for eight hours a day), the lease charge of $1,000 per day, and the cost of supplies at $800 per day. The total daily expense for treating eight patients thus is $9,400. The revenue from treating eight patients is $2,500 × 8 = $20,000 per day. The net profit is $10,600 per day.

It is clear that the workload is highly unbalanced. The laboratory technicians are only used 28 minutes in a 60-minute cycle, whereas the physician is used 100 percent, from 8:00 a.m. to 4:00 p.m. Suppose that management wants to cut costs (improve profits) and decides to work with just one laboratory technician. By working with one laboratory technician, the workload is more balanced because the one remaining technician is now occupied for 56 minutes in a 60-minute cycle.

The only apparent challenge is to schedule the laboratory technician so that he can carry out the prep and monitor activities without delaying the physician. In this example, the scheduling is easily accomplished as follows: instead of having the technician complete the prep and monitor on patient 1 before starting the prep on patient 2, the technician completes the prep on patients 1 and 2 before beginning the monitor activity on patient 1. Thereafter, the technician always performs the prep activity on patient $n +$ 1 before performing the monitor activity on patient n. As seen from Table 8.1, this simple trick allows the clinic to work with one laboratory technician without any problem when activity times are deterministic.

The laboratory technician now works for nine hours a day from 7:30 a.m. to 4:30 p.m. He is paid $1,000 per day (eight hours worked on regular time at $100 per hour plus $200 for an hour worked on overtime). Since the clinic was formerly paying the two technicians a total of $1,600 per day, it is now saving $600 every day. The other expenses remain the same, so the total expense drops from $9,400 to $8,800 per day. Hence the profit for the Frontier City Clinic increases from $10,600 per day to $11,200 per day.

The Impact of Variation on Dependent Events

No doubt such a deterministic situation is highly unlikely even with scheduled patient arrivals because there will be some variation in activity times. Let's revisit Frontier City Clinic and consider a slightly more realistic situation with variation in the activity times.

To keep it simple, let's continue to assume that patients arrive exactly at their scheduled times. In other words, arrival times are still deterministic, with patients arriving every 60 minutes starting at 7:30 a.m. Assume that the prep and monitor activities take 20 minutes each for 50 percent of the patients and 36 minutes for the other 50 percent of the patients. The average prep and monitor activity times thus are still 28 minutes each. Assume, too, that the test activity takes 50 or 70 minutes, each with probability 0.50. Figure 8.2 shows the distribution of these activity times.

While the physician and the laboratory technician still have sufficient capacity to complete their activities in isolation, the dependency between the activities in the presence of variation makes scheduling much harder than in the deterministic case. Table 8.2 presents the actual realization of activity times for eight patients scheduled on a given day. Suppose that the scheduler has advance knowledge of this realization of activity times. How effectively can the physician and the single laboratory technician be scheduled now? Can the physician still complete eight patients a day by 4:00 p.m. as before?

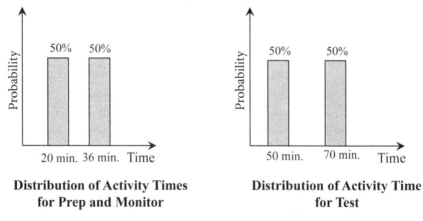

Distribution of Activity Times for Prep and Monitor

Distribution of Activity Time for Test

Figure 8.2 Distribution of activity times for the clinic.

Table 8.2 Actual Realization of Activity Times on a Given Day

Patient	Prep	Test	Monitor
1	36 minutes	70 minutes	36 minutes
2	36 minutes	50 minutes	36 minutes
3	36 minutes	70 minutes	36 minutes
4	36 minutes	50 minutes	36 minutes
5	20 minutes	70 minutes	20 minutes
6	20 minutes	50 minutes	20 minutes
7	20 minutes	70 minutes	20 minutes
8	20 minutes	50 minutes	20 minutes

As before, the physician is the bottleneck (and also the more expensive resource). So the clinic tries to schedule the laboratory technician as well as it can and in such a way that it keeps the physician utilized as much as possible. Table 8.3 presents such a schedule. This schedule ensures that the elapsed time between the completion of one activity and the start of the next activity on a patient never exceeds one hour.

The reader should note that this schedule is based on full knowledge of activity times for all patients, and this helps to generate a good schedule. Of course, activity times for patients usually are not known in advance, so the schedule that unfolds in practice very likely will be much worse than the schedule presented in Table 8.3.

Table 8.3 Schedule for Variable Activity Times—One Laboratory Technician

Patient	Arrival time	Prep Start	Prep Finish	Test Start	Test Finish	Monitor Start	Monitor Finish
1	7:30	7:30	8:06	8:06	9:16	9:16	9:52
2	8:30	8:30	9:06	9:16	10:06	11:06	11:42
3	9:30	9:52	10:28	10:28	11:38	12:02	12:38
4	10:30	10:30	11:06	11:38	12:28	12:58	1:34
5	11:30	11:42	12:02	12:28	1:38	1:38	1:58
6	12:30	12:38	12:58	1:38	2:28	2:28	2:48
7	1:30	1:54	2:14	2:28	3:38	3:38	3:58
8	2:30	2:48	3:08	3:38	4:28	4:28	4:48

In any case, note that both the physician and the laboratory technician work overtime with this schedule. The physician works overtime for 28 minutes, and the laboratory technician works overtime for 78 minutes (because his normal work schedule is from 7:30 a.m. to 3:30 a.m.).

The total wage paid to the physician is $6,700 (for eight hours at $750 per hour on regular time plus 28 minutes on overtime at $1,500 per hour). The total wage paid to the lab technician is $1,060 (eight hours at $100 per hour on regular time plus 78 minutes on overtime at $200 per hour). As before, the lease charge is $1,000 per day, and the daily cost of supplies is $800. The total expense incurred by the Frontier City Clinic on this day is $9,560. The revenue is $20,000 as before (8 patients at $2,500 per patient), so the net profit for the day is now only $10,440.

The schedule provided by Table 8.3 raises a number of issues for discussion. It shows that variability and dependency can degrade performance significantly. The degradation is observed even with *no variation* in patient arrival times. While the first patient did not have to wait for any time between activities, the second patient waits for a total of 70 minutes (10 minutes between prep and test; 60 minutes between test and monitor), the third patient waits for 66 minutes, and so on.

The combined waiting time, across all eight patients, is 336 minutes, resulting in an average waiting time of 42 minutes per patient. Furthermore, the flow of patients through the system is quite uneven. Even though patients arrived exactly every 60 minutes, nearly two hours elapse between the time the first patient leaves the clinic and the time the second patient leaves the clinic. The elapsed time between the departure of the fourth and fifth patients is only 24 minutes. Are the uneven flow and the large lead time due to factors beyond management control?

No doubt the variation in activity times causes lead times to increase. However, the main reason for the uneven flow in this example is because management operated in the cost world and attempted to balance the capacities of the two resources, the physician and the laboratory technician(s). By so doing, they have virtually created two bottlenecks—both resources have been loaded close to 100 percent.

This situation is similar to one discussed in Chapter 3, where an analogy was drawn between a set of processes and a chain. Suppose that a chain consists of 10 links, and one of them is the weak link (the bottleneck). The ability of the chain to pull or lift objects is limited by the weakest link. The throughput world will focus on strengthening that link.

Suppose, instead, that management works in the cost world—it is unhappy with the cost of maintaining nine strong links and "right-sizes" the chain by selling the nine heavy links, replacing them with nine links that have the same capacity as the weakest link. On first glance, this is a truly efficient chain because every link is capable of carrying exactly the same load. What is the problem here? The problem is that there are now 10 weak links, any one of which can break.

To return to the hospital clinic example, as a result of the action undertaken with a cost world perspective, not only is the physician a bottleneck, but the laboratory technician is now very close to becoming a bottleneck. In the context of the load chart discussed in Chapter 7, both resources are now loaded at or close to 100 percent. There is no wiggle room to accommodate any variation or schedule disruptions.

Yes, the goal is to ensure that all resources work at the same pace—and no doubt that pace is dictated by the bottleneck resource—the physician in this example. However, the products—the patients in this example—also should flow as smoothly as possible.

Let's assume that it is not possible to eliminate the variation. What would improve flow in this example? Suppose that the clinic had stayed with two laboratory technicians. In this case, scheduling would have been far simpler, *and* the experience for the customer would have been far superior. Table 8.4 presents the schedule that would have developed if the clinic had

Table 8.4 Schedule for Variable Activity Times—Two Laboratory Technicians

Patient	Arrival time	Prep Start	Prep Finish	Test Start	Test Finish	Monitor Start	Monitor Finish
1	7:30	7:30	8:06	8:06	9:16	9:16	9:52
2	8:30	8:30	9:06	9:16	10:06	10:06	10:42
3	9:30	9:30	10:06	10:06	11:16	11:16	11:52
4	10:30	10:30	11:06	11:16	12:06	12:06	12:42
5	11:30	11:30	11:50	12:06	1:16	1:16	1:36
6	12:30	12:30	12:50	1:16	2:06	2:06	2:26
7	1:30	1:30	1:50	2:06	3:16	3:16	3:36
8	2:30	2:30	2:50	3:16	4:06	4:06	4:26

stayed with two laboratory technicians. With this schedule, the physician works overtime for only six minutes. The laboratory technicians each work less than 7.5 hours a day and do not incur overtime.

The total wage paid to the physician is $6,150 (eight hours at $750 per hour on regular time plus six minutes on overtime at $1,500 per hour). The total wage for the two laboratory technicians is $1,600 (two people for eight hours each at $100 per hour on regular time). As before, the lease charge is $1,000 per day, and the daily cost of supplies is $800. The total expense for this day is $9,550. Since the daily revenue is $20,000, the Frontier City Clinic makes a net profit of $10,450 for the day. Thus, in this example, the profit actually increases by a small amount when the clinic reemploys the second laboratory technician.

In addition, with two laboratory technicians, the average waiting time per patient drops from 42 minutes down to 13 minutes. Furthermore, there is a steady flow of patients departing the clinic. In summary, instead of working in the cost world and trying to balance capacities, by hiring an additional technician and focusing on throughput, the clinic was able to do the following:

▲ Create a smooth flow of patients through the system
▲ Dramatically reduce the waiting time for patients
▲ Increase profits—albeit by a small amount

The next Lean Supply Chain Principle summarizes the lesson provided by the Frontier City Clinic exercise:

Lean Supply Chain Principle 14

Do not focus on balancing capacities. Focus on synchronizing the flow.

To reiterate, the objective is not simply one of balancing capacities or improving the utilization of all equipment and human resources. The objective is to synchronize flow so that products (or customers) move through the enterprise as smoothly and quickly as possible. By operating in the cost world, the clinic no doubt saved on the salary paid to one laboratory technician. However, the decision to only hire one technician created a scheduling nightmare for the clinic, resulted in some very unhappy customers, and required the physician *and* the laboratory technician to work overtime. In general, with a set of dependent activities and more than one of the resources operating at close to 100 percent, the system will experience serious interference and congestion, especially if processing times are variable.

Even this small example with two resources demonstrated the disruptive effect of variation in the system. A number of important measures of system performance, such as lead time, WIP, and flow, are affected by variation. As noted in Chapter 7, Taiichi Ohno is believed to have stated that "Inventory is the root of all evil." A more precise statement is, "Variation is the root of all evil."

The Frontier City Clinic example also can be used to show how TOC and Lean can work in concert to obtain better flow and increased throughput. With its systems perspective, the TOC Five-Step Focusing Process can be applied first to leverage the bottleneck. Since the test activity requires the largest time to complete, can the average test activity time be reduced, by using improved technology/equipment? Can the physician offload some of her activity time to a technician?

Lean now can try to address variability in test times, perhaps in conjunction with Six Sigma techniques. Lean and Six Sigma also can address the variability in the prep and monitor activities and work on removing any wasteful activities performed by the physician and the laboratory technician(s).

What are some steps enterprises can take to minimize the impact of variation? The following sections discuss two specific ways by which enterprises can reduce variability in the system and improve flow: work with small batches, and apply pull.

As observed earlier, when products are produced and shipped in large batches, the bullwhip effect is pronounced, impeding flow in the supply chain significantly. So the first step is to consider setup-time and batch-size tradeoffs. Next, some methods are presented for reducing variation and enhancing flow using pull signals. A simulation called the *dice game* is also presented that shows how a production line is managed much more effectively using pull signals. The chapter concludes with a explanation of why pull systems have an inherent ability to reduce system variation.

Creating Flow: The Impact of Batch Size

The impact of setup times on the flow of products through the enterprise has not been discussed so far. It is difficult to overestimate the impact of setup times because they affect batch sizes. No doubt Lean aims at reducing setup times, but in many cases setups cannot be eliminated. When setup times are fairly significant, many enterprises end up making wrong batch-sizing decisions. For instance, the manager is driven to consider building products using a variant of the economic order quantity (EOQ) formula.

The EOQ formula is arguably the result of a local optimization mind-set. The mind-set typically operates as follows: large-batch production results in few setups and therefore incurs less setup cost. However, large-batch production increases inventory and inventory holding costs. Conversely, producing small batches increases setup costs but results in lower inventory holding costs. The EOQ formula computes a batch size that optimizes the sum of the setup costs plus the inventory holding costs.

Rules such as those prescribed by the EOQ formula divert attention from the objective of creating flow. Such rules tend to force managers to work around the problem rather than work through the problem. For example, one problem with the EOQ formula is that it assumes that setup costs are given. The manager may blindly accept the setup times or costs and not consider the fact that setups could be reduced, perhaps by significant amounts. The EOQ formula thus results in inventory decisions that almost always err on the high side—it usually results in batch sizes that are larger than necessary. As a consequence, the inventory levels are higher, as are lead times and operating expenses.

It must be noted that batch-sizing decisions are not solely restricted to the manufacturing industry. The notion of economies of scale, which drives the EOQ formula, occurs in the service industry as well. In a service-industry context, batching can occur if an operator who attends to requests from multiple categories of projects or customers decides to serve all customers from a certain category before switching to the next category of customers.

Cost-based batch-sizing decisions result in local optima that may be suboptimal for the enterprise. Large-batch operation increases the variation in the system, creating unnecessary work stops and starts as products move through the enterprise in large batches. Batch-sizing decisions therefore must be made in the context of what is best for the performance of the enterprise or the supply chain as a whole. These decisions must consider the synchronous flow of products through the enterprise or supply chain.

In many situations, however, there may be some compelling reasons for producing products in relatively large batches. What can the enterprise or supply chain do to work with such constraints?

To answer this question, it is necessary to distinguish between two types of batches, the *process batch* and the *transfer batch*.

Process Batch Versus Transfer Batch

What is the batch size in a dedicated assembly line that produces a single product? The process batch size is the size of the entire production run, often a large number. However, to maintain flow, products are moved as soon as they leave the assembly line. From the product's perspective, each unit processed is moved individually, so the batch size appears to be just one. This is the transfer-batch size. The notion of a transfer batch was introduced in Chapter 7 in the context of one-piece flow. By definition, one-piece flow relates to moving products one at a time between workstations. In other words, it relates to a transfer batch of size one. (*One* even could refer to one pallet.) Formally, the definition of process batch and transfer batch are as follows:

▲ *Process batch:* The quantity of a product processed at a resource before the resource is set up to make another product.
▲ *Transfer batch:* The number of units that are moved at a time from one resource to the next.

Differentiating between the process batch and the transfer batch makes it convenient to promote flow even when the resources are forced to produce in large batch sizes. Ideally, the process batch at nonbottleneck resources should be kept as small as possible to keep the flow of materials smooth and balanced. However, when setup times at the nonbottleneck resources are significant, care must be exercised to ensure that these setups do not result in the nonbottleneck resources becoming constraints.

At bottleneck resources that have significant setup times, the process batch generally will be larger. In such cases, it is still possible to have a smooth flow with small transfer batches. However, in a number of instances, a transfer batch of size one is either not possible or is impractical. For example, as discussed in Chapter 7, if the upstream process is a heat-treatment operation that necessarily has to produce a batch at a time, it may not be very meaningful to move these parts one at a time to the next process because they are removed from the furnace all at once. Similarly, if the downstream operation requires a setup each time it begins work on a new product, then moving parts to this operation with a transfer batch of size one may be pointless.

The flow of products through the enterprise is affected by the manner in which raw materials are released into the production line and by the manner in which the various resources are scheduled. A system consisting of a series of dependent processes is used to gain further insight into why systems that use pull signals to control job releases into the system work so much more effectively than comparable systems that use push methods.

Controlling Flow Using Pull*

A simple serial production process that operates on a single product is used to compare and contrast different methods for releasing raw materials and scheduling the resources. More specifically, a traditional method of scheduling production using a push system is compared with techniques that respond to pull signals. Examples of systems that respond to pull signals include the *kanban* system covered in Chapter 7 and the Drum-Buffer-Rope Technique presented in the next section.

A Serial Production System

The serial production process considered consists of a number of resources, denoted by R_1 through R_6, as shown in Figure 8.3. Raw materials are received and processed by resource R_1, after which they are processed by resources R_2 through R_6. When the unit completes processing at resource R_6, the raw materials become a finished product.

Each resource has a different average processing capacity. The resource with the lowest average processing capacity is resource R_3. While the average

---

*The material in this section is inspired by E. M. Goldratt and R. Fox (1986), *The Race*, North River Press, Great Barrington, MA.

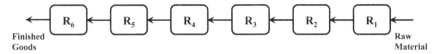

Figure 8.3 A serial production process with six resources.

processing capacity for a resource is constant over time, the processing capacity at any given instant may vary owing to several factors, such as breakdowns, changeovers, and so on.

To contrast the differences in scheduling production using a push system and various pull systems, it is convenient to replace the six-resource production line with an analogous model consisting of a fleet of six operators. This fleet of operators could represent a set of material handlers moving packages, a fleet of truck drivers moving cargo, or a convoy of troops. Figure 8.4 presents the model.

In this figure, the operator on the extreme right, operator 1, models resource R_1, whereas the operator on the extreme left, operator 6, models resource R_6. Each operator moves from left to right, and the height of the operator models the average processing capacity of the resource; the shorter the operator, the lower is the average processing speed. Thus the shortest operator models the bottleneck resource. The bottleneck in the figure is operator 3. Processing times can be variable. That is, the speed at which an operator walks is not necessarily constant.

This model works as follows: consider operator 1. Each time this operator takes a step forward (moves to the right), he increases the distance

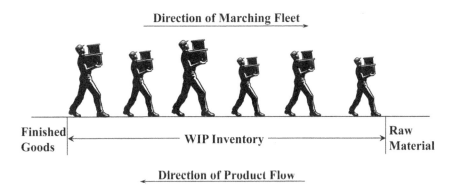

Figure 8.4 A fleet analogy.

between himself and operator 2 (assuming that operator 2 has not moved during this time) by one step. The analogy is that each time operator 1 steps forward, he processes one unit of raw material and puts it behind him in his output buffer (the input buffer for operator 2). Operator 2 now has an additional unit of WIP waiting to be processed. Thus, when operator 6 takes a step forward, he effectively creates one unit of finished goods inventory.

Suppose that there is initially exactly one unit of WIP between each operator. If all the operators move forward at the same pace, there will be just one unit of WIP between each operator at all times. However, since the six operators can walk at different (variable) rates, the number of units of WIP between each operator varies over time. Even though the pace of an operator may vary over time, his average speed is constant. Thus a taller operator immediately to the left of a shorter operator is usually close on the heels of his colleague, often having to wait for his colleague to move foreword.

Over time, the gap between operator 2 and bottleneck operator 3 will continue to widen. This gap corresponds to an increase in inventory between resources 2 and 3. Thus, when the fleet of operators spreads out, it corresponds to an increase in inventory in the system. The task of the scheduler is to contain inventory, namely, ensure that the fleet remains as close together as possible. How can the scheduler achieve this?

The Goal[2] uses a similar analogy, except that a troop of boy scouts is used in place of the fleet of operators. The slowest Boy Scout in *The Goal* is Herbie, and the troop leader, Alex Rogo, wishes to keep the troop as closely packed as possible. So Alex asks Herbie to move to the front of the line and rearranges the troop so that they are in increasing order of height following Herbie. Figure 8.5 shows such a rearrangement of the fleet.

While such a rearrangement works for a troop of Boy Scouts and may well work with a fleet of operators, it is unlikely to work if the fleet of

Figure 8.5 Rearranging the fleet.

operators models a production shop. It is usually not possible to rearrange equipment to have capacity constraints at the front of the shop and the equipment with the highest processing capacity performing the last operation. Precedence constraints in a manufacturing operation may specify that operation 2 must be completed before operation 3, and so on. Even if the sequence of operations could be rearranged, it may not be possible to move equipment to line them up in that same sequence. For example, it is usually not possible to move heat-treatment furnaces. So alternate ways of keeping the fleet close together have to be considered.

Using a Push System to Address Flow

One option is to have a drummer set the beat that all operators should follow. To further ensure that everyone keeps pace, it is possible to employ a conductor who will urge everyone to move at the same pace. Such an arrangement is depicted in Figure 8.6.

The book, *The Race*,[3] points out that such an arrangement is merely the Material Requirements Planning (MRP) System in operation. The conductor is the expeditor, constantly trying to ensure that every resource functions as per plan. The drummer is the materials management system, assisted by a computer, which pushes raw materials onto the shop floor and lets each operator work more or less independently as long as there is work to be done.

The MRP System does not tell each operator when to stop. As long as there is material in front of a resource, the resource typically continues to

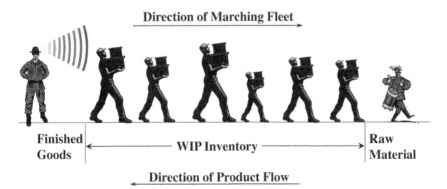

Figure 8.6 Trying to close the gap: a push system.

operate. As a result, not all the operators work according to the drum beat, and typically, the gap between the operators will continue to widen if left unchecked. The MRP System tries to close the gap through overtime, moving operators around, and so on.

There are several signaling mechanisms that can control the pace of the operators to ensure that no one steps too far out of line. These signaling mechanisms basically use pull signals and are referred to as the *kanban*, the *constant work-in-process* (ConWIP), and the *pull-from-the-bottleneck mechanisms*. Each one of these signaling mechanisms is examined using the fleet analogy.

Controlling Flow Using Kanbans

One way to prevent the fleet from spreading is to tie a rope between each pair of operators. To accommodate variation in the pace of the operators and to prevent them from constantly bumping against each other, some slack is provided for each rope segment. The amount of slack allowed determines the maximum number of steps that the upstream operator can advance ahead of his downstream colleague. To ensure that the fleet of operators does not march independent of customer demand, a rope is tied between the last (most downstream) operator and the customer. The length of the rope between the last operator and the customer has a similar interpretation as the length of the rope between each pair of operators: it represents the maximum amount of finished goods inventory allowed in the system.

Figure 8.7 presents such an arrangement. As the caption to the figure states, this arrangement represents, in principle, the *kanban* system of operation. More specifically, it is the in-process *kanban* system discussed in Chapter 7.

In this figure, if a downstream operator starts to fall behind, the rope between this operator and the neighboring upstream operator becomes tight, forcing the upstream operator to stop. In the same manner, with a *kanban* system, the length of the rope represents the maximum inventory that is allowed to accumulate between two resources. If this maximum amount is reached, then the upstream resource will stop operating until the downstream resource consumes some of the WIP inventory.

The release of jobs into this system is determined by the slack in the rope between operators 1 and 2. As long as there is slack in the rope, the

Direction of Marching Fleet

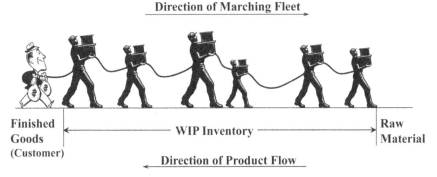

| Finished Goods (Customer) | ← WIP Inventory → | Raw Material |

Direction of Product Flow

Figure 8.7   Closing the gap: the *kanban* system.

pace of the first operator corresponds to the rate at which jobs are released into the system. If the rope is tight, operator 1 stops, corresponding to a temporary stoppage of jobs released into the system.

What will the effective pace of this system be? If the system is capable of producing parts at a faster rate than the customer is demanding them, the bottleneck is the customer. In that case, the rope tying the last operator to the customer will become tight, eventually stopping further processing by the operators. On the other hand, if the customer is demanding products faster than the system can produce them—because there is an internal bottleneck—then the rope tying the last operator to the customer usually remains slack because the customer picks up finished goods almost as soon as the last operator puts them out.

How much inventory will this system accumulate? The maximum distance between the first and last fleet operators (the maximum amount of WIP inventory in the system) will be the sum of the lengths of the ropes between each pair of operators. Thus a cap is placed on WIP, and this drives all the benefits of pull systems. As Little's Law indicates, the lead time is directly proportional to the inventory in the system. Thus, placing a cap on WIP, in turn, places a cap on lead times.

By tying a rope between each pair of operators, observe that each operator is essentially pulled by his downstream operator—the operator behind him. Tying a rope between each pair of operators may constrain the system a little too severely. If any one of the operators becomes disabled, the rest of the fleet will quickly come to a halt. All the ropes upstream of this operator will become tight, and all the operators downstream of this operator will catch up with their upstream partner and not be able to move forward. The next method discussed, ConWIP, is not as restrictive.

Controlling Flow Using ConWIP

In the ConWIP technique, a rope is tied between operator 1 and operator 6. There is also a rope tied between operator 6 and the customer (the finished goods inventory buffer). The ConWIP mechanism takes its name from the fact that the WIP inventory level in the system is usually constant, as determined by the lengths of the ropes between the first and last operators and the last operator and the customer. Figure 8.8 presents the fleet analogy for this model.

With the ConWIP mechanism, operator 1 is forced to stop when the rope between operator 6 and operator 1 becomes tight. This rope can become tight in one of two ways. Either operator 6 cannot move forward because the rope between him and the customer has become tight—because the customer has not picked up finished goods inventory—or operator 1 has moved too far ahead of operator 6. In either case, operator 1 now can resume moving forward only when operator 6 makes a move.

As with the *kanban* system, the drum beat is set by the customer. If there was no rope tying the last operator to the customer, the drum beat would have been set by the last operator. In fact, the reader may have observed that instead of having two ropes, a single rope could have tied the first operator to the customer without violating the ConWIP mechanism. However, this may result in a less disciplined system.

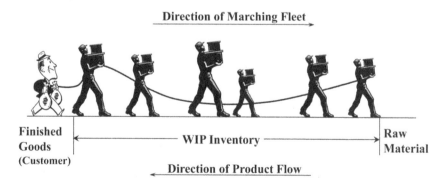

Figure 8.8   Closing the gap: the ConWIP mechanism.

Unlike the *kanban* system of operation, the other operators proceed in a less restricted manner because they are not constrained by any ropes. They stop only if they bump up against their upstream operator. The ConWIP mechanism generally is *self-balancing*. Each operator, except the first, essentially works at his own pace so long as there is a gap between him and the upstream operator. In other words, the only pull signal is from the last operator (or the customer) to the first operator, with the rest of the operators working in a push mode. The ConWIP mechanism thus is a *hybrid* of push and pull. However, it must be observed that this mechanism also places a cap on WIP. Therefore, the ConWIP mechanism generally should perform as well as the *kanban* system and, in many instances, even better than the *kanban* system because the ConWIP mechanism does not restrict the activity of the operators as much as the *kanban* system does.

The danger with the ConWIP mechanism is that when there are many operators in the fleet, the ConWIP system may not have as much discipline as a *kanban* system. Unlike the *kanban* system, which ties a rope between each pair of operators, the ConWIP implementation only has one rope tying the first and last operators. With the *kanban* system, ropes are likely to get taut more quickly relative to the ConWIP system because there is a rope between each operator pair. Thus the *kanban* system tends to focus attention on removing process variability faster than otherwise would occur with a process that uses the ConWIP system.

Controlling Flow by Pulling from the Bottleneck

The *pull-from-the-bottleneck system* ties the rope from the first operator to the operator that is the bottleneck (the bottleneck could be the customer). Thus the bottleneck sets the pace for the entire system. However, an adequate amount of slack (rope) is provided to ensure that the bottleneck never has to stop. The rationale is that the bottleneck should be allowed to continue moving even if one of the upstream operators is temporarily disabled. As noted by Lean Supply Chain Principle 3, time lost at bottleneck resources translates to lost revenue. Figure 8.9 presents the fleet analogy for this model.

In this figure, the pace at which the operators can move is set by the bottleneck. While there is a pull from the bottleneck to the first operator, the remaining operators in the system are not similarly constrained. This model

Direction of Marching Fleet

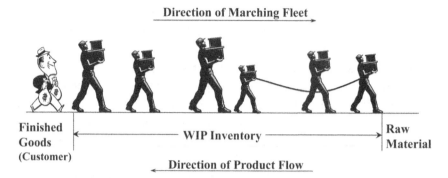

Finished		Raw
Goods	**WIP Inventory**	**Material**
(Customer)	**Direction of Product Flow**	

Figure 8.9 Closing the gap: the pull-from-the-bottleneck system.

is, like the ConWIP system, also a hybrid system in the sense that it has elements of both push and pull.

In the figure, the implicit assumption is that the bottleneck is an internal resource, so the rope is tied to the resource constraint. When the bottleneck is internal and not the market demand, it is unnecessary to tie the rope between the last operator and the customer. However, when the constraint is the market, the rope in the pull-from-the-bottleneck system is tied to the customer through the last operator, just as in the case of the ConWIP system.

The *pull-from-the-bottleneck system* is very similar to the Drum-Buffer-Rope (DBR) Model that was referenced earlier. The DBR Model is now explained.

The Drum-Buffer-Rope Model

The DBR Model balances the flow through a detailed Master Production Schedule that matches customer demand with the system's constraints. Figure 8.10 presents the Drum-Buffer-Rope Model for a system with an internal constraint.

The starting point for the DBR Model is identification of the most heavily loaded resource within the system—the constraint resource. The constraint resource determines the throughput of the system, and it is the only resource scheduled in the DBR Model. The schedule for the constraint is called the *drum* because it sets a drum beat that dictates the pace of system operation. All the other resources operate according to this drum beat to ensure that the constraint is used productively.

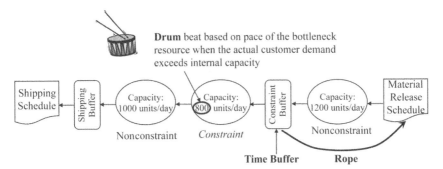

Figure 8.10   The Drum-Buffer-Rope Model.

The constraint is the only resource scheduled in the DBR Model because it is the only resource that cannot recover from any unexpected disruptions. For this reason, the nonconstraint resources are not buffered. However, while nonconstraints have sprint capacity and can catch up after a disruption, subordination of these nonconstraint resources can be a nontrivial task, as noted in Chapter 3 when discussing the Five-Step Focusing Process. In general, any resource that can compromise the throughput of the system if its capacity is not managed carefully is referred to in the TOC literature as a *capacity-constrained resource* (CCR). Special attention is needed for managing CCRs.

The *buffer* is a period of time used to protect the drum from any random or unplanned disruptions that may occur upstream from the constraint. The DBR Model uses two buffers—a *constraint buffer* and a *shipping buffer*. The constraint buffer is a lead-time offset used to schedule the release of materials that are processed by the constraint. The constraint buffer reduces the likelihood that any variation in the upstream processes will cause the constraint to idle. The shipping buffer is another time buffer that protects against any disruptions that may take place after the products move past the constraint.

The two buffers compensate for any process variation and help to make DBR schedules more stable. The buffers also eliminate the need for very accurate data—accommodating the fact that many manufacturing enterprises find it very difficult to obtain accurate data to let them arrive at good schedules.

The final component of the DBR Model is the *rope*. The rope refers to the mechanism that releases work into the production process. The rope is essentially a communication device from the constraint to the beginning of the process. For example, if the constraint is due to start work on an order at 4:30 p.m., and the constraint buffer is eight hours, then material for this order is released at 8:30 a.m., eight hours before it is due at the constraint. The rope ensures the proper subordination of the nonconstraints—it ensures that orders are not introduced onto the shop floor at a rate faster than the constraint is able to handle them, even if the nonconstraints do not have work to do.

If the constraint is not internal but is external market demand, then the rope ensures that the raw materials are not introduced onto the shop floor at a rate faster than the customer demand rate. To implement the rope, the drum provides the material release points with a detailed schedule that itemizes the materials to be released along with the sequence of these releases.

Time Buffers Versus Inventory Buffers

The DBR Model is unique in the sense that it uses *time buffers* rather than *inventory buffers*. It is customary to think of a buffer as an inventory of units that may protect a resource from being starved for work. However, if a process operates on multiple products, it is difficult to quantify the protection for the constraint in terms of units of inventory, especially when the processing times for dissimilar items could be quite different. In such situations, there is a compelling reason for setting the buffer in terms of time units rather than as inventory units.

For example, consider a simple case where the constraint processes two types of products, one requiring 5 minutes per unit and the other requiring 30 minutes per unit. To maintain an inventory buffer, the number of jobs of each type required in front of the constraint has to be specified. However, if the goal is to ensure that the constraint is always used productively, it is enough to specify that there should be, say, 60 minutes of work buffered between the material release point and the constraint. The 60 minutes of work buffered could represent a combination of units of the two product types that could vary over time. Thus time is a common denominator that clearly identifies the amount of protection desired.

DBR was developed originally and applied to a build-to-order (BTO) environment. In the BTO environment, the focus is on timely deliveries of the right products. While having inventory in front of the constraint will ensure that the constraint is always busy producing some product, the constraint may not be producing the right product based on customer due dates. The time buffer promotes timely deliveries of the right products by specifying the raw materials release sequence and subordinating nonconstraint activities. In a serial production process, the constraint buffer and the shipping buffer provide adequate protection from unplanned disruptions.

For more complex flows, earlier DBR Models required an assembly buffer to be located at the point where an assembly operation requires parts that flow through the constraint. The assembly buffer was used to ensure that any assembly component that did not flow through the constraint arrived at the point of assembly early enough so that the assembly operation could proceed smoothly. Thus the goal was to ensure that parts that flowed through the constraint did not get held up at the assembly process by these other components. The assembly buffer is no longer used in the DBR Model.

Determining Buffer Size

Determining the correct buffer size can be a nontrivial task. The total buffer size can be expressed as the sum of the processing times, the setup times, the constraint buffer, and the shipping buffer. The smallest possible buffer size is clearly the sum of the processing times and the setup times, but this is obviously an impractical buffer size. At the other extreme, the current production lead time could be a possible choice of buffer size.

In essence, the time buffer increases the planning lead time from the absolute minimum value required to process the products to one that can accommodate disruptions that are likely to occur. If the buffer size is too large, the resulting increase in lead time will lead to the system having larger WIP levels, making it difficult to manage flow. In particular, there is a real possibility that the constraint now will not have clear guidance on what product to work on next.*

Goldratt has recommended setting the size of the time buffer initially equal to half the current lead time. The DBR Model uses a buffer

---

*A similar situation exists in the service world. When the quantum of work in the system increases, the service to individual customers gets delayed, resulting in more frequent customer complaints.

management process to modify the buffer size, if necessary. Buffer management is discussed in a subsequent section.

This discussion of the DBR Model is summarized as follows:

▲ The system constraint and any other possible CCRs are identified. This step corresponds to step one in the Five-Step Focusing Process.

▲ The drum beat—the schedule of the work at the constraint—is developed. The drum is essentially the exploit step—step two—in the Five-Step Focusing Process. *Exploit* means that the schedule makes sure that the constraint works only on products that have a market demand, that the constraint is able to work without breakdowns or interruptions as far as possible, or that the constraint processes only products that have no known defects.

▲ The throughput of the system is protected from random disruptions through time buffers that protect the constraint and the shipping point. The time at which work is released is determined based on the constraint buffer.

▲ Logistical ropes are tied to the drum. The ropes synchronize nonconstraints to ensure the timely release of material into the system. This step corresponds to the subordinate step—step three—in the Five-Step Focusing Process and can be a challenging step.

The DBR Model is simple in concept. Goldratt emphasizes that the drum does not have to be sophisticated. Setting priorities for the different orders is less important than simply having a drum, although some consideration for sequencing work can be given based on urgent orders, orders requiring more lead time from the constraint to the shipping point, and so on. Implementation of DBR depends, to some extent, on the plant configuration. A comprehensive treatment of the DBR Model for different plant configurations is provided in the book, *Synchronous Management*, by Srikanth and Umble.[4]

As noted earlier, the DBR Model was developed for the BTO environment. The DBR Model also assumes the presence of an internal resource constraint. At the time the model was developed, capacity was still a limiting factor in a number of industries. In today's customer-centric world, where capacity outstrips demand in the majority of industries and the market is the constraint, a simpler version of the DBR Model, the *Simplified Drum-Buffer-Rope Model* is used.

The Simplified Drum-Buffer-Rope Model

The Simplified Drum-Buffer-Rope (S-DBR) Model was proposed in the year 2000 by Schragenheim and Dettmer in their book, *Manufacturing at Warp Speed.*[5] The S-DBR Model does not use a constraint buffer. The only buffer maintained is the shipping buffer. In the S-DBR Model, the shipping buffer is referred to as the *production buffer.*

The drum beat in the S-DBR Model comes from the market—it is based on firm orders. The rope is tied to the market—in other words, the material release schedule is generated directly by firm orders received, as shown in Figure 8.11.

The S-DBR Model has some advantages. It does not require any specialized software, which can be a significant benefit for enterprises that might be unwilling or unable to invest in specialized DBR software. The S-DBR Model can use an enterprise's existing MRP or Enterprise Resource Planning (ERP) software, and which can be a significant benefit for enterprises that might be unwilling or unable to invest in specialized DBR software.

The S-DBR Model is particularly appropriate for the build-to-stock (BTS) environment, where the market is implicitly the constraint. The model is also appropriate for the make-to-availability (MTA) environment, where the enterprise guarantees availability of the product to the customer.

In general, it can be argued that the S-DBR Model is appropriate even if there is an internal resource constraint. Two characteristics of market demand make the market the major practical constraint in most cases. First, customers do not like to be subordinated to their supplier's internal constraint. These customers may choose to work with a supplier that is more responsive to their needs. Second, as noted by Schragenheim in an

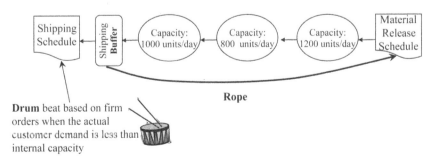

Figure 8.11   The Simplified Drum-Buffer-Rope Model.

article on S-DBR in the *Theory of Constraints Handbook*,[6] a worthy candidate for a strategic constraint is a resource whose capacity is difficult to elevate.

Taking this observation a step further, note that even if the constraint is internal, the enterprise still can have a market constraint if there is not enough demand for the product that the enterprise would really like to produce and sell with its limited capacity. For the Crossley, Steele, and Nice exercise presented in Chapter 3, the enterprise had a limited capacity of 1,000 labor hours, with demand outstripping capacity. However, the demand for the most preferred service, plumbing, was only 250 jobs per month. If Crossley, Steele, and Nice had generated more demand for plumbing, they could have made more profits by giving up other home-maintenance services and applying the limited 1,000 hours of capacity to do more plumbing jobs.

The fact that time buffers result in additional delays presents another powerful reason for limiting the number of buffers. In the DBR Model, the constraint buffer arguably disrupts flow because it initiates early release of parts that, on average, reach the constraint and then wait for their turn to be processed.

The DBR and S-DBR models represent the planning aspect of the process. To execute this plan in a simple and effective way, these models use a *buffer-management mechanism* that monitors the operation of the plan. Buffer management uses a visual display system that controls the progress of orders, adjusting buffer sizes as necessary.

Buffer Management

Buffer management (BM) is a feedback mechanism used during the execution phase to guide the manager on what work needs to be prioritized. BM also identifies situations where the protective capacity is insufficient or excessive so that buffers can be resized appropriately. BM is discussed here in the context of the S-DBR Model. The same approach applies for the DBR Model as well.

In the S-DBR Model, every order has a production buffer and a due date. The material release schedule for the orders is determined based on their due dates minus the production buffer length. While the orders are being processed, the BM system evaluates the percentage of buffer consumed. The percentage of buffer consumed determines the buffer status. The production buffer is divided into three equal zones: green, yellow, and red. If less than 33 percent of the buffer is consumed for the order at a point in time, the order is in the green zone. A buffer status between 33 and 67 percent places the order in the yellow zone, and a buffer status greater than 67 percent places the order in the red zone.

Records are maintained indicating any reasons why orders have moved into the red zone. This information is used to direct continuous-improvement efforts. If an order remains mainly in the green zone as it progresses to completion, this is an indication that the production buffer was set too generously and that it needs to be sized down for the next comparable order.

The discussion so far underscores the need for enterprises to develop control mechanisms for releasing materials and monitoring their progress through the process steps. In a perfectly deterministic world, any reasonable control mechanism can be applied. However, the variability in the system results in some approaches being less effective than others. For example, in the presence of variability, push systems result in poorer performance than systems that respond to pull signals.

To someone who has not experienced the differences between push and pull systems, simply stating that pull systems perform better than push systems does not present a convincing argument. The *dice game* is an experiential simulation that can be used to compare push and pull systems. The dice game also provides better understanding of how variability and dependency affect flow in the supply chain.

The Dice Game

The dice game was used originally in the context of a manufacturing operation but since has found widespread use to demonstrate the effects of process dependencies and process variability in a number of other contexts, notably in service, logistics, and supply chain operations. The process has six to eight sequential operations that process work as shown in Figure 8.12. This process is simulated with a team of six to eight players. Typically, a number of teams play the game simultaneously, providing a spirit of friendly competition among the teams.

The first operation is a scheduling operation, denoted in the figure as the *scheduler*. The scheduler schedules work into the system and has an

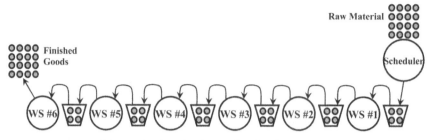

Figure 8.12   The layout for the dice game.

unlimited amount of raw materials available. Each workstation has four units of WIP inventory in its input buffer. The raw materials and WIP inventory can be simulated using poker chips. The configuration shown in Figure 8.12 has one scheduler and six operators for a total of seven players. Each player is provided with a single six-sided die.

The dice game typically is run for 20 days. At the start of each day, the scheduler rolls her die to determine how many jobs need to be scheduled that day (an excellent forecasting system). At the same time, each operator rolls a die to determine the production capability at his workstation on that day. Depending on the outcome of the die roll, the production capability on a given day is anywhere from one to six jobs per day. A high roll of the die means that the workstation has few problems that day and, correspondingly, a higher capacity. The workstations thus are modeled as unreliable resources with high variability.

Each operator now determines the number of jobs that can be processed that day at his workstation and moved downstream—to a higher-numbered workstation—at the end of the day. The number of jobs moved downstream is the smaller of the number of jobs in the operator's input buffer and the roll of his die. The scheduler always schedules the number of jobs provided by the roll of her die because it is assumed that there is an ample supply of raw materials available to the scheduler.

The scheduler and the operators move jobs downstream to their respective output buffers at the end of each day. The scheduler moves raw materials into the input buffer of workstation 1, and the operators at the workstations move their jobs into the input buffer of their immediate downstream workstation. The operator at the last workstation moves jobs into the finished goods buffer. Transfer of work to downstream processes takes place only at the end of each day. Operators are not allowed to steal jobs from their upstream operation. In other words, the pieces processed at workstation n on any given day cannot be used by the operator at workstation $n + 1$ on that same day.

At the start of the simulation, each workstation has four units of WIP inventory in its input buffer, as indicated earlier. Thus, with six workstations, the WIP inventory at the beginning of the game is 24. The system-wide WIP inventory and the system throughput are monitored using a scoring sheet as shown in Table 8.5. Typically, the player from each team who is operating the last workstation is asked to keep score. In the table, the initial WIP of 24 units is identified as the WIP at the end of day 0. The WIP at the end of each subsequent day is simply calculated as follows:

WIP at the end of day = WIP at end of previous day + jobs released – jobs completed

Table 8.5 Dice Game Score Sheet: Push Simulation

Day	Jobs released	Jobs completed	WIP at the end of the day
0	—	—	24
1			
2			
.			
.			
.			
20			

The number of jobs released into each day is simply the face value of the die rolled by the scheduler because the scheduler has ample raw materials, as noted earlier. The number of jobs completed each day is the actual number sent to finished goods, and it is the smaller of the number of jobs in the input buffer of the last operator and the roll of his die.

The throughput of this system is the sum of all the jobs completed over the 20 days. What would this throughput be? Since the roll of a die can result in any number between one and six with equal probability, the average of these numbers is 3.5. It is tempting therefore to conjecture that the system will produce 70 units on average over the 20 days. However, on some days the operator at a workstation may roll a number greater than the WIP inventory in his workstation's input buffer. Thus the total number of jobs shipped at the end of 20 days of simulation typically is much lower than 70. The ending WIP inventory is usually significantly higher than the WIP inventory at the beginning of the game.

The game, as described, simulates a *push* system; the scheduler pushes jobs into the system based on a forecast—namely, the roll of a die. The results from the dice game will validate Lean Supply Chain Principle 14, showing that a balanced system will not produce a smooth flow of products if products are pushed through the system in the presence of variation. The flow is very uneven, and WIP inventory accumulates at different points in the production line at different times. Furthermore, when the game is run with multiple teams, the throughput and amount of inventory accumulation at the different tables will be significantly different. In sum, the dice game shows that *push systems are neither stable nor predictable.*

Variations on the Dice Game

There are a number of variants to the dice game that bring about other learning points. One such variant is to introduce a bottleneck workstation by giving one of the players a four-sided die. It is possible to incorporate overtime as well, by allowing one or more players an additional roll of the die each day.

Another version of the game is to simulate a production line with reduced variation. A die roll of a one, two, or three represents a production capability of three units that day. A dice roll of a four, five, or six represents a production capability of four. These assumptions effectively simulate a reduced-variation setup where each resource has the capability to produce either three or four jobs every day. The impact of reduced variation on throughput and flow will be dramatic, validating Lean Supply Chain Principle 11.

The dice game also demonstrates the differences between push and pull systems. The game can simulate the ConWIP system or the pull-from-the-bottleneck mechanism. The following discussion presents the simulation of the ConWIP system.

Simulating the ConWIP System

The dice game provides a number of additional learning points when it simulates the ConWIP system. As with the standard version of the dice game, the ConWIP simulation is initialized with four units of WIP inventory in front of each operator. With the ConWIP simulation, all the operators roll their individual dice each day, but the scheduler does not roll a die. On the first day, the scheduler moves four units of raw material into the input buffer of the first workstation. After that, she simply releases the number of jobs that were completed by the system at the end of the previous day.

Such a scheduling mechanism keeps the WIP level fairly constant. The WIP level is not the same every day because there is a one-day information lag for information to be transferred from the last station back to the scheduler. Thus the WIP level stays around 24, with a small variation around this number.

Table 8.6 presents the score sheet for this simulation. This score sheet is essentially as before except that four jobs are released on day 1.

Table 8.6 Dice Game Score Sheet: ConWIP Simulation

Day	Jobs released	Jobs completed	WIP at the end of the day
0	—	—	24
1	4		
2			
.			
.			
20			

The results from the dice game with the ConWIP system are usually quite revealing. No doubt the results will differ from one game to the next because of the variability in the rolls of the dice. However, it will become clear to the participants that the variation in the system is considerably reduced. The throughput numbers as well as the WIP levels across the different teams will be fairly close to one another. This simulation thus will reveal that *pull systems are more stable and predictable* than push systems.

Pull Systems Are More Stable and Predictable Than Push Systems

What makes pull systems more stable and predictable? It is due to the reduced variation in a pull system. As noted in Chapter 7, there are two types of variation in the system, system variation and process variation. In the dice game, the process variation is simulated by the roll of the dice. Each workstation has a variation in production capability each day. The other type of variation—the system variation—is not as apparent. Pushing products through the system produces a higher system variation than with a system using pull signals.

By definition, the WIP level in the ConWIP system is fixed. When the WIP level is fixed in the system, it introduces a *negative correlation* between the WIP levels at the different workstations. For example, suppose that the WIP level in the system is fixed at 20 jobs. When there is variation in the processing times at the different workstations, the number of jobs present at the various workstations will vary over time. Suppose that on a given day all 20 jobs are at workstation 1—perhaps there was a breakdown at workstation 1. Then it is known with certainty that there will be no jobs at any of the other workstations. Thus, knowledge of the WIP level at workstation 1 results in perfect information about WIP levels at other workstations.

Even the knowledge that there are 10 jobs at workstation 1 provides information that the other workstations collectively have 10 jobs. In general, with the ConWIP system, if the number of jobs at a set of workstations is high, there will be a smaller number of jobs at the other workstations. Such a negative correlation between the WIP levels tends to dampen the variation in lead times.

In contrast, in a push system, the WIP levels at individual workstations are more or less independent of one another. In other words, the knowledge that the WIP level at workstation 1 is high provides no information on whether the WIP level at workstation 4 is high or low. It is possible for WIP levels at several stations to be high—or low—simultaneously. In other words, the variation in WIP levels typically is higher in push systems. Since WIP levels are proportional to lead times as per Little's Law, lead times generally are more variable in a push system than in an equivalent pull system.

Comparing Pull and Push Systems for Efficiency

In general, a pull system is more efficient than a push system, implying that it is preferable to run the system as a pull system wherever possible. It can be shown, using fairly rigorous analysis, that for the same level of throughput, the push system will have more WIP than a comparable pull system. Similarly, for a given level of throughput, the push system will have longer average lead times than a comparable pull system. These results are stated here without proof. For a detailed discussion and analysis, refer to the book, *Factory Physics*, by Hopp and Spearman.[7]

ConWIP Efficiency Law

For a given level of throughput, a push system will have more WIP than an equivalent ConWIP system.

Corollary to the ConWIP Efficiency Law

For a given level of throughput, a push system will have longer average lead times than an equivalent ConWIP system.

Conclusions

The concept of flow is central to managing the lean supply chain. It is instructive to use a river analogy when considering how to flow the products through the supply chain. The river should flow smoothly, all the way from the mountain to the ocean, without having it collect in dams along the way. Dams are analogous to pockets of inventory; they impede the smooth flow of product through the value stream, decrease throughput velocity, and increase lead times.

▲ Flow is enhanced by reducing lead times. Reduced lead times and improved flow go hand in hand, creating a virtuous cycle.

From a systems perspective, the intent is to

▲ Focus on the bottleneck resources because they control the flow. The idea is to synchronize flow by first scheduling (focusing on) the bottleneck resource so that it works on the most productive product family. The nonbottleneck resources then can be scheduled to march in step with the bottlenecks.

▲ Take care when allocating workload to the resources—especially in the presence of variation. In particular, if all resources end up having similar workloads, variation can wreak havoc and significantly increase lead times. It is therefore imperative to work on reducing variation in the supply chain. In the presence of variation, the focus should be on synchronizing or balancing the flow, not on balancing capacities.

▲ From an operational perspective, flow can be enhanced in a number of ways.

▲ Work with small batches. Large batch sizes impede flow. They also result in increased variation. If large batch sizes are deemed necessary, then use process batch sizes and transfer batch sizes judiciously to move the product through the supply chain. The process batch size can be large at the bottleneck in order to minimize the setups. However, in that case, the transfer batch size should be made as small as possible. In any case, the batch size for nonconstraints can be small because they have additional capacity by definition.

▲ In general, variation in the system will reduce flow—and correspondingly increase lead times.

▲ A pull system has less variation than a comparable push system. As a consequence, a system operated with pull signals will have better flow, less lead time, and less WIP than a comparable system that uses a push mode of operation.

References

1. R. Moore and L. Scheinkopf (1998), "Theory of Constraints and Lean Manufacturing: Friends or Foes?" Chesapeake Consulting, Inc.
2. E. M. Goldratt and J. Cox (1984), *The Goal: Excellence in Manufacturing*, North River Press, Great Barrington, MA.
3. E. M. Goldratt and R. Fox (1986), *The Race*, North River Press, Great Barrington, MA.
4. M. L. Srikanth and M. Umble (1995), *Synchronous Management*, Spectrum Publishing Company, Wallingford, CT.
5. E. Schragenheim and H. W. Dettmer (2000), *Manufacturing at Warp Speed: Optimizing Supply Chain Financial Performance*, CRC Press, Boca Raton, FL.

6. E. Schragenheim (2010), "From DBR to Simplified-DBR for Make-to-Order," in *Theory of Constraints Handbook*, J. F. Cox and J. G. Schleier (eds.), McGraw-Hill, New York.

7. W. Hopp and M. Spearman (2001), *Factory Physics*, 2nd ed., Chap. 10, Irwin McGraw-Hill, New York.

CHAPTER 9

Managing Projects the Theory of Constraints Way

Every organization manages projects. With the collective experience these organizations have garnered from managing countless projects over all these years, why do they still find project management to be such a complex process?

Part of the complexity is due to the fact that project management requires the simultaneous management of three elements: *scope, time,* and *cost.* The relationship among these three elements is sometimes referred to in project management literature as the *project management triangle* (Figure 9.1).

A suggested refinement to the project management triangle is to separate out performance quality from scope and add *performance quality* as the fourth element. Balancing these three—or four—elements can present conflicting priorities across the duration of a project. Typically, people want high-performance quality in a short amount of time at the lowest possible cost. However, it would appear that if the project duration has to be reduced, more resources must be deployed, which will result in increased costs.

Conventional wisdom would also dictate that if one or more of these elements is nonnegotiable, the other elements will need to be adjusted. Accordingly, priorities must be determined among these elements for whatever project the organization undertakes. For example, if the scope and cost are fixed, then the scheduled completion time will have to flex accordingly unless quality is compromised. Pursuing this line of thought, the project management triangle would help to determine the drivers and the tradeoffs necessary for project success.

But what if it were possible to improve on all these elements simultaneously? Recall the discussion on the productivity frontier presented in Chapter 5. That discussion centered on how the enterprises identified as world-class were able to improve their process-execution performance

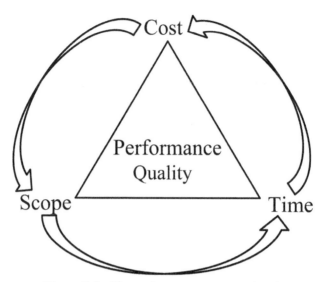

Figure 9.1 The project management triangle.

simultaneously along multiple dimensions such as cost, quality, and delivery. Is it possible to affect the elements in the project management triangle in a similar manner?

The answer is yes. These questions are addressed satisfactorily by a relatively new technique called *Critical Chain Project Management*, introduced later in this chapter. Let's first discuss the characteristics of projects and the challenges faced with project management. This discussion will also review a traditional, well-known project management technique called *Program Evaluation Review Technique/Critical Path Method* (PERT/CPM) that has been in use since the 1950s.

Characteristics of Projects

What is project management? More specifically, what is a project?

The Project Management Institute (PMI)* defines a *project* as a temporary group activity designed to produce a unique product, service, or result.

---

*PMI is the world's leading not-for-profit membership association for the project management profession, with more than half a million members and credential holders in 185 countries.

The project is identified as temporary because it has a distinct beginning and end in time and a definite scope and cost. The PMI definition for a project includes the word *unique* to indicate that a project is a unique set of tasks or operations designed to accomplish a singular goal. The project team often includes team members that typically do not have to work together. These members can come from different organizations drawn from different parts of the world. Examples of projects include bridge construction, processing insurance claims, and expanding sales into a new geographic market. *Project management* is the application of knowledge, skills, and techniques to execute projects effectively and efficiently.

The PMI definition suggests that project management has the following characteristics:

- A nonroutine activity intended to achieve a specific outcome
- Has defined start and end dates
- Requires completing a set of possibly interdependent tasks
- Involves tasks executed by people who do not always work together all the time
- Involves tasks typically having long durations
- Involves a lot of uncertainty in estimating task durations

The last-named characteristic, uncertainty, is arguably the most distinguishing characteristic of projects. This characteristic presents some of the biggest challenges to project management.

A typical project consists of a quantum of work that is predictable and known in advance. Projects also require a certain amount of work that is known in advance, although the time required by the work is not very predictable.

However, the real challenge stems from the work that is completely unforeseeable or unknown. Consider the repair and overhaul of aircraft; this represents a project because each aircraft can have unique repair and overhaul requirements. The unknown work in these projects can appear in the form of unexpected cracks in the aircraft's skin or problems that might be encountered from a previous repair. Uncertainties surrounding project management can also be caused by new projects that tend to shift priorities.

The Impact of Variation on Project Completion Times

How do managers cope with these uncertainties? Figure 9.2 presents two simple projects. Assume that all the tasks in these two projects have task durations that are uniformly distributed in the range [5, 25] days resulting in an average task time of 15 days for each task. In each project, the project manager has three workers, resources *A*, *B*, and *C*, assigned to work on the various tasks.

The project in Figure 9.2*a* requires three tasks to be completed: the first performed by resource *A*, the second by resource *B*, and the third by resource *C*. The letters and numbers in each box represent the resource that performs the task and the average task time. The average completion time for this project is simply the sum of the three average task times, which is 45 days, and there is a 50 percent probability that the project will be completed in 45 days.

The project in Figure 9.2*b* requires both tasks 1 and 2 to be completed by the two resources *A* and *B* before tasks 3 and 4 can start. Similarly, resource *C* can start task 5 only after both tasks 3 and 4 are completed. Note that this project will complete in 45 days if there is no variation in task completion times. With the uniformly distributed task times, a simulation of this system shows that the average project completion time is about 52 days. The probability that the project will complete in 45 days with the variation in task times is now less than 25 percent.

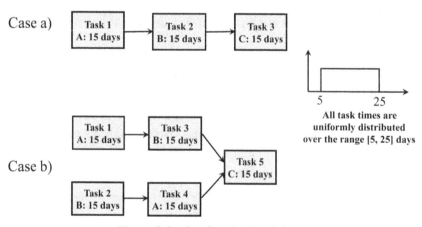

Figure 9.2 Synchronization delays.

Even for the simple five-task project presented in Figure 9.2*b*, a project that would have taken 45 days with deterministic task times now takes an average of 52 days to complete because of task time variation combined with resource and task dependencies. If the manager of the project were aware of the variation in task times, she certainly would not promise the customer a project completion time of 45 days because the probability of that outcome is less than 25 percent. What would her promised due date be?

The safest estimate would be to assume the worst-case scenario of 25 days for every task and quote a 75-day project completion time. Perhaps the manager might think such an estimate to be overly conservative. Suppose that instead she promises the customer a 69-day project completion time. The simulation reveals that there is about a 98 percent probability that she will meet the 69-day promise. The manager now gives each resource 23 days to complete their respective tasks and initiates the project with a strong conviction that the project will complete by the promised due date.

How will this play out? Almost surely the project will exceed 69 days. In fact, it is very likely that the project will take even more than 75 days to complete. To understand why, let's review how projects are managed traditionally using PERT/CPM.

Project Management with PERT/CPM

PERT is an acronym for *Program Evaluation Review Technique*, a technique that originated in 1958 when the Special Project Office of the Department of the Navy and the consulting firm Booz Allen Hamilton developed this project management technique for managing the Polaris nuclear submarine program. *CPM* is an acronym for the *Critical Path Method* technique that was developed by DuPont in 1957 to manage the overhaul of its chemical plants.

PERT and CPM are very similar techniques, even though they were designed for somewhat different reasons. CPM was developed for projects with a set of commonly performed tasks where the task times were fairly well known, whereas PERT was developed for projects with tasks where scientists had little prior experience with these tasks and could not estimate their times with much certainty.[1] The primary difference between the two techniques was that the PERT model buffered tasks times to account for uncertainty while the CPM model did not. Since these techniques were very similar in their approach, they were merged subsequently into one technique, PERT/CPM.

In the PERT/CPM technique, task times typically are buffered to accommodate uncertainty. Thus, for the five-task example provided in Figure 9.2, each task probably would be allocated a task time of 23 days.

The PERT/CPM technique identifies the *critical path* in a project network, which is the longest path in the network. The critical path determines the shortest time in which the project can be expected to be completed. Tasks on the critical path receive the most attention in a project because any delays on this path can delay the project completion time.

Determining the Critical Path

The PERT/CPM technique is best illustrated with an example. Consider the launch of a new program by the center for executive education in a business school. This project starts by identifying the tasks required to complete the launch. Figure 9.3 shows the tasks involved in the launch.

Next, the estimated time required for each task in the project is determined. Figure 9.4 shows the estimated task times. These task times have been buffered to account for any uncertainty in the task times.

To identify the critical path and to monitor progress on the project, PERT/CPM uses a set of five different time values associated with each task on the network: the *actual task time estimate*, the *earliest start time* (EST), the *earliest finish time* (EFT), the *latest start time* (LST), and the *latest finish time* (LFT), as shown in Figure 9.5.

Task	Description	Immediate Predecessors
A	Design program and scope	-
B	Identify program location	-
C	E-mail program catalog to prospects	A
D	Identify the course faculty	A, B
E	Accept participants	C
F	Get faculty to select text	D
G	Receive course material from faculty	F
H	Reserve and prepare seminar room	E, G

Figure 9.3 Tasks required for the new executive program launch.

Task	Time Estimate in Weeks (buffered for uncertainty)
A	6
B	2
C	3
D	4
E	10
F	6
G	8
H	2

Figure 9.4 Task times for the new executive program launch.

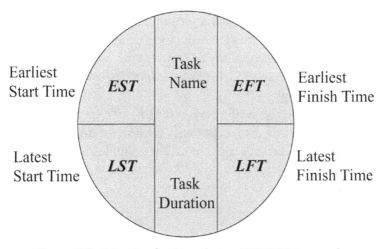

Earliest Start Time — *EST*

Task Name

EFT — Earliest Finish Time

Latest Start Time — *LST*

Task Duration

LFT — Latest Finish Time

Figure 9.5 Notation for the tasks in a PERT/CPM network.

Using the information presented in Figures 9.3 and 9.4 and the notation presented in Figure 9.5, the PERT/CPM technique draws the project network. The resulting network diagram is presented in Figure 9.6. The diagram shows each of the tasks as a node in the network. The arrows in the network capture the precedence requirements. A dummy node, labeled "Start," is introduced to start the network, and this node is connected to any task that has no preceding task.

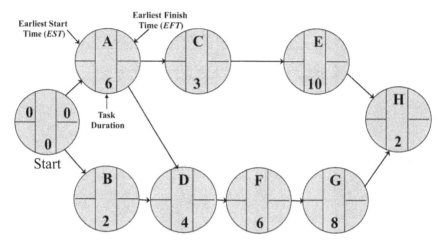

Figure 9.6   Network diagram using the notation.

The technique now executes a *forward pass* to determine the earliest start and earliest finish times for each task. The EST for a task that has no predecessor is set to zero, and the EFT for this task is simply the task time. So the technique sets the EST for tasks *A* and *B* equal to zero and fills in their EFTs accordingly.

The EST for each succeeding task is the EFT of its predecessor task. If a task has more than one predecessor task, the EST for the task is the largest among the EFTs of its predecessor tasks. For example, the EST for task *D* is the larger of the EFTs for tasks *A* and *B*. Figure 9.7 shows the PERT/CPM

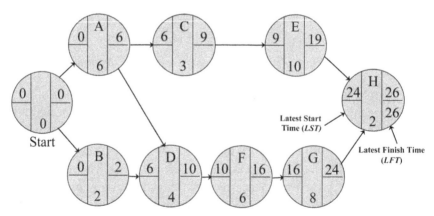

Figure 9.7   Finding earliest start and finish times.

network with the earliest start and finish times filled in for each node in the network.

The EFT for the last task, task *H*, is 26 weeks. PERT/CPM sets the EFT for the final task equal to the LFT for that task. So the LFT for task *H* is also 26 weeks (see Figure 9.7).

The PERT/CPM technique now executes a *backward pass* to fill in the latest start and finish times, starting with task *H*. Since the time estimate for task *H* is 2 weeks, if this task must finish in 26 weeks, then its LST should be 26 − 2 = 24 weeks. This LST becomes the LFT for any task that immediately precedes task *H*.

In the backward pass, any task that has more than one successor task will receive a latest finish time that is the smallest of the latest start times for the successor tasks. The LFT for task *A* thus is the smaller of the LSTs for its successor tasks *C* and *D*.

The backward pass is repeated until the dummy node is reached, at which point all the EST, EFT, LST, and LFT values have been filled in, as shown in Figure 9.8. This figure also identifies the critical path, *A-D-F-G-H*, which is the set of tasks that have the same EST and LST values or, alternately, the tasks that have the same EFT and LFT values. This diagram shows the slack associated with each task, which is simply the difference between the LFT and EFT values (or, alternately, the difference between the LST and EST values). All tasks on the critical path have zero slack.

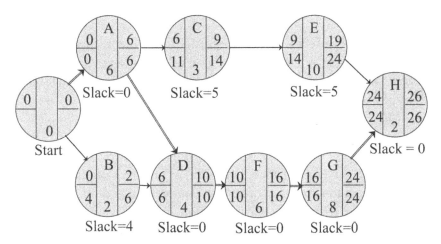

Figure 9.8 The critical path for the center for executive education program.

After the critical path is determined, the project is launched. The necessary resources are deployed to carefully manage the critical path. In summary, the PERT/CPM technique proceeds as follows:

▲ The tasks and their precedence relationships are identified
▲ Task times and resource requirements are estimated
▲ Task times are buffered to protect against uncertainties
▲ The project network is developed, and the critical path is determined, along with the earliest start, earliest finish, latest start, and latest finish times for each task
▲ These times are broadcast to everyone involved in the project: the customer, the project manager(s), and the project supervisors

Returning to the example presented earlier, the dean of the center for executive education is promised a scheduled launch of the program in 30 weeks—a four-week buffer has been added to the projected project completion date in case Murphy* strikes.

How likely is it that this project will complete in 30 weeks? Surprisingly, the answer is that it is very likely that the project will take more than 30 weeks, even though the task times have been buffered for uncertainty and the critical path is carefully monitored throughout the entire project duration. To understand this phenomenon, let's examine the possible sources of project delay and their underlying causes.

There are many factors that contribute to project delays: the project scope changes, there is inadequate funding, resources are not available, there is no management support, or the due date promised to the customer is unrealistic. Some of these factors are outside the project manager's control and could well result in unavoidable project delays. However, there are many factors that result in needless project delays that the project manager can anticipate and correct.

Causes of Avoidable Project Delays

Multitasking, as it is understood here, is the act of setting aside a task before it is completed to work on another task. This definition of multitasking is a little different from an alternate definition of multitasking that describes

---

*Murphy's Law states that if anything can go wrong, it will.

the act of working, or trying to work, on multiple tasks at the same time. Regardless of how it is defined, multitasking is one of the biggest causes for project delays.

Multitasking

Consider a resource that has to complete three tasks, A, B, and C, each one of which requires three days of work from the resource. Suppose that all three tasks are available to be worked on at the start of day 1.

If the resource completes these tasks one at a time, say, in the order A, B, C, then task A is completed at the end of day 3, task B is completed at the end of day 6, and task C is completed at the end of day 9. Pictorially, the nine days spent completing these tasks can be represented by the sequence A-A-A-B-B-B-C-C-C.

Suppose that the resource instead engages in multitasking and completes one day of work on each task, switching to the next task at the start of each following day. The sequence of work performed by the resource is now A-B-C-A-B-C-A-B-C.

When a task is set aside to perform another task, the resource performing the task has to reset itself, either mentally or physically, to work on the next task. Even if it is assumed that the time to switch between tasks is negligible, multitasking delays task completions and increases lead times. Task A now is completed at the end of day 7, task B is completed at the end of day 8, and task C is completed by the end of day 9.

It is true that the total time needed to complete all three tasks remains the same if switchover times are assumed to be negligible. However, the lead times for tasks A and B now have increased by a significant amount.

This simple example makes it clear why multitasking results in project delays, but the practice of multitasking is still prevalent because its impact on project delays is not well understood. In fact, multitasking sometimes is celebrated as a desirable skill for managers in an increasingly complex world that requires the manager to manage multiple tasks simultaneously.

When people multitask between multiple tasks or projects, they invariably build in additional safety buffers into their task time estimates to accommodate their multitasking behavior. Building in such safety buffers promotes other behavioral problems such as *Parkinson's Law*, the *Student Syndrome*, and *sandbagging*.

Parkinson's Law

As noted earlier, task times typically are padded with a safety buffer to accommodate the uncertainties inherent in projects. Sometimes task times are also inflated as a result of negative experiences with similar projects in the past. Regardless of the underlying reasons, inflating task times promotes a well-known behavioral phenomenon often referred to as *Parkinson's Law* ("Work expands to fill the time available").[2]

Parkinson's law promotes project delays in two ways. When a worker is given a generous amount of time to complete work, a time period that he knows to be generous, there is a tendency for him to slow down the effort to complete a task no matter how well intentioned he may be.

Parkinson's law also promotes project delays through the *continue-to-polish syndrome*. The continue-to-polish syndrome is essentially driven by the notion that it is not quality work if a task is completed well before its prescribed task completion time. A task may be completed well ahead of its allotted time for a variety of reasons: the customer was not as demanding as a typical customer, or the product requiring service was in near-perfect condition. However, the worker serving the customer or servicing the product may feel compelled to provide the same level of service for every customer or product.

The worker also may be under the impression that when more time is spent on a task, it must result in a better-quality product. Alternately, there may be a perception that if there is time left over after completing the task, the customer would benefit if the worker provided a few extra finishing touches to the product or service.

The Student Syndrome

The *Student Syndrome* refers to the tendency for people to put off working on a task until the due date draws near. The Student Syndrome, together with Parkinson's Law, promotes procrastination due to the perception that task times are padded with considerable safety buffers. When work eventually begins on the task, there is now very little room for any error or for any unplanned activities that may affect the task duration. The result is that the actual task completion time often exceeds the planned task completion time.

Sandbagging

Sandbagging takes place when workers do not notify the project manager as soon as they complete their assigned tasks. Sandbagging can take place especially when there is a perception that reporting an early task completion will result in a corresponding reduction in the time allowed for that task the next time it has to be performed. The workers may have fought hard with management to secure the amount of time currently allowed for performing these tasks, in which case they may be reluctant to acknowledge that a task was completed earlier than planned.

To sum up the discussion so far, Parkinson's Law and the Student Syndrome promote delays in task completion times, while sandbagging results in any potential gains from early task completions to go unreported. In sum, Parkinson's Law, the Student Syndrome, and sandbagging combine to waste the safety buffers built into the tasks and extend task completion times beyond the time allotted for the tasks.

This discussion provides compelling reasons for not providing any safety buffers for tasks. Yet, at the same time, there is a compelling need to provide this safety to protect against any uncertainties, especially because Murphy's Law is ubiquitous. The resulting conflict is presented by the cloud in Figure 9.9.

Examining the cloud in Figure 9.9 provides the direction of the solution by highlighting the root cause: the focus on getting tasks completed on time. The implicit assumption is that the project will complete on time if the individual tasks in the project are completed on time. The pressure to keep tasks on schedule, especially tasks on the critical path, is often intense. Paradoxically, such a pressure contributes to project delays because project

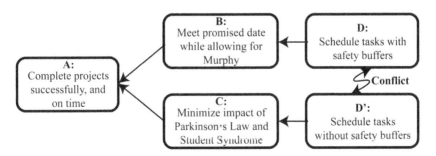

Figure 9.9 The task safety buffer cloud.

managers often lose focus on what really matters—completion of the project. Goldratt says, "It is not important to complete each task on time. It is essential to complete the project on time."* This fundamental observation provides the fifteenth Lean Supply Chain Principle.

Lean Supply Chain Principle 15

Focus on project completion times rather than task completion times. To ensure timely project completions, buffer the project, not the task.

Goldratt's statement urging project managers to focus on project completions instead of task completions captures the essence of *Critical Chain Project Management* (CCPM). CCPM is a proven technique that has produced dramatic results for many organizations. This chapter concludes with a case study on a CCPM implementation by the Marine Corps Logistics Base (MCLB) at Albany, Georgia. This CCPM implementation resulted in a 60 percent reduction in lead times across all product lines and a 50 percent reduction in the number of assets being serviced.

Critical Chain Project Management

The CCPM technique was introduced by Goldratt in 1997 in a book called *Critical Chain*.[3] CCPM is based on a number of key principles, some of which go counter to traditional intuition. CCPM views the project as a system, not as a collection of tasks. With such a systems perspective, the most important date is the project due date. Instead of promoting Parkinson's Law by buffering individual task times, CCPM prescribes removing the safety buffers used to pad individual tasks and replacing them with a buffer that protects the project. Replacing task safety buffers with a project buffer exploits the statistical law of aggregation discussed in Chapter 4, which shows that the same amount of protection is provided by an

---

*TOC Insights into Project Management and Engineering, software available for download from the Goldratt Marketing Group.

aggregated project buffer that is significantly smaller in size than the sum of the safety buffers for the individual tasks on the critical path.

CCPM uses aggressive task-duration estimates to determine the project completion time. The technique recommends cutting the task durations in half, essentially removing most of the safety embedded in the task. This recommendation has some theoretical basis. The resulting reduced task times are termed *aggressive-but-possible task times.** The technique then proceeds to draw up the project plan to determine where attention must be focused during execution of the project.

CCPM distinguishes between the planned schedule and the actual schedule. A fundamental rule in CCPM is that project tasks and resources should not be scheduled precisely while the project plan is being drawn up. The actual schedule will unfold eventually during execution, using buffer management to drive priorities, in a manner very reminiscent of the Drum-Buffer-Rope (DBR) Models discussed in Chapter 8. Buffer management in CCPM is described in a subsequent section.

While drawing up the planned schedule, CCPM eliminates any conflicts that may arise from using shared resources required for multiple tasks. Such conflicts may arise within and across projects. For ease of exposition, the development of the CCPM planned schedule is first explained within a single-project environment. The planned schedule for a multiple-project environment is discussed in a subsequent section.

Planning the CCPM Schedule in a Single-Project Environment

The technique is best illustrated with an example. Consider the project network presented in Figure 9.10. This network has two parallel paths of tasks that must be completed before the final task is executed. Each task in the figure is represented by the resource used and the time it takes the resource to complete the task. It is assumed that these task times have been buffered to account for uncertainties.

The network in Figure 9.10 includes two tasks that must be performed by resource X, each of duration 20 days. If the resource contention for this

*It may not always be possible to cut task times in half. For example, if a significant part of the task is machine-dependent, the extent to which the task time can be cut may be limited.

V	W	X
12 days	12 days	20 days

		Z
		24 days

Y	X
16 days	20 days

Note: All time durations have been buffered for undertainty.

Figure 9.10 Project network for the CCPM plan.

task is mistakenly ignored, the PERT network will develop a critical path that includes the upper parallel path and the final task performed by resource Z, projecting a planned project duration of 68 days.

Each task time is now cut in half to determine the aggressive-but-possible task times. Figure 9.11a shows the network with the aggressive-but-possible task times.

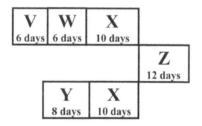

a) Determine aggressive but possible times

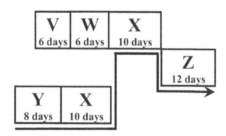

b) Accommodate resource dependencies and identify the longest path of dependent events

Figure 9.11 Setting up the critical chain.

Staggering the Start Times

Conflicts that may arise with resources used in multiple tasks are resolved by *staggering* the start times of these resources for the various tasks. Figure 9.11*b* shows the network where the potential conflict for resource X is resolved by sequencing resource X to perform the task on the lower parallel path first before it begins to work on the task in the upper parallel path. The longest path of dependent events, Y-X-X-Z, is the *critical chain*, the critical path when resource dependencies are considered explicitly.

Half the safety removed from tasks along the critical chain then is placed at the end of the project as a *project buffer* that protects the whole project from late delivery. Each secondary parallel path or subproject is planned using the same aggressive task durations with an associated *feeder buffer* that is set equal to half the safety removed from the tasks in the subproject. The feeder buffer is inserted at the point where the subproject connects to the critical chain and serves to protect the project from any delays that may occur on the feeder tasks. The start time for the subproject is set equal to the latest possible time that will accommodate the estimated subproject duration and the feeder buffer. Figure 9.12 shows the critical chain with the project buffer and feeder buffer.

It may be noted that the length of the project buffer prescribed by CCPM equals half the critical chain project duration, so the prescribed project buffer length equals a third of the total buffered project duration. While this is the prescribed project buffer length, in actual implementation, the project duration and the project buffer duration may have to be adjusted based on the extent to which task times can be cut.

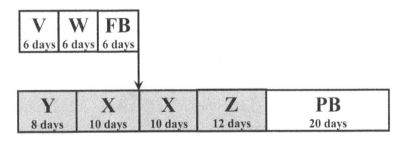

Provide the Project Buffer (PB) and the Feeding Buffers (FB)

Figure 9.12 The critical chain.

The aggressive-but-possible task times essentially minimize the project delays that result from Parkinson's Law. CCPM also minimizes the Student Syndrome by not displaying due dates or milestones. Instead, CCPM uses visual signals to highlight the progress of the project and to identify any tasks that need attention, without providing specific due dates. Only the starting times of the project and the subprojects are fixed. During execution, tasks are encouraged to start as soon as their preceding tasks are complete; this is the *relay runner* work ethic, a work ethic that plays a key role in minimizing the Student Syndrome.

Planning the CCPM Schedule in a Multiproject Environment

With multiple projects, the projects are staggered in a manner similar to the staggering approach used in a single-project environment. The approach is to identify the most loaded resource. This resource will set the *drum*, and the schedule is drawn based on the drum. The planned schedules for the different projects now are set according to the schedule of tasks performed by the drum. At this stage, it is important to get agreement on the planned schedules from the project managers for the different projects.

Executing the CCPM Schedule Using Buffer Management

CCPM requires the manager to gather periodic updates on task status during execution. A daily update is recommended. At these updating epochs, every task team is expected to provide their best estimate of the time remaining on the task on which they are working—a rough estimate of how much more time the team expects the task will take before it completes. These periodic updates are necessary for *buffer management*. Buffer management works as follows:

During execution, individual tasks may complete sooner or later than their planned aggressive-task-time estimates. If the sum of the actual completion times of tasks exceeds the sum of the task times in the planned-aggressive schedule, the expected completion time is pushed past the end of the aggressive schedule and starts to eat into the project buffer. This is called *buffer penetration.*

The status of the project is determined by the extent of buffer penetration. Buffer penetration provides a leading indicator of project status and warns the project manager of difficulties far enough in advance to allow for corrective actions. The buffer penetration is measured by the *buffer burn rate*, which is defined as the ratio of the percentage project buffer consumed to the percentage project completed.

A simple example will clarify the buffer burn rate concept. Suppose that the aggressive project duration is 120 days, and the project buffer is 60 days. Suppose, too, that at the end of day 78, the project has completed 48 days of actual work and used up 30 days of the project buffer. The project has completed 48 ÷ 120 = 40 percent of the required work, but it has consumed 30 ÷ 60 = 50 percent of its project buffer. The buffer burn rate thus is 50 ÷ 40 = 1.25. The project is likely to be in jeopardy because it is consuming the buffer at a rate significantly faster than it is completing work. This project will typically be color-coded red to denote that it needs immediate attention. A project with a buffer burn rate of less than one will typically be color-coded green to denote that it is progressing well.

In general, teams that take a longer amount of time beyond the planned aggressive task time should provide valid reasons for task delays. The project supervisor does not take these teams to task but instead works with them to bring the project back on schedule. By not penalizing teams for late completions, the project manager will minimize reasons for sandbagging.

The Fever Chart

CCPM uses a *fever chart* to track projects. This chart, which plots the percentage of project completed against the percentage of buffer consumed, is used to track either the progress of a single project over time or present a snapshot of the status of multiple projects at a point in time. Figure 9.13 presents a fever chart that tracks a single project over time.

The fever chart has three zones—green, yellow, and red. The green zone represents the zone within which the project is expected to operate if the project is proceeding smoothly without any major problems. When a project is in the green zone, it is probably advisable for management to let the project continue without any intervention. It is noted, however, that if projects generally remain in the green zone most of the time, it is a signal that the task times may not have been set aggressively enough.

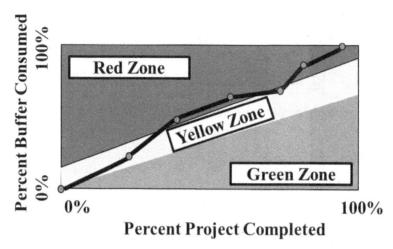

Figure 9.13   The fever chart used in CCPM.

The yellow zone represents the zone where there is normal, or moderate variation. In a sense, the yellow zone relates to common-cause variation in projects. While there is no need for alarm when the project is in the yellow zone, management should be alert and prepared to devise action plans for recovering buffer penetration.

When a project enters the red zone, it is time for management to take action. In a sense, the red zone represents special-cause variation. The project could have been delayed for numerous reasons; it may even be a result of a lack of adequate attention.

Buffer penetration gives the project manager an idea of where to focus resources to keep the project moving toward completion. In multiproject environments, buffer management compares the buffer penetration between projects and sets priorities for allocating resources correctly between projects as follows:

Suppose that a resource must choose on which task to work next from among multiple tasks on different projects and feeding chains. Within a project, the rule is to set priorities according to the type of buffer consumed, with tasks on a critical chain receiving priority over tasks located on a feeding chain. Across projects, the priority is given to the project that has a greater percentage of its project buffer consumed. CCPM thus provides a systems perspective toward determining how projects—and the tasks within each project—should be prioritized so as to complete projects in a minimum amount of time.

An Un-common Sense Minute

Executing projects with CCPM provides an un-common sense minute: "In order to complete projects faster, delay their start times." CCPM prescribes the release of new work into the system based on the availability of the most loaded resources because these constraining resources limit the amount of work that can be completed. The rule is to not release any new work into the system if the constraining resource is already overloaded, even if some of the other resources are idle.

On first glance, this rule may appear to go counter to an objective that aims to complete work as soon as possible. However, releasing work prematurely into the system results in overloading already constrained resources and thus at best serves only to distract the focus on completing projects in a timely manner. This approach is captured by the sixteenth Lean Supply Chain Principle.

Lean Supply Chain Principle 16

To reduce bad multitasking, let the bottleneck resource pace the release of projects into the system.

The approach recommended by Lean Supply Chain Principle 16 is reminiscent of the pull principle advocated by the DBR Model. Limiting the number of projects that are worked on will result in fewer disruptions and interruptions.

The key ideas underlying the CCPM methodology are summarized as follows:

▲ Remove safety from individual tasks, and develop aggressive-but-possible task times.
▲ Identify the longest path of dependent events. This is the *critical chain*. The safety removed from individual tasks is aggregated into a consolidated project buffer to protect the overall project.

▲ Create a project plan with firm start times for the beginning tasks in each leg of the project, but do not schedule start times for the individual tasks after the beginning tasks, and do not display milestones.

▲ Work on each task as soon as possible using the relay-runner work ethic. Resolve any conflicts using buffer management to arrive at a single priority system for all projects.

▲ Avoid multitasking resources to the extent possible by reducing the amount of work in the system and having a single global priority system provided by buffer management. New work is released into the system only at the rate at which the system actually can perform.

Sustaining the Change

After a few projects are completed with CCPM, the resources will get more confidence in the technique and get used to a situation where bad multitasking is reduced dramatically. They will begin to feel more comfortable that their task time estimates are no longer regarded as commitments and so will more readily provide the correct task time estimates instead of padding them with safety. At this stage, the path forward will be to continue to work on reducing the total project completion time. However, there is a big caveat—cutting task times in half will no longer be an effective approach. The best approach at this stage may be to set the project buffer equal to a third of the current total lead time.

Providing Frequent Updates

The importance of continuing to focus on daily updates cannot be overstated. With CCPM, the key to managing projects and avoiding the Student Syndrome is to have the project managers perform a daily walk-around, querying the status of all the tasks currently in progress. This activity can be a difficult one, at least at the outset. Project teams in traditionally managed projects detest even a weekly progress reporting because it so vividly manifests their lack of progress, and there is a real fear that they will be taken to task for these delays. However, once the project team is provided with an assurance that the real purpose of the walk-around is to determine where to focus resources, the resistance to daily reporting will become much less pronounced.

CCPM is a proven, effective approach for managing large projects, and there are numerous case studies that document the significant benefits realized from CCPM. CCPM uses extensive management attention and computer software for managing the projects. However, this level of management oversight may be excessive for a vast number of projects. What most people need is an easy-to-use focusing mechanism that:

▲ Helps management to identify the true capacity available during project execution
▲ Provides management with a WIP status
▲ Gives guidance to management on when to release additional work into the system
▲ Allows management to deploy resources on the projects that need them the most

These needs are addressed by Visual Project Management (VPM).[4] VPM is a new approach that follows the basic principles and concepts of CCPM. VPM is especially applicable when projects do not have many feeder chains or when projects have relatively shorter task durations that do not span multiple days.

Visual Project Management*

VPM is a visual, simple, and easy-to-use project management system. There are three steps to VPM:

1. Create a firm, aggressive plan for each project.
2. Provide frequent reporting of completed tasks.
3. Create an Expert Resource Bench.

A Firm, Aggressive Plan

Everyone needs a plan for effective project execution, but a detailed plan is seldom made for a variety of reasons:

---

*The material presented in this section is drawn from the white paper, "How to Get Things Done: Visual Project Management," by J. Holt and M. Srinivasan.

▲ Plans change too quickly to be helpful
▲ Managers believe that they already know what needs to be done
▲ It is harder to draw up a plan than to execute the project
▲ It is a waste of time to make plans that will not be followed anyway

All these reasons may have some basis, but the fact remains that effective project execution requires a sound plan. The solution, then, is to devise a simple project plan that is "good enough" to capture the tasks in the project at a general level. Such a plan can be developed regardless of the manner in which the project is presented—whether it is presented in a PERT/CPM format, as a CCPM plan, or just based on a simple listing of the tasks that must be executed to complete the project.*

The resulting plan is treated as a firm plan in the sense that the planned starting time for the initial set of tasks—which could represent either the start of the project or the start of any subprojects that connect to the project—stays firm. Each task in the plan is now assigned an aggressive task time estimate. The definition of *aggressive* is based on the opinion of the resources executing the work.

The aggressive task time estimates for tasks along the critical path or critical chain are added up to arrive at the planned *project duration*. A project buffer equal to 50 percent of the planned project duration is used to buffer the variation in the task times. The output from this step is the *project plan*, which consists of a list of tasks with the aggressive task times, the project duration, and the project buffer. The predicted project completion time is the sum of the project duration and the project buffer.

Frequent Reporting of Completed Tasks

Effective management of the project plan requires knowledge of the project status. Project status is important but often hard to evaluate because there are many factors competing for consideration. For example, to obtain a full picture of project status, there is a perceived need to estimate the additional time required for all partially completed tasks. Ignoring such distractions, there is only one item of information required—the tasks on the project plan that have been completed.

---

*Experienced project managers may find it peculiar to let a simple list of tasks be considered a project plan. With VPM, having just a list is acceptable.

Like CCPM, VPM requires periodic updating of the project status. However, unlike CCPM, VPM requires only task completions to be reported, not the time remaining on tasks in progress. Task completions should be reported frequently (daily or at least weekly). From this single bit of information, the percentage of the project completed is computed simply as:

$$\text{percent project completed} = \frac{\text{sum of estimated task duration times for completed tasks}}{\text{project duration}} \times 100$$

The project duration is the sum of the estimated task duration times for tasks along the critical path/critical chain. It does not include tasks executed in parallel to the critical path or critical chain; nor does it include tasks in subprojects. Similarly, the completed tasks in the numerator of this equation relate only to critical tasks.* The percentage of time consumed by the project so far is also easily computed by looking at the calendar:

$$\text{percent time consumed} = \frac{\text{current time} - \text{start time}}{\text{project duration}} \times 100$$

No additional information is needed.

Visual Display of Project Status

During execution, VPM provides a visual display of project status that makes it obvious to all observers when a project needs help and when it is progressing smoothly. This status is provided early enough for managers to be able to help with problems while there is still time.

VPM uses a simple green light (okay) and red light (not okay) approach to project status. Over the life of a project, there are zones where a certain amount of deviation from the plan is acceptable and other zones where deviation is not acceptable.

If the project is in the green zone, it is progressing well. Management should continue to offer support, facilitating and providing resources as

---

*If the project plan is just a list of projects, the project duration includes the total time of all tasks, and completed tasks include any of the tasks on the list. Both the project duration and the completed task times used in this equation are based on the planned task time estimates and not on the actual time of the project. This greatly simplifies reporting.

planned. No extraordinary effort is required, and management should stay out of the way.

Management's role changes if a project is in the red zone; it must take action to help the project return to the green zone. Resources must be redirected to a project that is in the red zone. Resources may come from other projects, from internal experts, or from outside. The variable nature of project tasks, the dependency between project tasks, and the inability to closely manage parallel projects or various subprojects require prompt actions from management to move the project toward the green zone. An example visual display is shown in Figure 9.14.

Project status is displayed by plotting the project's progress based on the percent project completed and the percent buffer consumed. The percentage buffer consumed is calculated by the simple equation

percent buffer consumed = 2 x (percent time consumed – percent project completed)

When the percent time consumed exceeds the percent of project completed, the project buffer gets consumed. For a 10-day project, every day the project is delayed results in a 10 percent delay for the project. The one-day delay penetrates into the project buffer by one day. Note that the project buffer is initially set to 50 percent of the project duration. Since the

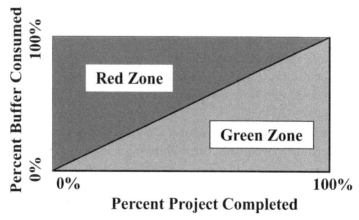

Figure 9.14 Project status chart in VPM.

project buffer for a 10-day project is 5 days, a 10 percent delay in the project will consume 20 percent of the project buffer.

The preceding expression shows that if 100 percent of the project buffer is consumed by the time the project is completed, then the percent time consumed will be 150 percent. The expected completion time, the date given to the customer, should be the 150 percent time—the aggressive estimate plus the 50 percent project buffer.

The project status chart in Figure 9.14 has a ratio of two units wide to one unit high to depict the correct scale along the *x* and *y* axes in the chart (the project buffer is 50 percent of the aggressive project duration). This chart can be used to track the progress of a single project or to report a snapshot view of many projects. Figure 9.15 shows the project status of a single project over time.

In this figure, each small circle indicates the status of the project at a specific reporting epoch (a moment in time). The first data point starts at 0 percent complete with 0 percent of the buffer consumed. The second data point shows about 25 percent of the project completed and about 5 percent of the buffer consumed. This means that the tasks completed between the first and second reporting periods took only slightly longer than the estimated time (about 5 percent more than expected). While the tasks did take longer than expected, it was not a problem. VPM allows for up 50

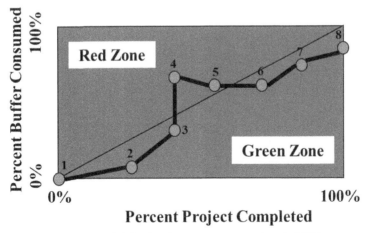

Figure 9.15   Single-project status chart in VPM.

percent buffer consumption rate for the project. The project is in the green zone at the second reporting epoch.

At the third circle, the next reporting epoch, the project is still in the green zone. However, the buffer consumption rate has increased. The slope of the line between the second and third circles is greater than the slope of the line dividing the green zone and the red zone, which is ½. The implication is that during the time interval between the second and third reporting epochs, the completed tasks reported took more time than estimated—more than 150 percent of the estimated time. However, at this point in time, the project is not in jeopardy. It is in the green zone. No heroic actions are needed. On the other hand, the project status is approaching the red zone, and this may be a cause for concern. Management should be ready to respond if necessary.

From the third circle to the fourth circle (the next reporting epoch), there is a vertical line. The implication is that during this period of time, no progress was made on the project; no additional tasks were reported as completed. The clock continued to run, but the percentage of completed tasks did not increase. This situation could arise if the resources working on the project are performing a long-duration task that was not completed before the end of the reporting period. Perhaps there was some difficulty associated with completing a task, or it could be due to some bad multitasking that pulled the resources away from the project. The result is the same: the project has moved into the red zone.

The Expert Resource Bench

When a project is in the red zone, VPM suggests that management act immediately to move the project back to the green zone. The first line of response is the Expert Resource Bench, a team of highly skilled people that are charged with responding to emergencies. The Expert Resource Bench is about 20 percent of the resource pool.

The Expert Resource Bench can be likened to a SWAT team or a "first responder." When a project enters the red zone, the Expert Resource Bench arrives to assist those working on the project, to help get tasks completed, and to put the project back into the green zone. The efforts from the Expert Resource Bench may include help with the work, offloading some of the work, training, or Socratic inquiry. Additional resources beyond the Expert Resource Bench may also be necessary in some cases.

From the fourth circle to the fifth, there is a significant recovery in buffer consumption. Perhaps a long-duration task was completed in this period, or other tasks were completed in less than the estimated time. The project status is much better, but the project is still in the red zone and still demands attention from management.

From the sixth circle onward, the project stays in the green zone. The project finally completes after using about 90 percent of the project buffer (about 145 percent of the aggressive project schedule).* Figure 9.16 is a project status chart for many projects. This chart shows the current status of all the individual active projects at a moment in time.

In this figure, most projects are progressing well, with buffer consumption ranging from 0 percent for projects that are near completion but using less than 100 percent of the project buffer. There are four problem projects (projects 1421, 1541, 614, and 644).

A multiproject status chart such as the one shown in Figure 9.16 provides important additional management information. Too many projects in the red zone suggests that the organization is unable to keep up with projects in progress and communicates to management the need to choke or hold

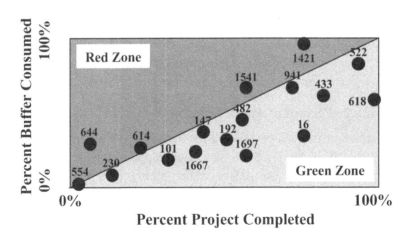

Figure 9.16 Multiproject status chart in VPM.

*If the project had progressed from start to finish according to the aggressive task estimates, the project status chart would show a row of circles moving across the chart in a horizontal line from 0 percent to 100 percent complete along the *x* axis without any buffer consumption.

back the release of new projects into the system. Conversely, having no projects or too few projects in the red zone suggests to management that more projects can be inserted into the system.

Allowing no more than about 10 percent of projects in the red zone prevents too many projects in the system (and the bad multitasking that it causes). The Expert Resource Bench is sufficient to assist return of about 10 percent of the projects from the red zone back into the green zone.

The multiproject status chart also identifies which projects are progressing routinely. Projects well into the green zone (such as projects 16 and 1697) can be a source of resources needed for projects in the red zone (such as projects 1421 and 1521). Management can easily make informed assignments of resources based on buffer consumption status.

Implementing VPM

There are four steps to implementing VPM:

1. Freeze 25 percent of all currently active projects.
2. Plan the 75 percent remaining projects (the remaining uncompleted part of these projects) with PERT, CCPM, or the list of tasks with a firm, aggressive project duration plan. Add the 50 percent project buffer to the project duration to get a predictable delivery date.
3. Plot project status on all active projects frequently (by recording completed tasks daily or at least weekly) on the project status chart.
4. Take management actions in accordance with the project buffer status.

Freezing 25 Percent of Active Projects

The most controversial part of VPM is freezing a portion of the currently active projects. However, this is a necessary step. In most project environments, the workers are overloaded. If the system is loaded with more work than the resources can deliver, it would not be surprising if work backs up, and projects are late and lack valued content.

Freezing projects means that these projects are removed from the active project workload. The decision on which projects to freeze depends on the system and the customer. The frozen projects typically are low-priority work or future work that does not have to happen right now. Management may choose to freeze even more than 25 percent of current work to get down to a reasonable workload.

Implementing VPM without removing low-priority work will drive many projects into the red zone immediately. It is a much better idea to freeze the lower-priority projects and thaw them (release them again) at a controlled rate to which the system can respond. In the end, with VPM, the frozen projects will be completed at about the same time or sooner than they otherwise would have if they had been left unfrozen.

Planning Projects

Planning the remaining 75 percent of the active projects is the same as defined earlier. The remaining work can be planned, ignoring the previously completed work. Again, a 50 percent project buffer is included for the project to absorb variations in different tasks and to protect the project as a whole. The aggressive estimates used in VPM remove much of the local safety from individual tasks. That safety is aggregated and moved to the project buffer. A 50 percent project buffer is more than sufficient for projects when buffer management is used.[5] To move projects quickly and predictably, new work is released into the system only at the capacity that the system can deliver.

Plotting Project Status

Plotting project status is important. It helps to track progress for individual projects and gives management the correct feedback when all projects are examined together. Frequent plotting is helpful so that management decisions based on buffer consumption rate will be correct.

Management Actions—the Expert Resource Bench

The Expert Resource Bench provides two main roles. One role is to help recover projects in the red zone. As noted earlier, the Expert Resource Bench acts as a first responder or an emergency medical crew to help complete tasks and move projects from the red to the green zone. In fulfilling this role, the bench does Just-In-Time training (people really want to learn when they are faced with an immediate, tough problem they could not solve), becomes a short-term added resource, or can assist in bringing other resources to the task.

The Expert Resource Bench has another role. The Expert Resource Bench is made up of experts who know a lot about the processes, the tasks, and the techniques needed to complete the projects. About 50 percent of the Expert Resource Bench's time should be spent observing the system.

When projects are in the green zone, the Expert Resource Bench simply watches progress without interfering. The experts ponder and analyze, "Why is the buffer being consumed so rapidly without progress? How can we improve this process so that it is easier, better, faster? What is the underlying cause of the many different problems we see? How can we improve the system as a whole?"

It is the Expert Resource Bench's responsibility to develop better methods and techniques and to report to management about how and when such improvements should be made. The Expert Resource Bench is the foundation of the learning organization.

Special Cases in VPM

When first implementing VPM, the existing projects that are underway may be late already, or adding the 50 percent project buffer to the remaining work of existing projects may push them past the promised delivery date of the project. Alternately, the project may be on a very tight schedule. In such situations, there is a tendency to try to eliminate the project buffer and just press forward with the project the best way possible. But there is a better way.

In such situations, the project buffer is still calculated the same way as before and is inserted at the end of the (aggressive) critical path/chain. The end of the project buffer (which should be the expected date promised the customer) is now pushed back earlier in time to the currently promised delivery date. The amount of pushback time is factored into the determination of percent time consumed. Thus, when calculating the percentage of time the project has consumed, the pushback time is simply added to the start time for this project. This will correctly show the real status of the late project on the project status chart.

$$\text{percent time consumed} = \frac{\text{current time} + \text{pushback} - \text{start time}}{\text{project duration}} \times 100$$

This minor adjustment to the percent time consumed, in turn, adjusts the percent buffer consumed and positions the project correctly on the project status chart. It will show that with 0 percent of the project complete, there is already consumption of the project buffer. The project will be in the red zone, and management will give it the necessary attention.

Another special situation occurs when the project buffer is completely consumed (exceeds 100 percent). When the project buffer is more than 100 percent consumed at any time during the project, the project will be late. Actions should be taken to either notify the customer right away or cancel the project. In theory, it is possible to recover a project that has over 100 percent of the project buffer consumed if it is early in the project. However, if the VPM buffer status guidelines have been followed and a project has consumed more than 100 percent of the project buffer even after management attempts to bring the project back into the green zone, caution is warranted. Such a project may have some peculiar problems that very likely may not be resolved by the promised delivery date.

This chapter concludes with a case study highlighting the implementation of CCPM at the Marine Corps Logistics Base in Albany, Georgia.

CASE STUDY

CCPM at a Marine Corps Logistics Base[6]

The maintenance center at the Marine Corps Logistics Base (MCLB) in Albany, Georgia, repairs and overhauls a wide variety of equipment required by the Marine Corps for combat readiness. The items repaired and overhauled at the maintenance center include small arms, amphibious vehicles, light armored vehicles, fuel tankers, trucks, earthmoving equipment, and logistics vehicle systems.

In 2001, the maintenance center was struggling to complete equipment repairs on time and was coping with an increasing backlog of work. Asking for "plus-ups," or additional time to complete the work, had become a normal way of doing business. The repair and overhaul of the MK-48, a heavy-duty hauler for the Marine Corps, presented a classic example of the problems the center was facing. The center was repairing and overhauling 5 units a month, whereas the customer demand was for 10 units per month. The customer was threatening to divert the business to the private sector.

The Repair Process at the Base

The repair and overhaul process starts by disassembling each vehicle to determine its *work scope*, which is the amount and nature of the work

CASE STUDY

to be done on the product. The work scope also identifies the parts that can be repaired and the parts that need to be replaced. Repairable parts are routed through a series of support shops that include cleaning, blasting, painting, machining, body work, and weapons work. Parts that need replacement are either replaced from existing spare-parts stock or ordered from an external source.

In 2001, the scheduling of the repair and overhaul process was based on a Manufacturing Resource Planning (MRP II) system, a push system. The MRP II push system introduced products into the shops as and when they arrived at the base, without regard to the status of the resources in the shops, leading to false starts and delays, increased inventories, and lowered throughput. The practice was to send disassembled parts immediately to the support shops to allow as much time as possible for the parts to move through the repair cycle. Consequently, many of the resources were resorting to multitasking.

The center's management team reviewed alternate approaches to schedule the repair and overhaul process and picked CCPM. It contracted with Vector Strategies* to implement CCPM on the MK-48s. The pilot project proved successful, and the center began implementation of CCPM plantwide in April 2002. Used in conjunction with Lean, this implementation has generated dramatic improvement in performance.

Applying CCPM

The maintenance center's management sought input from employees throughout the organization on where they perceived bottlenecks to exist. Opinions varied, but every major resource in the center was believed to be an important bottleneck by at least someone in the facility.

The center analyzed the capacity at the main shop and the support shops. Contrary to everyone's expectation, the analysis revealed that the facility had adequate capacity to meet the customer demand for 10 MK-48s per month.

---

*www.vectorstrategies.com.

CASE STUDY

Further analysis revealed that the root cause for the consistent shortfalls and high inventory levels was the choice of scheduling system—the MRP II system used to schedule the repair and overhaul. The scheduling system was pushing products out to the shop floor without regard to the status of the resources.

The analysis revealed that the center could easily meet the customer demand for 10 MK-48s a month with properly timed material releases. This discovery allowed the center to model the main shop where products were disassembled and subsequently reassembled as the critical chain. The center used the Simplified Drum-Buffer-Rope (S-DBR) Model to schedule the tasks in the support shops. As discussed in Chapter 8, the S-DBR Model is used when the market is the constraint. The S-DBR Model was implemented as follows:

When orders are received, a quick check is made on the total load at the capacity-constrained resources (CCRs), which are the support shops. If the CCR is not too heavily loaded, the order is accepted and released into the system for processing. The corresponding material release schedule then is generated by the MRP II system. The MRP II system thus facilitates the S-DBR schedules. The MRP II database also stores data on lead times for items supplied by vendors.

Results from the Implementation

A corporate plan was developed to implement Lean activities for supporting the new process. The center undertook a 6-S* activity and a reengineering of the supply warehouse. The 6-S activity resulted in a significant increase in available shop floor space. Hundreds of person-hours associated with the testing and repair of cables on the amphibious and land-assault family of vehicles were saved. Tools in excess of $200,000 were turned in for redistribution and future use. The process flows in production work centers were streamlined.

---

*Chapter 7 discussed the 5-S activity. Many organizations include a sixth S to the 5-S activity to incorporate Safety.

CASE STUDY

A major benefit from the convergence of Theory of Constraints (TOC) and Lean was that it resulted in increased employee morale and made the facility a cleaner and safer place in which to work. The center has become extremely flexible and better positioned to meet its responsibilities for regeneration and reconstitution of critical supplies. It was able to meet a customer demand for the repair and overhaul of 23 units in one month without incurring overtime.

The magnitude of culture change was greatest in the support shops. Withholding disassembled parts instead of releasing them prematurely and cluttering the support shops met with substantial resistance at the outset from employees who feared it would delay the repair process. This aspect of the implementation was the last part of the culture change accepted and accomplished by the maintenance center, when the employees saw significant improvement with every other aspect of the implementation.

Conclusions

The project management triangle defines the relationship among three elements—scope, time, and cost. A fourth element—performance quality—is sometimes added to separate out performance quality from scope. Conventional wisdom dictates that it is not possible to improve on all these elements simultaneously. CCPM, however, shows that such tradeoffs may not be needed and that it is possible to satisfactorily address all these elements simultaneously.

CCPM uses a visual tracking method called a *fever chart* to identify the progress of tasks and projects at different points in time, and it is based on the following key ideas:

▲ Remove safety buffers from individual tasks and instead buffer the project
▲ Do not display milestones for task completions
▲ Release new work into the system at the rate at which the system can perform; release work based on the workload at the most heavily loaded resource

▲ Avoid multitasking resources to the extent possible
▲ Do not schedule start times for the individual tasks, but allocate resources to tasks based on priorities
▲ Complete each task as quickly as possible once it begins using a relay-runner work ethic.
▲ Update the expected task completion times for tasks in progress frequently—daily if possible—by performing a daily walk-around.

VPM is a simple, visual project management system that facilitates predictable project completions without the need for extensive project management plans. Even a simple listing of tasks is adequate.

▲ VPM does not need expensive software to operate the system.
▲ VPM requires only a single item of information to be reported—the completed tasks—to evaluate project status.
▲ The project status is visual. Project status charts indicate whether the project is in the green zone or the red zone. These charts tell management, at a glance, whether the system is overloaded or starved.
▲ The project status charts alert both the project manager and management about any projects that need attention. This alert comes early enough to enable corrective action.
▲ An Expert Resource Bench is used to respond quickly to help move any troubled projects back to the green zone. The Expert Resource Bench serves to analyze and help implement systemic improvements.

References

1. W. L. Winston and S. C. Albright (2008), *Practical Management Science*, South-Western College Publishing, Boston.
2. C. N. Parkinson (1987), *Parkinson's Law*, Ballantine Books, Reissue edition, New York.
3. E. M. Goldratt (1997), *Critical Chain*, North River Press, Great Barrington, MA.
4. J. R. Holt and M. M. Srinivasan (2011), "Seeing How to Get Things Done: Visual Project Management Shows the Way," *APICS Magazine*, January–February 2011, pp. 38–41.
5. E. M. Goldratt (1997), *Critical Chain*, North River Press, Great Barrington, MA.
6. M. M. Srinivasan, D. Jones, and A. Miller (2005), "Corps Capabilities," *APICS Magazine*, March 2005, pp. 46–50.

INDEX